Contents

Welcome!

*The Royal Air Force Memorial,
Victoria Embankment, is one
stunning example of public sculpture,
the commemorative art form
English Heritage is celebrating
in the year 2000 (see also p. 6-7).*

AD · ASTRA

On March 31 2000, I step down as Chairman of English Heritage after eight stimulating – and exhausting – years. Much has changed since I joined. But there has been one constant – the enthusiasm and dedication of our ever increasing number of members.

When I joined we had 110,000 members; now we have 480,000. Our members are at the core of what we do. We know, because you've told us, that most of you become members and remain members because you believe in the importance of our work, and not only because you are entitled to visit our sites and events free of charge.

Every year your subscriptions help us to do more to conserve our environmental heritage, regenerate our historic cities, towns and villages. One example has been our Conservation Area Partnership Scheme whereby, in the last five years, we have, in partnership with 357 local authorities, invested £36 million, and attracted over £170 million in additional funding from other sources. This scheme has been superseded by our Heritage Economic Regeneration Scheme, which targets England's 'humble heritage' and areas listed high on the government's index of deprivation.

Our Register of Buildings at Risk this year identified 1615 grade I and II* buildings at risk from dereliction and decay. With your backing, we can at last begin to save some of these most important English historic houses and monuments. And we have protected our architectural heritage in other ways – some controversial – by recommending post-war buildings for listing in specific categories. For our heritage is not only about the past, it is also about the best of modern architecture and innovative new design.

I am particularly proud of our plans to build over the next five years contemporary gardens at ten of our historic properties. The first two open this summer. They are the Walled Garden at Osborne House, Isle of Wight and the South Moat at Eltham Palace in south east London.

Meanwhile, the Secretary of State has asked me to continue to be closely involved with the Master Plan for Stonehenge, which will, I hope, transform our greatest archaeological monument from being a 'national disgrace' into one of the wonders of the world and fully worthy of its status as a World Heritage Site.

If you are not an English Heritage member, please join. Your membership will enable us to increase the range of our work, which is to conserve England's glorious heritage wherever it is at risk. Each year you will receive your own copy of this Handbook, every three months you will receive a copy of your own magazine, *Heritage Today*, and you will be free to explore and enjoy the best of England's heritage.

I am confident that I am leaving England's heritage in the safe hands of our committed Commissioners and staff, and you, our members.

SIR JOCELYN STEVENS
Chairman

Regions

The properties included in this book are listed alphabetically within nine regions. Each region is colour-coded, with the maps on pages 232–242 showing the area each region covers. Each entry also includes the property's county and its map reference.

South East
Berkshire
Buckinghamshire
Hampshire
Kent
Oxfordshire
Surrey
East Sussex
West Sussex
Isle of Wight

London

South West
Bristol
Cornwall
Devon
Dorset
Gloucestershire
Somerset
Wiltshire
Isles of Scilly

East of England
Bedfordshire
Cambridgeshire
Essex
Hertfordshire
Norfolk
Suffolk

East Midlands
Derbyshire
Leicestershire
Lincolnshire
Northamptonshire
Nottinghamshire
Rutland

West Midlands
Herefordshire
Worcestershire
Shropshire
Staffordshire
Warwickshire
West Midlands

Yorkshire
North Yorkshire
South Yorkshire
West Yorkshire
East Riding of
　Yorkshire
North East
　Lincolnshire
North
　Lincolnshire

North West
Cheshire
Cumbria
Greater Manchester
Lancashire
Merseyside

North East
Co. Durham
Northumberland
Tyne & Wear
Teesside

What's new in 2000

Left, Ranger's House, one of many properties where a new exhibition will take place this spring. Bottom, Eltham Palace, where a new garden has been designed, as part of the Contemporary Heritage Gardens project.

You will notice that this year's Handbook once again contains a number of **themes** providing background information and general comment on a variety of subjects; from archaeology to Victoriana, from windmills to deserted medieval villages ... all designed to help you enjoy the heritage even more.

Exciting **new exhibitions** are also planned for 2000 at Richmond Castle, Dartmouth Castle and Rievaulx Abbey. From 23 March to 31 May at Ranger's House a group of Greenwich-based artists will exhibit their work, and, at Kenwood, the spectacular exhibition *Eat, Drink and Be Merry, the British at Table 1600-2000* will take place from **27 June to 24 September.**

The year 2000 will also see a new audio tour and Discovery Centre for children and families at Bolsover from May, a new decorative scheme in the Dining and Music Rooms at Kenwood from April, and a new garden and Table Decker's Room at Osborne from late spring.

The **Year of the Artist** is a unique project starting in the South West region in 2000 and continuing into the new Millennium. It is designed to celebrate Britain's artistic achievements, focusing on the work of living artists, and highlighting the vital contribution that they make to our quality of life. Our built heritage will provide inspiration for this project as three artists take up residence at Tintagel Castle, Cleeve Abbey and amidst the ruins of Hailes Abbey during the summer.

Last April English Heritage announced **Contemporary Heritage Gardens**, a £1.5 million programme to create ten contemporary gardens in historic settings managed by English Heritage. You can now enjoy the winning designs for Queen Victoria's walled garden at Osborne, on the Isle of Wight, and for the South Moat garden at Eltham Palace, in South London. Many of our sites house wonderful collections and we are pleased to be part of the Museum and Galleries Month 2000 in May, which enables you to rediscover the joys and benefits of around 1,000 museums across the country. Look out for the details in the March 2000 issue of our members' magazine, *Heritage Today.*

Heritage Open Days 2000 (16 & 17 September) will offer a very special opportunity to visit and explore some of England's most fascinating buildings not normally open to the public. **London Open Houses 2000**, which will be on 24 and 25 September, will offer the same opportunity for sites in London. Again, you will find details in future issues of *Heritage Today.*

Public sculpture

YEAR OF PUBLIC
SCULPTURE

Public sculpture is *the* commemorative art form. It expresses society's desire to celebrate and remember its achievements and aspirations in a way which leaves a visible and often dramatic mark on the built

Public sculpture is often the most exuberant element of the historic built environment for which English Heritage is responsible. It is everywhere: in streets, squares, and parks, in shopping centres and on the façades of the country's public buildings and stately homes. It touches the lives of everyone, celebrating the heroes and events which have marked our history.

England is endowed with a rich national collection of public sculpture ranging from Celtic crosses of the 4th century AD to fine contemporary works, but it is often forgotten, or unseen. English Heritage, with its teams of conservation specialists, architects, researchers, engineers and traditional craftsmen is there to protect and promote this art form.

The year 2000 marks an important step forward in the role that English Heritage will play in the country's public art: 47 statues in London have been given to us to care for, including the Wellington Arch – one of the largest outdoor sculptures in the country, which is to undergo major restoration – the Cenotaph, the statues of Edith Cavell and Florence Nightingale, those of the Duke of Wellington and Charles II, and also war memorials such as the Royal Artillery Memorial and the Crimea Memorial.

Guards Division Memorial, Horse Guards Rd, SW1.

Mount Grace Priory's Madonna of the Cross.

Two Piece Reclining Figure Number Five, *by Henry Moore, Kenwood House.*

environment. The role of English Heritage is to care for and protect that heritage. Its aim is to preserve our past, not only in the form of ancient castles, grand houses or World Heritage Sites, but in everything from bridges and romantic ruins to public monuments and sculptures.

But the work of English Heritage is not limited to the preservation of existing works already established as part of the country's historic collection. The Jerwood Sculpture Park at Witley Court is due to open in the spring, and will be a major showcase for work by famous sculptors such as Dame Elisabeth Frink and Lynn Chadwick as well as those established British artists who, as yet, may not be known to the wider public. Belsay Hall will see a 'Sitooteries' (summerhouses) exhibition by 12 of the country's

Above, statue of Edith Cavell, St Martins' Place, WC2. Left, Walking Man by Dame Elisabeth Frink, Witley Court. Below, Gurkha Regiment Memorial, Horseguards Ave., SW1.

most dynamic artists, designers and architects that will bring thoroughly contemporary interpretations of the traditional English summerhouse and pavilion to the grounds of the hall.

Sculpture has long been an interest and a concern here at English Heritage – see Henry Moore's works at Kenwood, *The Warriors* at Helmsley Castle, the statue of Richard III at Middleham, and the Madonna at Mount Grace Priory, to name a few – but this year also there will be an exhibition of works by Fenwick Lawson at Brinkburn Priory in Northumberland; in Yorkshire medieval sculptures will be on display at Rievaulx Abbey; Osborne House on the Isle of Wight will house an outdoor exhibition of sculpture involving fine arts students from Southampton; and the annual Children's Festival at Bolsover will take sculpture as its theme.

Commissioning new works, and encouraging the vision required to create them, will ensure that this public art form, which belongs to us all, continues to be available for all of us to enjoy.

Throughout the year 2000 a number of English Heritage properties will participate in a nationwide promotion and celebration of public art in all its forms – refer to *Heritage Today* for details as the year progresses.

Planning your visit

All opening times and admission prices in this handbook are valid from 1 April 2000 to 31 March 2001

Opening times

- Full details of opening times are shown under each property.
- Over 70 staffed properties are open **all year round.**
- Some properties may only be visited by **prior arrangement:** if so, contact details are given.
- A few properties have **keykeepers**. Please either contact them or ring the numbers shown under the properties. Every effort will be made to provide access, but we strongly recommend that you check well in advance of your visit to avoid disappointment.
- When a property is described as open at '**Any reasonable time**', please visit only during daylight hours. This is for safety reasons and also to avoid disturbance.

Thinking of visiting a site on 1 Jan 2001? Some staffed English Heritage properties will be open on 1 Jan 2001, however, we strongly advise that you ring the individual property beforehand to check.

Admission charges

- Admission to all properties is free to members unless otherwise stated. Most special events are also free to members.
- For non-members, charges vary from site to site. There are three

levels: Adult/Concession/ Children under 16. Throughout the Handbook these are shown as follows: **£2.50/£1.90/£1.30.**

- Concessions are available for senior citizens, unemployed people on production of UB40 and students on production of student union card.
- Children under five are admitted free.
- The Family tickets available at some of our major properties are a great money saver for a family day out.
- Disabled visitors (see p. 11). Each entry will show you the following information to help you make the most of your visit:

Open: opening times, including whether closed for lunch.

Entry: admission charges.

Site tel no: given in bold type.

Access: how to get there by car followed by the OS reference.

Remember to bring your membership card along, otherwise the normal admission charge will apply. We regret that no refunds can be made.

Our new Customer Services telephone number is 01793 414 910

Bus/Train: public transport details and finally, the symbols showing **facilities** available on site such as:
P (parking) 🍴 (refreshments) 👶 (baby changing facilities)

The Big Number changeover day

New area codes and eight-figure local telephone numbers were introduced this year for Cardiff, Coventry, London, Portsmouth, Southampton and Northern Ireland. After 22 April 2000 only the new codes will operate. For details ring a free BT helpline on 0800 731 0202.

Other historic attractions

As well as giving you free entry to our own properties, becoming a member of English Heritage allows you to enjoy half- or reduced-price admission to numerous other historic attractions throughout Britain. See page 243 for further details.

Welcome to visitors on bicycles

More and more people are travelling to our properties by bicycle. To find out more about which routes are convenient for our sites, call Sustrans on 0117 929 0888 or visit their website at **www.sustrans.org.uk**

Some questions and answers

How do I get there?
- Road and public transport details are shown under each entry.
- We are grateful to Barry S. Doe for providing the public transport information once again. Please call him with any comments on 01202 528707.

Can anyone come?
- We welcome families with children of all ages. However, inside some of our grander properties we regret that babies cannot be carried in back carriers (it increases the risk of damage to house contents). Alternative baby carriers are provided free of charge.

How about a picture?
- Non-commercial photography is welcomed in the grounds of all our properties. For conservation reasons, photography is not permitted inside certain properties. Ask on arrival.

May I smoke?
- Smoking is not permitted inside any of the properties.

Where's the toilet please?
- Some of our more remote properties, or those where the historic fabric of the property is sensitive, do not have toilets. Custodians will be happy to direct visitors to the nearest conveniences.

Can I bring my dog?
- We aim to welcome dogs at as many properties as possible. Symbols are shown under each entry. We would be grateful if dog owners would clear up any mess their dogs make. Some sites are provided with bins for the purpose. Guide- and hearing-dogs are welcome at all our properties.

Should I ring first?
- Unforeseen closures of our properties are extremely rare. However, to avoid possible disappointment we do advise that you check by ringing the site before your visit.

What about group discounts?
- Discounts of 15% are available at most properties for groups of 11 or more. If you are a group organiser or a tour operator, call Customer Services on 01793 414 910 for a free copy of our *Group Visits Guide*.
- Student and school groups are admitted free to properties provided they book in advance. For further information on this and our other educational services, please call 01793 414 910 Our *Windows on the Past* teachers' membership scheme offers many valuable benefits including free admission for up to four teachers – call Customer Services for further details on 01793 414 910.

Make the most of your visits

Guides and tours
- *Souvenir Guidebooks* 🖽 are on sale at almost all the properties where an entrance fee is charged or through our postal sales service on 01536 533500.

- From April to October 2000, we host a programme of *Special Events*, most of which are especially suitable for children (see page 14).

the help of reconstruction drawings or interactive displays.
- Other properties host temporary exhibitions of paintings and sculptures.

- *Personal stereo guides* 🎧 are available this year at 47 of our sites.
- *Interactive audio tours* allow you to control the information you hear as you move around. At some sites, we regret the audio tour is not available on days when special events are being held.

Early learners
- Many of our sites have special features, exhibitions or educational facilities 🇪. Look out for properties with *free children's activity sheets*.
- Baby changing facilities 🖼 may also be available.

Shops
- Many properties have shops 🖽 offering an attractive range of souvenirs, gifts and books 🖽. And if all that makes you hungry…
- Refreshments are available at many properties. Our restaurants 🍴 or tearooms ☕ are often located within the historic buildings themselves. Visitors are also welcome to picnic ⛱ in the grounds of many sites.

Displays and exhibitions
- At most properties, display panels explain how the property appeared in the past, often with

A special welcome to visitors from overseas
- Visitors from overseas can gain unlimited free access to English Heritage properties for one week or two, with our *Overseas Visitor Pass*. It's great value, with prices from as little as £12.50 for an adult for the whole week. Family and two adult passes are also available. Call Customer Services on 01793 414 910.

Access for all!

**A warm welcome to visitors
with disabilities**

We at English Heritage are eager to
ensure that our historic attractions
are accessible to everyone who
wishes to enjoy them. We therefore
aim to make our properties open to
people with disabilities of all kinds
wherever possible. Look for the ♿
symbol, indicating that much of the
property is easily accessible.

A *Guide for Visitors with
Disabilities* is available. For a free
copy call Customer Services on
01793 414 910 or send us an email at
members@english-heritage.org.uk
It is also available in large print
versions, tape or disk, and Braille.

For anyone with access to
the World Wide Web, the guide is
also available on our website at
www.english-heritage.org.uk.

The guide highlights features
ranging from perfumed gardens
to elaborate stone carvings.
We have tried to provide as honest
an assessment of services and
facilities as possible. This includes
hazard warnings of such obstacles
as steep steps, slippery car parks
on rainy days and uneven ground.
The guide also informs visitors
with disabilities where it is
advisable to take a companion.
**Admission is free for the
assisting companion of a
visitor with disabilities.**

at many properties are personal-
stereo guided tours for wheelchair
users or visitors with a visual
impairment. At some, there are
personal-stereo tours in basic
language for visitors with learning
difficulties.

Staff will be pleased to assist
visitors with special needs.
We recommend you contact
the property in advance so that
preparations can be made to
ensure you have a rewarding visit.

If you have any comments,
or suggestions following a visit to
one of our sites, we would like to
hear from you. Please call us on
01793 414 910.

Women in England's heritage

It is indisputable that history tends to have been written by men from a male viewpoint – perhaps understandable given the overwhelming influence of traditionally male pursuits like politics and war on the conduct of affairs. But the other side of the coin is that the crucial impact of half the human race on the broad brush of history has frequently been overlooked.

Some of the obvious examples stand out head and shoulders above many of their male contemporaries – queens like Elizabeth I and Victoria, for instance, both formidable figures under whose leadership Britain thrived.

Victoria, who reigned for nearly 64 years, became an icon and symbol of her age. In her role as queen, she demonstrated shrewdness, a firmness of will and an innate political flair but these qualities were combined with a fierce loyalty and an abiding devotion toward her children and her husband (to whom, incidentally, *she* made the proposal of marriage).

Elizabeth I, likewise a resolute and courageous monarch, was regarded as something of an oddity for choosing to remain unmarried. She was only too aware, however, that her flouting of convention in this way strengthened her position; to be assured of the continued attentions of many distinguished and powerful men was an invaluable tool. She once described herself as having the body of a weak and feeble woman but 'the heart and stomach of a king'.

Women who asserted their independence were regarded as hard and vicious, a reputation attributed for many centuries after her death to the formidable Bess of Hardwick. Accumulating vast wealth as a result of her four marriages, she set about refurbishing Hardwick Old Hall before moving on to the New Hall she was building next door, which was completed in the 1590s. Mistress not only of Hardwick but also of Chatsworth, Bess left her legacy in the mighty dynasty she founded.

But it is not only those women with great wealth or those in positions of power who are worthy of note. There were many others

Left, Whitby Abbey. Below, Virginia Courtauld. Below left, Emma Darwin. Opposite page top, Queen Elizabeth I and bottom, Queen Victoria.

Left, Whitby Abbey. Below, Virginia Courtauld. Below left, Emma Darwin. Opposite page top, Queen Elizabeth I and bottom, Queen Victoria.

whose place in history might seem less obviously important but who defied the traditions of their time and, nevertheless, made their mark. Those once exclusively male professions, such as medicine, may have remained impenetrable to women were it not for the likes of Elizabeth Garrett Anderson. Resolute in her defiance of the male medical establishment, her perserverance led her, in the 19th century, to become the first woman formally to qualify as a doctor.

Earlier in history, the chance of a powerful and rewarding 'career' could sometimes be open to women through the church. Abbess Hilda of Whitby was someone who recognised the influence she might have on the institution which, after all, underpinned society. She was widely revered for her devotion and learning, so much so that her abbey was the venue for the Synod of Whitby in AD664, called to settle several matters of dispute between the two forms of Christianity in the country.

For some women in history it was in adversity that their truly formidable qualities were given the chance to shine. Take Lady Blanche Arundell, known for her spirited defence of Old Wardour Castle during the Civil War. At 60 years of age, and with only a few men at her command, she withstood 1300 rebels for several days, more than proving her heroism and loyalty.

In more recent times, Emma Darwin, wife of Charles, proved herself a veritable 'power behind the throne'. Her husband consulted her on all his work before circulating it more widely, though, less harmoniously,

they are said to have argued over the wallpaper at Down House.

Finally there are those who are best remembered for a certain eccentricity of character – although they exerted a positive influence, all the same. Mad Madge of Newcastle made known her objections to the inferior lot of women in her society at the cost of being treated with great suspicion and accused of dangerous peculiarity.

In the 1930s, Virginia Courtauld and her husband, Stephen, built a magnificent Art Deco home within the remains of the medieval palace at Eltham. Virginia's tatooed ankle and pampered pet lemur, Mah-Jongg, were a celebration and assertion of her individuality. Just one of the many inspiring women who have populated English Heritage sites.

Let us entertain you!

Millennium events to enjoy

To mark the Millennium our events programme is even bigger and better, with over 1,000 top quality re-enactments, displays, family entertainments, and much more running from April to October. The highlight of the year is *History in Action 2000* at Kirby Hall on 12-13 August, the biggest international multi-period historical festival in the world. Featuring more than 100 displays every day on an enlarged site, this top event cannot be missed! Kirby Hall also hosts a major 'civil war battle spectacular' on 28-29 May, with specially constructed earthworks in an outstanding setting – perhaps one of the most exciting and photogenic shows of the year.

Throughout July and August visitors can enjoy a festival of mini events every weekend at over 25 properties around the county – ideal for keeping the family entertained.

The season kicks off with special Easter and St George's Day events, including the St George's Festival at Wrest Park, and ends with a spectacular re-enactment of the Battle of Hastings. Full details of these and over 700 other events taking place this year – nearly all of them free to English

... and some wonderful weekend concerts

Picnic in the grounds of some of the most beautiful properties in the care of English Heritage and enjoy world-class performances by acclaimed orchestras, soloists and conductors.
• Kenwood Lakeside, Hampstead, Sat/Sun from 1 July to 26 August.
• Marble Hill House, Twickenham, Sat/Sun from 23 July to 20 August
• Audley End, Saffron Walden, weekends of 29–30 July and 5–6 August. For further details, please ask for the 2000 Concert Brochure

Heritage members – can be found in the *Events Diary 2000*, available at all properties or from Customer Services on 01793 414 910.

by calling the Concert Information Line on 020 8233 7435 or email **concerts@imgworld.com**, or pick up a brochure at concert venues. Members of English Heritage are entitled to a discount on concert ticket prices.

Top, Battle Abbey re-enactment with Lord Montagu. Above, Kenwood lakeside concert with fireworks. Left, medieval tournament at Beeston Castle.

Images of England
Creating an internet home for England's listed buildings

Tudor palaces and Victorian town halls, 1960s tower blocks and Norman castles, Saxon chapels and Art Deco cinemas, watermills and windmills, farms and factories, piers and pigeon lofts . . . more than 360,000 structures around England are 'listed' to protect them for future generations.

Now, a ground-breaking project, the brainchild of the National Monuments Record, the public archive of English Heritage, is capturing the diversity and richness of these treasures for the future.

Over the next three years, Images of England will be working with hundreds of volunteer photographers around the country to capture new images of these buildings. The resulting 'snapshot in time' of our built heritage at the beginning of the new Millennium will be made accessible to the widest possible audience through the internet.

Financial support for this major project is being provided by a generous grant of more than £3 million from the Heritage Lottery Fund through the Millennium Festival Fund.

When completed in 2002, the Images of England digital database will provide an unparalleled overview of the best of our built environment. Local history and heritage groups, conservation professionals, family historians, property owners, and above all the education sector will have an invaluable new resource at their fingertips. The Images of England website will offer contemporary photographic records of each listed building, linked to accompanying text, with the potential to study designs and materials and compare examples throughout the country. All at the click of a mouse!

The photographers taking part in this project are the key element in tackling the project's mammoth target of 360,000 images. When complete, the photographic record created by the Images of England project will stand as a testament to the skills and determination of the volunteers from all over England who are taking part.

For more information please visit the Images of England website at **www.imagesofengland.org.uk**

Top left, Inn sign, White Horse Inn, Tattingstone, Suffolk. Grade II listed carved wooden figure of a white horse erected in the 18th century.
Above, New Tyne Bridge, Newcastle upon Tyne, Grade II listed, the largest single-span steel arch bridge in Britain at the time of its construction (1925-8).
Below, Belle Tout lighthouse, built 1831, Beachy Head, Sussex, Grade II listed.

English Heritage grants schemes

The work English Heritage does to protect and conserve our architectural and archaeological heritage, and to educate and inform the public about it, is varied and diverse.

Buildings and monuments in our care range from major World Heritage Sites such as Stonehenge and Hadrian's Wall to smaller, less well-known but still fascinating and significant prehistoric sites,

medieval abbeys and industrial buildings.

But this is the tip of the iceberg. Over half the work we do, and the money we spend, goes towards the identification and conservation of

buildings and monuments not in our direct care. We are the custodians of the statutory lists of listed buildings, scheduled monuments and conservation areas in England, and our specialists are constantly involved in updating, revising and adding to those lists. We give over £36 million a year in repair grants to listed buildings, scheduled monuments, conservation areas, churches and cathedrals. We also devote about £10 million a year to archaeology.

A great deal of our conservation work in the last few years has been directed towards identifying historic buildings and monuments at risk from neglect and decay.

For the last two years we have produced a Register of Buildings at Risk, which has identified and published details of all Grade I and II* listed buildings and above – ground scheduled monuments known to be at risk or vulnerable.

In order to help owners of such buildings and monuments to repair and maintain them, we recently announced our intention to offer over £40 million in grant aid over the next three years to buildings at risk and Grade I and II* historic parks and gardens. Priorities will be:

- Buildings and monuments on, or eligible for inclusion in, our Register of Buildings at Risk.
- Grade I and II* parks and gardens included in our Register of Historic Parks and Gardens.
- Privately-owned houses which have, or once had, associated land and which have been in the same family ownership for 30 years.
- Projects which demonstrate significant social or economic regeneration benefits.

A sample of the amazing variety of skills necessary to care for our properties. Above, work on the fireplace in the library of Danson House, Bexley. Below, laying of the roof tiles, again at Danson House. Below left, work on the head of the newly gilded statue of Prince Albert, Albert Memorial, London.

Our commitment to regeneration is indicated by our new (summer 1999) Heritage Economic Regeneration Scheme (HERS). Grants within this scheme are aimed particularly at repair work which will enhance the character of conservation areas in the most deprived urban and rural parts of the country. The purpose is

Opposite page. An English Heritage grant was offered in July 1998 to Seaton Delaval Hall, Northumberland. Top, the rose garden in summer; bottom, view of the formal garden, both Seaton Delaval Hall.

English Heritage grants schemes

Before (above), and after conservation (right): The Moot, Downton, Wiltshire.

to support and encourage local employment, new housing and inward investment.

In April 1999 we relaunched our joint scheme with the Heritage Lottery Fund for churches and other places of worship. Grant aid here will be focused on roof work, including towers, spires and associated masonry repairs where historic fabric is at risk.

These are only some of the grant schemes we operate, both through our central London organisation and, mainly now, through our nine Regional Offices.

Details of addresses and telephone numbers of these offices are given on the inside back cover.
You are welcome to contact any of our Regional Offices to discuss particular conservation issues within that region.

Better still – demonstrate your commitment to supporting and sharing our work on the conservation of all aspects of our historic environment by becoming a member of English Heritage.

18

Membership

English Heritage membership

The valuable income from members' subscriptions helps fund much of the vital conservation work you will find described and illustrated within these pages. This ranges from the restoration of well-loved landmarks to supporting regeneration work in deprived areas and the painstaking cleaning and conservation of valuable historic artefacts.

Membership also means that you are entitled to many exciting benefits including:

· Free admission to over 400 historic attractions in the care of English Heritage.
· *Heritage Today*, members' quarterly magazine.
· Free or reduced-price entry to over 600 special events.
· Half-price admission to historic sites in Scotland and Wales.
· Discounts on tickets for our open-air concerts.
· The chance to enjoy a wide variety of members' activities including tours, breaks and cruises.
· A brand new, fully updated Handbook every spring.

Membership is excellent value for money at £28 for an adult and only £49.50 for a family, with many other categories to choose from.

Help us conserve more of England's heritage without costing you a penny

Please take advantage of our direct debit facility: it is convenient for you and will save us time and money on administration. At the same time you could take out a Deed of Covenant which allows us to claim back the tax you have already paid in your membership fee. Also, why not consider applying for the English Heritage Visa Card?

For further details on how to become a member, or any other information mentioned on this page please call **01793 414 910** or write to:

English Heritage Membership Department, PO Box 570, Swindon SN2 2YR
or send an email to:
members@english-heritage.org.uk

Give a present of our past

Searching for that special present? Then choose a gift of English Heritage Membership – a thoughtful and original present that lasts all year but can be given at any time of the year.

It comes in a stylish presentation pack that includes this Handbook, a map and a greeting card with a token that the recipient can use to start their membership whenever they choose.

If you are already a member then you'll know what a great gift this will make!

To order your gift membership simply call 01793 414 910.

London

Left, Lady Dorothy Cary, by William Larkin, one of the stunning
Jacobean paintings belonging to the magnificent Suffolk
Collection that can be seen at Ranger's House; in the background,
the south front of Kenwood House; right, James Stuart, Duke of
Richmond and Lennox, by Van Dyck, a painting from The Iveagh
Bequest, Kenwood House; far right, a bronze cast copy of
The Sentry by Jagger Charles Sargeant, bought by Stephen
Courtauld in 1924. It can be seen in the Library at Eltham Palace.

Kenwood

Chapter House

Albert
Memorial

Chiswick
House

Jewel
Tower

Ranger's House

Marble Hill
House

Eltham Palace

Down House

Albert Memorial

Kensington, London (p. 233, 6)
George Gilbert Scott conceived his Memorial to Queen Victoria's husband, Prince Albert the Prince Consort, as a gigantic bejewelled shrine protecting the gilt bronze sculpture of the Prince. Scott's vision far outstripped the technology of the time and by the 1990s the various materials – cast iron, lead, bronze, glass, mosaics and stone – were suffering severe structural problems. In 1994 English Heritage embarked upon one if its most ambitious conservation projects ever – to strip the Memorial back to its cast-iron core, conserve every element, and rebuild it. The restoration was completed a year ahead of schedule and the Memorial was reopened by Her Majesty the Queen on 21 October 1998.

Damage from World War II was also repaired, and the opportunity was taken to replace some of the gilding removed during World War I – including that on John Foley's stunning sculpture of the Prince which gives full meaning once again to Scott's vision.

The Albert Memorial is managed by The Royal Parks Agency.

Guided tours behind the railings: all year at 2pm and 3pm on Sun. Each tour lasts 45 to 50 mins. Group bookings at other times by prior arrangement. To book a tour please call 020 7495 0916 (10am–4pm).

Entry Adults: £3 Children/concs and English Heritage members on presentation of their card: £2.50.

Bus Frequent from surrounding areas. Tel 020 7222 1234.

Train Victoria 1½ m.

Tube South Kensington ½ m.

✛ Chapter House, Pyx Chamber
🕮 and Abbey Museum

Westminster Abbey, London (p. 233, 6м)

The Chapter House, built by the royal masons around 1250, contains some of the finest medieval wall paintings and sculpture to be seen. The octagonal building still has its original floor of glazed tiles. The 11th-century Pyx Chamber houses Abbey treasures and the Abbey museum medieval royal effigies.

Open 1 April–30 Sep: 9.30am–5pm daily. 1–31 Oct: 10m–5pm daily.

Westminster Abbey's Chapter House.

1 Nov–31 Mar 2001: 10am–4pm daily. Closed 24–26 Dec and 1 Jan 2001. Pyx Chamber: 10.30am–4pm all year. May be closed at short notice on state occasions.

Entry £2.50/£1.90/£1.30

Tel 020 7222 5897

Access Approach either through the Abbey or through Dean's Yard and the cloister.

Bus Tel 020 7222 1234.

Train Victoria and Charing Cross both ¾ m, Waterloo 1m.

Tube Westminster ¼ m; St James's Park ¼ m. 🅿 🎧 *small charge* 📷 🚫

Chiswick House

Chiswick, London (p. 232, 5M)

Surrounded by beautiful gardens, close to the centre of London, lies one of England's finest Palladian villas. It was designed by the third Earl of Burlington, a great promoter of the Palladian style first pioneered in England by Inigo Jones. Lord Burlington sought to create the kind of house and garden found in ancient Rome, and employed William Kent to design sumptuous interiors to contrast with the pure exterior. Admire the Blue Velvet Room, with its fabulous gilding, and the octagonal domed Saloon lit from the drum by windows derived from the Roman baths of Diocletian.

Enjoy the house's lavish interiors before stepping outside into the classical gardens – a perfect complement to the house itself.

An exhibition and video tell the story of the house, grounds and Lord Burlington.

The Servant, starring James Fox, was filmed here.

English Heritage Hospitality
Chiswick House is available for exclusive corporate and private events. Call the Hospitality Manager on 020 8742 1978. Please note that the house often holds wedding receptions from 3.30pm on Sat. which may mean that it is extra busy at this time.

Open 1 April–30 Sep: 10am–6pm daily. 1–28 Oct: 10am–5pm daily. 29–31 Oct: 10am–4.30pm daily. 1 Nov–31 March 2001: 10am–4pm Wed–Sun. Closed 24–26 Dec and 1–16 Jan 2001.

Entry £3.30/£2.50/£1.70.
Tel 020 8995 0508
Access Burlington Lane, W4.
Local Tourist Information
Tel 020 8572 8279.
Bus LT 190 Hammersmith–Richmond; E3 Greenford–Chiswick. Tel 020 7222 1234.
Train Chiswick ½m (trains every 30 mins from Waterloo).
Tube Turnham Green ¾m.
P (off westbound A4)
(access to both floors) (also available for the visually impaired, those with learning difficulties, and in French and German)
(Burlington Café, open daily in summer, weekends only in winter. Not managed by English Heritage.)
(restricted areas)

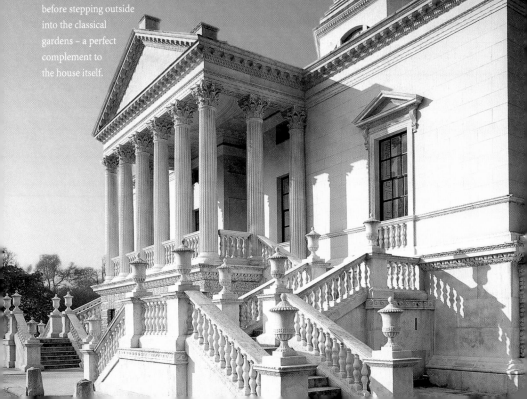

⊙ Coombe Conduit

Kingston-Upon-Thames, London (p. 232, 5M)
Two small buildings (one now a ruin), connected by an underground passage, which supplied water to Hampton Court Palace.

Open every 2nd Sunday, April–Sep.
Entry Free. (Property managed by the Kingston Society.)
Bus Frequent from surrounding areas. Tel 020 7222 1234.
Train Kingston-upon-Thames ¼ m.

*Below, Charles Darwin by an unknown artist. Below left, the grand piano in the Drawing Room, Down House.
Bottom, Jewel Tower and a recontruction painting of Jewel Tower and Westminster in the background.*

⊙ Danson House

Bexley, London (p. 233, 5M)
Built in 1762-7 for a city merchant, this Palladian-style house designed by Sir Robert Taylor has undergone essential conservation work to the fabric and the interiors of the four principal rooms. Further conservation work is due to take place in 2000.

For more information contact Customer Services on 01793 414910.

⊙ Down House:
✽ Home of Charles Darwin

Downe, Greater London (p. 233, 5N)
See p. 26-27 for full details.

⊙ Eltham Palace
✽

Eltham, London (p. 232, 5M)
See p 28-31 for full details.

⊙ Jewel Tower

Westminster, London (p. 233, 5M)
One of two surviving buildings of

the original Palace of Westminster, the Jewel Tower was built c.1365 to house the treasures of Edward III. The exhibition, 'Parliament Past and Present', shows how Parliament works and a touch-screen computer gives a virtual tour of both Houses of Parliament.

Open 1 Apr–30 Sep: 10am–6pm daily. 1–31 Oct: 10am–5pm daily. 1 Nov–31 Mar 2001: 10am– 4pm daily. Closed 24–26 Dec and 1 Jan 2001.
Entry £1.50/£1.10/80p
Tel 020 7222 2219
Access Opposite S end of Houses of Parliament (Victoria Tower).
Bus Frequent from surrounding areas. Tel 020 7222 1234.
Train Charing Cross ¾ m, Victoria and Waterloo, both 1m.
Tube Westminster ¼ m.

Kenwood

Hampstead, London (p. 232, 6M)
See p. 32-4 for full details.

*Far right, Portrait of the Artist
(c. 1663), by Rembrandt, which can
be seen at Kenwood House. Right,
engravings of some of Kenwood's
decoration. Bottom, left to right,
Marble Hill House, the Great Room,
and a painting of Henrietta Howard.*

London Wall

Tower Hill, London (p. 233, 6M)
The best-preserved piece of the
Roman Wall which formed part of
the eastern defences of London.

Open Any reasonable time.
Entry Free.
Access Near Tower Hill
underground station, EC3.

Bus Frequent from surrounding
areas. Tel 020 7222 1234.
Train Fenchurch Street ¼m.
Tube Tower Hill, adjacent.

Marble Hill House

Twickenham, London (p. 232, 5M)
A magnificent Thames-side
Palladian villa built 1724-29 for
Henrietta Howard, Countess
of Suffolk, mistress of King George
II, set in 66 acres of parkland.
The Great Room has lavish gilded
decoration and architectural
paintings by Panini. The house
contains an important collection
of early Georgian furniture and
paintings, and the Lazenby Bequest
Chinoiserie collection. There is
a display on the ground floor with
an introductory film about the
house, grounds, and the life and
times of Henrietta Howard.

Longitude, starring Jeremy
Irons, was filmed here in 1999.
• Free Children's Activity Sheet
  available.
• Pre-booked group tours available.
Open 1 April-30 Sep: 10am-6pm
daily. 1-31 Oct: 10am-5pm daily.
1 Nov-31 March 2001: 10am-4pm
Wed-Sun. Closed 24-26 Dec and
1-16 Jan 2001.
Entry £3.30/£2.50/£1.70.
Tel 020 8892 5115
Access Richmond Road,
Twickenham.

Bus Frequent from surrounding
areas. Tel 020 7222 1234.
Train St Margarets ¼m.
Tube Richmond 1m.
P (at Richmond end of Marble
Hill Park) (exterior & ground
floor only; toilets) (Coach
House Cafe, open March-Oct,
but closed Mon-Tue in March)
(restricted areas)

Down House: home of Charles Darwin

Charles Darwin was one of the most influential scientists of modern times. It was from his study at Down House that he worked on the scientific theories that first scandalized and then revolutionized the Victorian world, culminating in the publication of one of the most significant books of recent centuries, *On the Origin of Species by means of Natural Selection*, in 1859.

Darwin returned to Britain from his epic voyage on HMS *Beagle* around South America in 1836. He took up residence in London, but following his marriage to his cousin, Emma Wedgwood, and the first signs of his own poor health, he decided in 1842 to move into the peace and open space of the country.

At first he thought Down House was 'oldish and ugly' but it soon became apparent that the move to Kent offered him the freeedom and space to enjoy family life and to correlate the discoveries from which he formed his revolutionary theory of evolution.

Originally a farmhouse, the main structure was built in the late 18th century. The principal asset of the house is that it remains much as it was when Darwin lived there. On the ground floor, the Drawing Room, the Dining Room and the Study have been furnished and decorated to reflect the domestic life of the family. The Study –the centre of his life – contains his writing desk and chair, along with parts of the collection of 5,000 objects connected with his work. It also contains reminders of the vilification Darwin underwent when his theories were published. Going against the conceptions of the age, both scientific and religious, Darwin bore the brunt of the outrage with equanimity. He himself kept *Punch* cartoons that derided his theories and the cruellest caricatures from *Vanity Fair*.

Darwin's happiest years were spent at Down House. It was very much a family home as well as being the centre of his intellectual world. The landscape and gardens provided the focus for much of the research underpinning

Darwin's theories and writing, and they were a large part of family life too. Thus it is with a view to understanding both the life *and* work of Darwin that restoration is in progress to recreate the appearance and atmosphere of the grounds as they would have been towards the end of his life. The 'sand-walk' or 'thinking path' which Darwin walked daily can still be followed, and the greenhouses where he made his plant studies – especially on orchids and carnivorous plants – can also be viewed. The flower garden originally designed by Darwin's wife is another highlight of the restoration project, the beds planted to recreate as closely as possible Emma's designs.

With an interactive exhibition on the first floor capturing the essence of Darwin's life and work, – the huge original bound manuscript of the journal from his five-year voyage on HMS *Beagle* is on display there – Down House is a tribute to the memory and influence of this country's best-known scientist: a man who once modestly said, 'I have dabbled in several branches of natural history...'

★ Winner of 1999 London Tourism Board for Best Small Visitor Attraction of the Year award.

★ England for Excellence awards 1999, Silver.

Open 1 April–30 Sep: 10am–6pm Wed–Sun. 1–31 Oct: 10am–5pm Wed–Sun. 1 Nov–23 Dec: 10am–4pm Wed–Sun.
Closed 24 Dec–6 Feb 2001.
7 Feb–31 March 2001: 10am–4pm Wed–Sun. Open Bank Holidays.
Entry £5.50/£4.10/£2.80.
• **Visitors must pre-book from 12 July until 10 Sep unless travelling by public transport. Please call the house.**
• **Groups over 11 must pre-book at all times.**
Tel 01689 859119
Access In Luxted Road, Downe, off A21 near Biggin Hill. Limited parking for visitors is provided at the House throughout the open season. As Downe is a small village with limited capacity for traffic,

English Heritage encourages visitors to travel by public transport.
Bus LT 146 from ⇌ Bromley North and South; R2 from ⇌ Orpington. There is no Sunday service. Tel 020 7222 1234.
Train Orpington 3½ m.
🚻 🅿 📷 🖨 🎧 (available in French, German, Japanese and for those with sight or hearing impairments) 📹 ♿ (throughout) 🚫

Opposite page, top left, Charles Darwin in old age; left, the gardens and the greenhouse.
This page, top left, Darwin's 'Privy Corner', his study; above, the Dining Room. Above left, the interactive exhibition on the first floor.

Eltham Palace

Just 200 yards from Eltham's High Street, visitors will discover the remains of one of England's largest but least known medieval royal palaces which stands adjacent to a spectacular 1930s house, a showpiece of contemporary design.

Commissioned by Stephen and Virginia Courtauld and completed in 1936, the house stands as a testament to the couple's choice of interior design and reflects their leisure-filled lifestyle. Influenced by French Art Deco with echoes of Cunard ocean liner style, the rooms reflect the work of various architects and designers employed by the Courtaulds to create contemporary interiors.

Access to the Dining Room is through spectacular black and silver doors featuring animals and birds drawn from life at London Zoo. Even more exotic is Virginia Courtauld's vaulted bathroom lined with onyx and gold mosaic, complete with gold-plated bath taps and a statue of the goddess Psyche.

The combination of classical statuary and modern design was the height of Parisian vogue at the time. A measure of the Courtaulds' flamboyant nature is reflected in the sleeping quarters allocated to their pet ring-tailed lemur, Mah-Jongg, whose centrally heated cage is still on view in the house. Modern technology was employed to enhance the comfort and efficiency of the house: it was wired throughout for electricity which powered a central vacuum cleaner and loudspeakers to broadcast records on the ground floor. The main rooms were also linked by an internal telephone system.

The Courtaulds left in 1944 to escape the heavy bombing of South East London. Most of their collection of works of art and furniture is no longer in the house, but replica 1930s furniture has been carefully replicated in the main rooms, including the Entrance Hall, which contains a copy of the circular carpet specifically designed for the room by Marion Dorn. Missing wood veneer has been replaced, surfaces repainted to match the Courtauld paint schemes and appropriate soft furnishings introduced, while a restoration programme on the gardens is in progress in order to recapture the

'The new design and planting have been conceived to enhance some of the stunning features, such as the moat wall...' – Isabelle Van Groeningen, designer for Eltham Palace South Moat garden. Opposite page, the bridge over the South Moat.
This page, above, a sculpture relief overlooking the terrace. Below, the statuary bust of Virginia Courtauld, carved by F. Lovatelli in 1923. Left, the pergola.

luxurious appearance of the palace and its surroundings in the 1930s.

Visitors are invited to leave the modernity of the Courtauld house and enter the heart of the medieval palace. The Great Hall, although incorporated into the 1930s house, was built for Edward IV in the 1470s as a dining hall for the court. The hall measures an impressive 100 feet in length and when it was built it was the largest of its kind, with the exception of Westminster Hall, built in the 11th century.

In the 1500s, extensive work was undertaken at the palace for Henry VIII, including the building of new king's lodgings and a new chapel. The construction of a network of underground sewers was commissioned at this time and can still be seen.

Henry VIII was the last monarch to spend substantial amounts of time at Eltham, and after the Civil War the palace fell into disrepair and was sold. Many of the buildings were dismantled and the site became a farm. The Great Hall was used as a barn and its picturesque decay was recorded by Girtin, Turner and other artists

at the end of the 18th century. When, in 1827, George IV's architect announced plans to dismantle the roof of the Great Hall, interest in Eltham reached a peak and a successful preservation campaign was launched. The Great Hall was restored and became the Courtaulds' grand music room in the 1930s.

The moated Palace is set in beautiful parkland with expansive views over London and an exciting plantsman's garden. The amalgam

of 20th-century and medieval at Eltham Palace is a feature which will be maintained in the restoration programme planned for the South Moat garden.

As part of the Contemporary Heritage Gardens scheme launched in 1999 by English Heritage, whereby ten contemporary gardens will be created in historic settings over the next five years, three areas of the South Moat will be developed in the spirit of the Courtaulds' 1930s plantsman's garden. These areas are the 100-yard-long border, the White Wood and the Theatre lawn. Based on Art Deco principles to reflect the splendid interiors of the house, working with large bold groups and using contrasting colours, the planting design will bring vibrancy from Spring to Autumn to these parts of Eltham's wonderful gardens.

Open 1 April–30 Sep: 10am–6pm Wed–Fri & Sun. 1–31 Oct: 10am–5pm Wed–Fri & Sun. 1 Nov–31 March 2001: 10am–4pm Wed–Fri & Sun. Open Bank Holidays throughout the year. Closed 24–26 Dec and 1 Jan 2001. Pre-booked group tours available if booked at least 2 weeks in advance.

Opposite page, top, the Entrance Hall with the recreated Engströmer furniture and Dorn carpet. Below, Virginia Courtauld's bathroom, and bottom, a detail of a statue of Hospitality at the entrance.
This page, below and left, the Dining Room; middle picture, Virginia Courtauld's bedroom, and bottom, the roof of the Great Hall.

£5.90/£4.40/£3.
Gardens only: £3.50, £2.60, £1.80.
Tel 020 8294 2548
English Heritage Hospitality:
Eltham Palace is available for exclusive corporate and private events. Call the Hospitality Manager on 020 8294 2577.
Access Junction 3 on the M25, then A20 to Eltham, off Court Rd, SE9.
Bus Frequent from surrounding areas. Tel 020 7222 1234.
Train Eltham ½ m.
🚻 P (signed off Court Rd) 🚻🚻🚻
🎧 (also available in French and German)♿ (P ♿ via Court Yard Entrance) 🖼🍴

Kenwood

In splendid grounds beside Hampstead Heath, Kenwood, an outstanding neoclassical house, contains one of the most important collections of paintings ever given to the nation, with works by Rembrandt, Vermeer, Turner, Gainsborough and Reynolds. The house was re-modelled by Robert Adam between 1764 and 1773, when he transformed the original brick house into a majestic villa for the great judge, Lord Mansfield. Adam's richly decorated library is one of his masterpieces and English Heritage has restored his original colour scheme in the Entrance Hall. Later Earls of Mansfield redesigned the parkland and Kenwood remained in the family until 1922. When developers attempted to buy the estate, the house and grounds were saved for the public by the brewing magnate, the first Earl of Iveagh. In 1928, when he died, he bequeathed the Kenwood Estate and part of his collection of pictures to the nation. From then the house became better known as an art gallery.

Major developments at Kenwood

In order to present its fine collection of paintings and splendid interiors to their best advantage, the east and west wings of Kenwood House have been re-presented for the year 2000, with new decoration, controlled heating, re-designed lighting, and new seating for visitors. The Dining Room features deep red velvet and matching curtains in the style of the late 1820s. The furniture, which includes a pair of sideboards and two neoclassical pedestals originally made for the room provide the perfect surroundings for the masterpieces which have been re-hung there - amongst them Rembrandt's *Self Portrait* and Vermeer's *Guitar Player*. In the Dining Room Lobby, or Marble Hall as it is otherwise known, a painted floor-cloth has been created echoing the original marble floor that gave the room its name. The Music Room, originally created for the Countess of

Mansfield, has also been redesigned to complement the portraits of Georgian ladies now hanging there. The curtains have been replaced with green silk and the suite of seat furniture made for Moor Park by Robert Adams has been newly upholstered to match.

Above left , Robert Adam (1728–92) by James Tassie; above, the mirrored recesses in the Library introduce a more human scale to the grand classical saloon.
Opposite page, top left, Mary, Countess Howe by Thomas Gainsborough; top right, the Library or 'Great Room'.

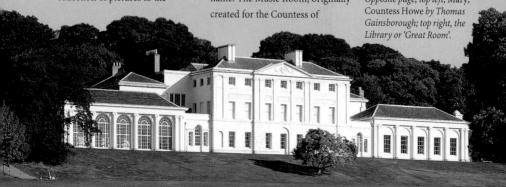

Eat, Drink and be Merry, The British at Table, 1600-2000

A forthcoming special event at Kenwood is the spectacular exhibition *Eat, Drink and be Merry, The British at Table, 1600-2000*. It will celebrate the changing attitudes to eating and drinking in Britain from the reign of Elizabeth I to that of Elizabeth II. Accompanied by paintings, prints and decorative arts borrowed from public and private collections throughout Britain, a series of set-piece displays will be created using period tableware and food. From the baroque splendour of a Royal Feast to the intimacy of a Nursery Tea of the 1930s, the table settings will reveal how the main meals of the day have developed over the past four centuries. Throughout the exhibition period the Brew House Café will be serving historic food to give you a chance to sample the mouthwatering delicacies which can be seen in the exhibition.

Eat, Drink and Be Merry, *paintings and displays from the exhibition: Above,* The Table, St Fagan's Castle, *1905 by Sir John Lavery. Left, see the Duke of Newcastle's Feast, a splendid display prepared for the duke in 1698.*

🎞 *Notting Hill* with Hugh Grant and Julia Roberts; Jane Austen's *Mansfield Park*.
• Pre-booked group tour
• Enjoy the summer concerts at the Kenwood Lakeside.

Mansion Cottage Visitor Information Centre

Information about the history, wildlife and importance of the Kenwood estate is available at the Mansion Cottage Visitor Information Centre . As well as informing visitors about specific projects and work in progress, the Centre produces a *What to look for at Kenwood* display each month, highlighting areas of special interest to the visitor. Whilst it is the aim of the Centre to open for at least five hours per day on six days each week, this is dependent on securing sufficient volunteer support.
Tel **020 7973 3893** for more details.
• Visit Lord Iveagh's coach and the gypsy caravan on summer Sunday afternoons.

• **Eat Drink and Be Merry, the British at Table 1600–2000** has been organised in association with York Fairfax House and Norfolk Museum Services
London: 27 June–24 Sep 2000
York: 26 Feb–24 Sep 2000
Norwich: 14 Oct–7 Jan 2001
Entry £3.50/£2.50.
For English Heritage members: free entry at Kenwood; £1 off at York, Fairfax House and the concessional rate at Norwich Assembly House.
The exhibition has been kindly sponsored by Waitrose.

Open 1 April–30 Sep: 10am–6pm daily. 1–31 Oct: 10am–5pm daily. 1 Nov–31 Mar 2001: 10am– 4pm daily. Closed 24–25 Dec. Open 1 Jan 2001.
Entry House and grounds free (park open later). Donations welcome.
Tel 020 8348 1286
English Heritage Hospitality:
Kenwood House will be available for exclusive corporate and private events from April 2000.
Call the Hospitality Manager on 020 7973 3494.
Access Hampstead Lane, NW3.
Local Tourist Information
Tel 0891 824 8844.
Bus LT210 ⇌ Finsbury Park– Golders Green. Tel 020 7222 1234.
Train Hampstead Heath 1½ m.
Tube Archway and Golders Green, then 210 bus, or Hampstead then

20 mins walk.
🏛 P ♿ (ground floor only; toilets) ⬛E📷🔲🔲 *small charge* ♿ (restricted areas) 🍽 The Brew House Café, open all year, serves delicious home-made food throughout the day: do not miss their exceptional breakfasts (*Time Out Good Food Guide 2000*). Call 020 8348 2528 for functions.

Top, The Guitar Player, by Jan Vermeer, c. 1672, one of the great paintings from Lord Iveagh's collection on display in the house. Left, the Brew House Café.

⊕ Ranger's House

Blackheath, London (p. 233, 5M)
A handsome red brick villa built
c. 1700, on the edge of Greenwich
Park, with a splendid bow-
windowed gallery. The house is also
home to the magnificent Suffolk
Collection of paintings, including
stunning full-length Jacobean
portraits .

• Pre-booked group tours of the
  House available.

• **Greenwich Open Studios
Exhibition** (23 Mar–31 May 2000).
For more than 25 years a group of 29
Greenwich-based artists have been
opening their studios to the public.
They work in a variety of media,
including painting and
photography, textiles and sculpture,
pottery and printmaking and many
are frequent exhibitors at the Royal
Academy. To celebrate their
achievements, English Heritage will
be hosting a millennium exhibition
of their work at Ranger's House.
Reasonable prices will allow plenty
of scope for the modest collector–
and there will be something to
appeal to all tastes. Entry to
exhibition is included in house
admission.

Entry £2.80/£2.10/£1.40
Open House: 1 April–30 Sep: 10am–
6pm daily. 1–31 Oct: 10am–5pm
daily. 1 Nov–31 March 2001: 10am–
4pm Wed–Sun. Closed 24–26 Dec
and 1 Jan 2001.

Entry £2.80/£2.10/£1.40.
Note: Ranger's House may close
Summer 2000/Winter 2001 for
major refurbishment. Please call the
house before your visit.
Tel 020 8853 0035
Access Chesterfield Walk,
Blackheath, SE10.
Bus LT53 Oxford Circus–
Plumstead. Tel 020 7222 1234.
Train Blackheath or Greenwich.
Ⓟ (in Chesterfield Walk) 🚻
Ⓔ 📷 ✗

*Top left, Diana Cecil, Countess of
Oxford by William Larkin. Top
right, Richard, 3rd Earl of Dorset,
by William Larkin, 1613. Both
paintings belong to the Suffolk
Collection.
Above, Time for Tea, Herb Garden,
Greenwich Park, by Frances
Treanor and above left, ceramics by
Marilyn Williams, some of the
works exhibited by the Greenwich
Studio artists.*

⊕ Winchester Palace

Southwark, London (p.233, 6M)
The west gable end, with its unusual
round window, is the prominent
feature of the remains of the Great
Hall of this 13th-century town
house of the Bishops of Winchester,
damaged by fire in 1814.
Open Any reasonable time.
Entry Free.

Access Near Southwark Cathedral,
corner of Clink St & Storey St, SE1.
Bus Frequent from surrounding
areas. Tel 020 7222 1234.
Train/Tube London Bridge ¼ m.

London Statues

In 1999 English Heritage assumed responsibility for the maintenance of 47 statues and monuments in central London on behalf of the Department for Culture, Media and Sport. A few monuments were government-funded, but the majority, although erected by private subscription, came into government ownership following the 1854 Public Statues (Metropolis) Act requiring new statues on public land in London to be accompanied by sufficient funds to ensure maintenance in perpetuity.

Of the statues on the list royalty is well represented, from Charles I, 1633, to Edward VII, 1921.

Most statues date from the 19th and early 20th centuries, but the continuing tradition of public sculpture and its diverse subject matter are well represented by the seven statues erected in the 1990s, which include those of Viscounts Slim and Alanbrooke, and Christopher Columbus.

Not surprisingly, the statues reflect the preoccupations of their time. Many of them are associated with wars and military campaigns, from the Napoleonic wars (represented by Marble Arch, Wellington Arch, and the statue of Wellington), and the Boer War (Carabiniers of 1906 by Jones), to the numerous works relating to the two World Wars, including Lutyens' Cenotaph and Nemon's Viscount Montgomery.

Non-combatant humanitarian involvement in war is represented by two monuments to women, Florence Nightingale by A.G. Walker and nurse Edith Cavell by Frampton.

Also honoured are two British heroes of Polar exploration who both died during expeditions: Sir John Franklin by Noble and Captain Scott by Kathleen Scott, his widow.

Charles I

The bronze equestrian statue of Charles I was privately commissioned in 1631 from the French sculptor Hubert le Sueur by Richard Weston, Lord Portland, the Lord High Treasurer. Charles sits proudly erect wearing contemporary costume. This is the first example of an equestrian statue of a ruler in Britain since Roman times.

Charles I, Whitehall

The Cenotaph, Whitehall

With the king's fall from power, it was ordered that the statue be sold for scrap, and it was reputedly melted down and made into souvenirs by a brazier called John Rivett. When the monarchy was restored in 1660 it was found that the statue had, in fact, been buried, and it was retrieved by Portland's heir, and eventually bought by the executed king's son, Charles II, in 1675. Sir Christopher Wren, Surveyor of the King's Works, designed the tall Portland stone plinth emblazoned with the Stuart coat of arms which was carved by Joshua Marshall, the King's Master Mason.

The Cenotaph

In June 1919 the architect Sir Edwin Lutyens was asked to produce a design for a temporary structure for the Whitehall site as part of the nation's Peace celebrations the following month. The resulting elegant Cenotaph (an empty tomb) atop a tall plinth was considered so appropriate that it was replaced in 1920 by the permanent Portland stone structure with stone wreaths modelled by Francis Derwent Wood. The Cenotaph was unveiled on 11 November 1920 as part of the burial ceremony of the Unknown Warrior in Westminster Abbey. The design for the permanent Cenotaph was extremely sophisticated. Lutyens followed the strict geometrical principles observed at the Parthenon in Athens, but the power of the monument lies in its simplicity and the brevity of the inscription, 'THE GLORIOUS DEAD', together with the dates 1914 and 1919 in Roman numerals, to which were subsequently added 1939 and 1945. Today, the Cenotaph remains the national memorial to those from the former British Empire and Commonwealth and their Allies who lost their lives during both World Wars, as well as in subsequent conflicts.

Christopher Columbus

In the south corner of Belgrave Square sits the bronze of a rather youthful Christopher Columbus holding a rolled maritime chart and looking westwards towards the Americas. The statue, a gift of the people of Spain, was sculpted by Tomás Bañuelos in 1992 and is mounted on a Portland stone base with two narrow grey granite bands. It is dedicated 'to all the peoples of the Americas in commemoration of the 500th anniversary of the encounter of the two worlds' – a reference to Columbus' expedition to the Americas in 1492 to claim territory on behalf of Spain.

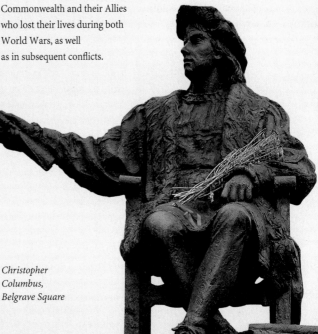

Christopher Columbus, Belgrave Square

Florence Nightingale, Waterloo Place

Wellington Arch

The Wellington Arch, one of London's most distinctive monuments, has had a very chequered career. In 1825 Decimus Burton was commissioned to design a pair of grand entrances to Hyde Park and Green Park, facing each other over Piccadilly. When it was decided that the Green Park entrance should serve Buckingham Palace (then being remodelled by John Nash), the requirements were for an altogether larger and more grand structure, but, unfortunately, Burton's lavish design was never completed, most of the intended sculptural ornament being omitted.

Worse was to befall the incomplete Arch, when, in 1838, the Wellington Memorial Committee decided that their intended national

Wellington Arch and Quadriga, Apsley Way

memorial to the 1st Duke of Wellington should be erected there. The resulting equestrian statue by Matthew Cotes was completely disproportionate to the size of the Arch, and was the cause of much controversy.

It was in 1882, in a drastic move to ease the growing traffic problems at Hyde Park Corner, that the decision was made to widen Piccadilly, which resulted in the demolition and subsequent re-erection of the Arch on its present site at the top of Constitution Hill. This provided an opportunity to rid the Arch of the over-sized statue of the Iron Duke, and and it was replaced, in 1912, by Adrian Jones' magnificent bronze group, the 'Quadriga of Peace'. English Heritage, having taken on responsibility for the Arch, is at present carrying out major structural repairs, and hopes to be able to open it to the public as a visitor centre for London's public statues and memorials.

Wellington Arch is due to open to the public in October 2000. Please phone Customer Services on 01793 414910 for more information.

Florence Nightingale

A.G. Walker's bronze figure of Florence Nightingale, unveiled in 1915, stands, appropriately, in a group with the memorials to her great ally Sidney, Lord Herbert of Lea, and to those of the Brigade of Guards who fell in the Crimean War. The heroic epoch of Florence Nightingale's life began in 1854 when she was sent with a party of 38 nurses to the Crimea. Her legendary compassion and care for the many suffering and dying British soldiers at the Scutari Military Hospital were combined with formidable intelligence and determination, and her immediate reforms at the hospital saved many lives. Throughout her life, she continued to exert an almost unrivalled moral and practical influence on medical reform. She received the Order of Merit in 1907, and died in 1910.

Edith Cavell

On 12 October 1915 Edith Cavell, a British-born nurse working in German-occupied Brussels, was shot by a German firing squad. She had coordinated a resistance group and helped perhaps as many as 600 Allied prisoners of war to escape from German captivity and return to Allied territory.

Her capture and execution stirred strong anti-German feelings and she became a national heroine. An appeal for a memorial was launched and the commission was awarded to the celebrated sculptor Sir George Frampton. The statue was unveiled by Queen Alexandra in March 1920. The moving inscription is taken from words spoken by Edith Cavell to Stirling Gahan, the only English priest remaining in Brussels, on the night before she died: 'Standing as I do in the view of God and Eternity I realise that patriotism is not enough. I must have no hatred or bitterness in my heart for anyone.'

George Washington

In front of the National Gallery is a bronze copy of Jean-Baptiste Houdon's celebrated statue of George Washington, founding genius and first President of the United States of America. The cast was presented to the nation by Washington's own state, the Commonwealth of Virginia, in 1921. The marble figure,

George Washington, outside the National Gallery

unveiled at the State Capitol in Richmond in 1788, is exactly life-size (6 ft 2 in) and shows Washington in the moment of retiring from his command, hanging up his riding cloak and sword and taking up his walking stick.

Below is the list of the 47 statues for which English Heritage is now responsible.

- *Belgian War Memorial*, Victoria Embankment
- *Simon Bolivar,* Belgrave Square, sw1
- *Duke of Cambridge*, Whitehall, sw1
- *Edith Cavell*, St Martin's Place, wc2
- *King Charles I*, Trafalgar Square, sw1
- *Clive of India*, King Charles St, sw1
- *Colin Campbell*, Waterloo Place, sw1
- *Lord Curzon*, Carlton House Terrace, sw1
- *Carabiniers Memorial*, Chelsea Embankment, sw3
- *Crimea Memorial*, Waterloo Place, sw1
- *Cenotaph*, Whitehall, sw1
- *Duke of Devonshire*, Whitehall, sw1
- *Edward VII*, Waterloo Place, sw1
- *General Eisenhower*, Grosvenor Square, w1
- *Sir John Franklin*, Waterloo Place, sw1
- *General Gordon*, Victoria Embankment
- *George II*, Golden Square, w1

- *George III*, Cockspur St, sw1
- *Earl Haig*, Whitehall, sw1
- *Duke of Kent*, Crescent Gardens (locked), Portland Place, w1
- *Baron Lawrence*, Waterloo Place, sw1
- *Machine Gun Corps*, Apsley Way, sw1
- *Montgomery*, Whitehall, sw1
- *Florence Nightingale*, Waterloo Place, sw1
- *Samuel Plimsoll*, Victoria Embankment
- *Lord Portal*, Victoria Embankment
- *Sir Walter Raleigh*, Whitehall, sw1
- *Royal Artillery Memorial*, Apsley Way W1
- *Captain Scott*, Waterloo Place, sw1
- *Lord Trenchard*, Victoria Embankment
- *Duke of Wellington*, Apsley Way, w1
- *William III*, St James's Square, sw1
- *Queen Charlotte*, Queens Square, WC1
- *Queen Anne*, Queen Anne's Gate, sw1
- *Sir Arthur Harris*, St Clements Dane, wc2
- *Lord Napier of Magdala*, Queen Anne's Gate, sw1
- *Lord Herbert*, Waterloo Place, sw1
- *Viscount Slim*, Whitehall, sw1
- *Viscount Alanbrooke*, Whitehall, sw1
- *General de Gaulle*, Carlton Gardens, sw1
- *James II*, outside National Gallery
- *George Washington*, outside National Gallery
- *Thomas Cubitt*, St George's Drive, Pimlico
- *Christopher Columbus*, Belgrave Square, sw1
- *General de San Martin*, Belgrave Square, sw1
- *Marble Arch*, w2
- *Wellington Arch and Quadriga*, Apsley Way, w1

South East

Left, 'Hurrah Henry' Event, a historical re-enactment at Dover Castle, in Kent; in the background, St Augustine's Abbey, in Kent, external view of the Great Abbey; right, one of a pair of cement copies of the Medici lions, which adorn a flight of steps on the Lower Terrace at Osborne House, on the Isle of Wight.

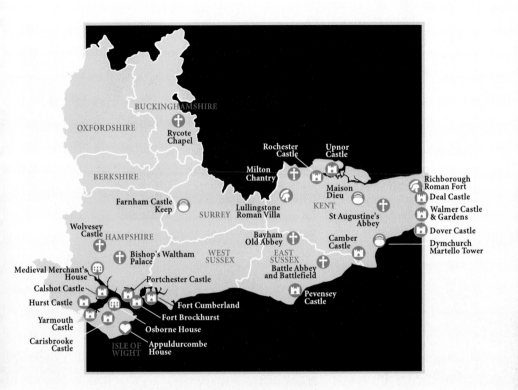

- BUCKINGHAMSHIRE
- OXFORDSHIRE
- Rycote Chapel
- BERKSHIRE
- Rochester Castle
- Upnor Castle
- Milton Chantry
- Maison Dieu
- Richborough Roman Fort
- Deal Castle
- Farnham Castle Keep
- SURREY
- Lullingstone Roman Villa
- KENT
- St Augustine's Abbey
- Walmer Castle & Gardens
- Wolvesey Castle
- HAMPSHIRE
- Dover Castle
- Bishop's Waltham Palace
- Bayham Old Abbey
- WEST SUSSEX
- EAST SUSSEX
- Camber Castle
- Dymchurch Martello Tower
- Medieval Merchant's House
- Calshot Castle
- Portchester Castle
- Battle Abbey and Battlefield
- Hurst Castle
- Fort Cumberland
- Yarmouth Castle
- Fort Brockhurst
- Pevensey Castle
- Carisbrooke Castle
- Osborne House
- ISLE OF WIGHT
- Appuldurcombe House

41

1066 Battle of Hastings Abbey and Battlefield

The one date in English history that everyone can remember is 1066: the date of the Battle of Hastings, when the conquering Normans vanquished the Anglo-Saxons on 14 October. There is just as much myth surrounding the conflict as known fact. The two armies did not even fight at Hastings, but at the place which became the town of Battle, 6 miles inland. There, on the valley slopes, it is possible to retrace the lines of conflict. In the ruins of the abbey that King William later built to commemorate the battle, you may imagine that you are standing on the very spot where the defeated King Harold fell. The battlefield itself provides an unparalleled chance to absorb the reality of the conquest. It was never a foregone conclusion that William would win. Only days before, Harold had won a famous victory in the north at Stamford Bridge against the King of Norway. William did win, but only after a great struggle.

Today a free interactive audio tour recreates the sounds of the battle, as you stand exactly where the English army stood, watching the Normans advance towards them. With the English occupying the high ground, the Normans were forced to fight uphill. They overcame this disadvantage by fighting both on foot and horseback, while the English dismounted, using swords or their huge two-handed axes. The course of the battle was reversed

when the Normans pretended to flee, but then turned back to cut down the English who had broken ranks in pursuit.

The final assault by William was preceded by a devastating volley of arrows. The Bayeux Tapestry depicts an arrow hitting Harold in the eye. He did not die directly from that wound, and some say that he was later cut down by a Norman sword. On Harold's death his army fled, the Normans in pursuit.

In 1070, when William ruthlessly crushed any opposition to his rule, he founded Battle Abbey to atone for the terrible loss of life at the Battle of Hastings.

Left, William the Conqueror, by an unknown artist. Below, the battlefield today. Above and far left, the re-enactment of the Battle of Hastings – an event that makes Battle Abbey great fun for the whole family.

A few portions of the abbey remain today, but little of the early Norman features. The best-preserved and most impressive part is the Great Gatehouse, finest of all surviving medieval abbey entrances, which was built around 1338. The great hall and other monastic buildings were incorporated into the Tudor and Georgian houses that occupied the

site after Henry VIII's dissolution of the monasteries. The battlefield, though, remains little touched: a generous gift from the USA enabled it to be purchased for the nation in 1976.

- Re-enactment of the Battle of Hastings on 14 and 15 October 2000.
- Discovery Centre – activity based exhibitions – makes finding out about Battle Abbey great fun. Available to booked school groups and open to families at weekends and during school holidays.
- Interpretation and exhibition on the run-up to the Battle of Hastings, 'The Prelude to Battle'.
- Exciting range of interactive displays and exhibitions.
- Family Discovery Pack available.

- Children's themed outdoor play area.
- Film/audio-visual – '1066, The Battle of Hastings'; Abbot's Hall open to the public during school summer holidays only.
- Superb Gift Shop.
- For details of the Battle Proms Concerts on 26 and 27 August, please call 01424 775 705.

Open 1 April–30 Sep: 10am–6pm daily. 1–31 Oct: 10am–5pm daily. 1 Nov–31 March 2001: 10am–4pm daily. Closed 24–26 Dec and 1 Jan 2001.

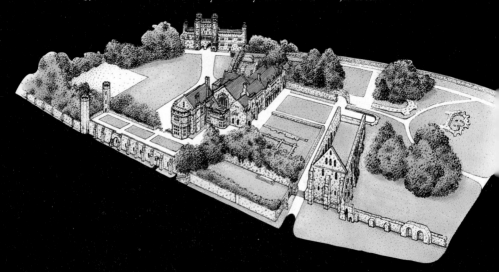

Entry £4/£3/£2. Family ticket
(2 adults & 3 children) £10.
Tel 01424 773792
Access In Battle, at S end of High
St. Battle is reached by road by
turning off A21 onto the A2100.
(OS Map 199; ref TQ 749157.)
Local Tourist Information
Battle (Tel 01424 773721) and
Hastings (Tel 01424 781111).
Bus Arriva Kent and East Sussex
4/5 Maidstone–Hastings;
Eastbourne buses 19,22 ⇌
Eastbourne–Battle.
Tel 01273 474747.
Train Battle ¼ m (10 mins' walk).
Inclusive rail + admission tickets
package available, ask at any
station.
P (charge payable) 🎧 *interactive*
also available for the visually
impaired, those in wheelchairs or
with learning difficulties, and in
French, German and Japanese;
braille guides in English only.)
Interactive tours will not be issued
on Special Events days.
🚻 E ♿ (some steps) 🚻 (nearby)
📷 🐕 (restricted areas)

*Opposite page, far left, tomb
of Sir Anthony Browne and
his wife Alice, in the Parish
Church. Top, the cloisters
and Priors Hall. Bottom,
bird's eye view of the abbey
and school.*
*This page, top, the Great
Gatehouse, from the south.
Right, interior of the 'novices'
chamber'.*

⊘ Abingdon County Hall

Oxfordshire (p. 232, 6K)

On the market place at Abingdon, a 17th-century public building was built to house the Assize Courts.

Open 1 April–31 Oct: 11am–5pm daily. 1 Nov–31 March 2001: 11am–4pm Tue–Sun. Closed 25–26 Dec.

Entry Free.

Tel 01235 523703

Access In Abingdon, 7m S of Oxford in Market Place.

(OS Map 164; ref SU 497971.)

Bus Cityline 35/A, Stagecoach Oxford 30 from Oxford (pass ⇌ Radley). Tel 01865 785400.

Train Radley 2½ m.

♡ Appuldurcombe House

Isle of Wight (p. 232, 3K)

The shell of Appuldurcombe, once the grandest house on the Isle of Wight, stands in its own ornamental grounds, designed by 'Capability' Brown. An exhibition of prints and photographs depicts the house and its history.

• Falconry Centre (additional admission charge).

Open 14 Feb–30 April 2000: 10am–4pm daily. 1 May–30 Sep: 10am–6pm daily. 1 Oct–15 Dec: 10am–4pm daily. 15 Feb–31 March 2001: 10am–4pm daily. Last entry one hour before closing time. (Property managed by Mr & Mrs Owen.)

Entry £2/£1.50/£1.

Tel 01983 852484

Access ½m Wroxall off B3327.

(OS Map 196; ref SZ 543800.)

Bus Southern Vectis 92/3 W Cowes –Ventnor, 7/A Ryde–Yarmouth. Tel 01983 827005.

Train Shanklin 3½ m.

Ferry Ryde 11m (Wightlink. Tel 0870 582 744); West Cowes 12m; East Cowes 12m (Red Funnel. Tel 02380 334010).

✪ Battle Abbey and Battlefield

♡ *East Sussex (p. 233, 4N)*

See p. 42–45 for full details.

✪ Bayham Old Abbey

♡ *East Sussex (p. 233, 4N)*

Ruins of a house of 'white' canons, founded in c.1208, in an 18th-century landscaped setting. The Georgian House (Dower House) is also open to the public.

Open 1 April–30 Sep: 10am–6pm daily. 1–31 Oct: 10am–5pm daily. 1 Nov–31 March 2001: 10am–4pm Sat–Sun. Closed 24–26 Dec and 1 Jan 2001.

Entry £2.10/£1.60/£1.10.

Tel 01892 890381

Access 1¼ m W of Lamberhurst off B2169.

(OS Map 188; ref TQ 651366.)

Bus Coastal Coaches 256 ⇌ Tunbridge Wells–Wadhurst. Tel 0845 769 6996.

Train Frant 4m.

✠ Bishop's Waltham Palace

Hampshire (p. 232, 4K)

This medieval seat of the Bishops of Winchester once stood in an enormous park. Wooded grounds still surround the mainly 12th- and 14th-century remains. Much was destroyed in a fire during the Civil War but the ground floor of the Dower House is intact. There is an exhibition on the Winchester Bishops on the first floor.

Open 1 April–30 Sep: 10am–6pm daily. 1–31 Oct: 10am–5pm daily. **Entry** £2/£1.50/£1. **Tel** 01489 892460 **Access** In Bishop's Waltham 5m from junction 8 of M27. (OS Map 185; ref SU 552173.)

Bus Stagecoach Hampshire bus 69 Winchester–Southsea (pass close ⇌ Winchester) Tel 01256 464501. Solent Blue Line/First Provincial 48 A/C Eastleigh–Fareham (pass close ⇌ Eastleigh) Tel 02380 226 235. All pass close ⇌ Fareham.

Train Botley 3½ m. 🅿️ ♿(grounds only) 🏠 🖼️ 🚻 (nearby in Bishop's Waltham) 🏞️ 🐕(restricted areas)

✠ Boxgrove Priory

West Sussex (p. 232, 4L)

Remains of the Guest House, Chapter House and church of a 12th-century priory.

Open Any reasonable time. **Entry** Free. **Access** N of Boxgrove, 4m E of Chichester on minor road off A27. (OS Map 197; ref SU 909076.)

Bus Stagecoach Coastline 702 ⇌ Chichester–Brighton (passes ⇌ Barnham) Tel 01243 783251. **Train** Chichester 4m. 🅿️ 🐕

◉ Bramber Castle

West Sussex (p. 232, 4M)

The remains of a Norman castle gatehouse, walls and earthworks.

Open Any reasonable time. **Entry** Free. **Access** On W side of Bramber village off A283. (OS Map 198; ref TQ 187107.) **Bus** Brighton & Hove 20 ⇌ Shoreham-by-Sea–Steyning.

Tel 01273 886200. **Train** Shoreham-by-Sea 4½ m. 🅿️(limited) 🐕

Carisbrooke Castle

From time immemorial, whosoever controlled Carisbrooke controlled the Isle of Wight. The castle sits at the heart of the island, and has been a feature since its foundation as a Saxon camp during the 8th century. Remnants of the Saxon wall running below the Norman keep still survive.

Enlarged by the Redvers family, who ruled the island until 1293, Carisbrooke was bought by Edward I on the death of Countess Isabella, whose individual taste is seen in the beautiful chapel she built.

During the English Civil War, Carisbrooke was prison to King Charles I who twice attempted escape. Lesser prisoners were made to tread the waterwheel (left), drawing water up the well's 49-metre (161-feet) depth until donkeys – still there today – were introduced in the 17th century.

Today, an interactive museum in the Old Coach House displays the history of the castle.

• Hands-on interpretation for children at the Donkey Centre.

Open 1 April–30 Sep: 10am–6pm daily. 1–31 Oct 10am–5pm daily. 1 Nov–31 March 2001: 10am–4pm daily. Closed 24–26 Dec and 1 Jan 2001.

Entry £4.50/£3.40/£2.30. Family ticket (2 adults & 3 children) £11.30.

Tel 01983 522107

Access 1¼m SW of Newport. (OS Map 196; ref SZ 486877.)

Local Tourist Information Newport (Tel 01983 525450) and Cowes (Tel 01983 291914).

Bus Southern Vectis 9 from Newport to Castle; otherwise 6, 7/A, 11/12 from Newport, Yarmouth & Ventnor to within ¼m. Tel 01983 827005.

Train Ryde Esplanade 9m; Wootton (IoW Steam Railway) 5m.

Ferry West Cowes 5m; East Cowes 6m (Red Funnel. Tel 02380 334010); Fishbourne 6m; Ryde 8m; Yarmouth 9m (Wightlink. Tel 0870 582 744).

🅿 🚻 🍴 (The Coach House Tea Room; open April–October)

♿ (grounds & lower levels only)

📷 🚻 Ⓔ 🏠

Above left, the well house treadwheel and winding mechanism, built in 1587. Below aerial view of Carisbrooke Castle.

◯ Calshot Castle

Hampshire (p. 232, 3K)

This century, the fort has been part of both a navy and an RAF base. Spectacular views of the Solent can be seen from the roof. Henry VIII built this coastal fort to command the sea passage to Southampton. The barrack room has been restored to its pre-World War I artillery garrison appearance.

Open 1 April–31 Oct: 10am–4pm daily. (Property managed by Hampshire County Council.)

Entry £2/£1. Family ticket (2 adults & 2 children) £5.

Tel 02380 892 023

When the castle is closed, phone 02380 892 077.

Access On spit 2m SE of Fawley off B3053. (OS Map 196; ref SU 488025.)

Bus Solent Blue Line X9, 39 Southampton–Calshot (passes ⇌ Southampton) to within 1m. Tel 02380 226 235.

🅿 🚻 ♿ ⎸(Keep: ground floor only; toilets) 📷 ✖

◯ Camber Castle

East Sussex (p. 233, 4O)

A rare example of an Henrician fort surviving in its original plan.

Open 1 July–30 Sep: 2–5pm Sat and Sun. Monthly guided walks round Rye Harbour Nature Reserve including Camber Castle. Please call the Reserve Manager on 01797 223862 for further information. (Property managed by Rye Harbour Nature Reserve.)

Entry £2/£1.50/£1. Friends of Rye Harbour Nature Reserve free.

Tel 01797 223862

Access by a delightful 1m walk across fields, off the A259, 1m S of Rye off harbour road. (OS Map 189; ref TQ 922185.)

Bus From surrounding areas to Rye, thence 1¼m. Tel 01273 474 747.

Train Rye 1¼m. ✖

◯ Carisbrooke Castle

Isle of Wight (p. 232, 3K)

See opposite page for full details.

◯ Conduit House

Kent (p. 233, 5P)

The Conduit House is the monastic waterworks which supplied nearby St Augustine's Abbey.

Open Any reasonable time. Exterior viewing only.

Entry Free.

Access From ring road turn right into Havelock St, right into North Holmes Rd, right into St Martin's Rd, right into Kings Park.

Approximately 5–10 mins walk from St Augustine's Abbey. (OS Map 179; ref TR 159585.)

Train Canterbury East or West, both 1½m.

⚙ Deal Castle

Kent (p. 233, 5P)

Deal Castle was built by Henry VIII as an artillery fortress to counter the threat of invasion from the Catholic alliance of France and Spain during the mid-16th century. Its huge, rounded bastions, designed to deflect shot, once carried 66 guns. It is a fascinating castle to explore, with long, dark passages, battlements and a massive basement with an exciting exhibition. Its remarkable coastal position affords breathtaking views out to sea.

- Interpretation exhibition.
- Free Children's Activity Sheet.

Open 1 April–30 Sep: 10am–6pm daily. 1–31 Oct: 10am–5pm daily. 1 Nov–31 March 2001: 10am–4pm

Reconstruction drawing by Alan Sorrell of Deal as newly completed in 1540.

Wed–Sun. Closed 24–26 Dec and 1 Jan 2001.
Entry £3/£2.30/£1.50.
Tel 01304 372762
Access SW of Deal town centre. (OS Map 179; ref TR 378521.)
Local Tourist Information
Deal (Tel 01304 369576).

Bus From surrounding areas. Tel 0845 769 6996.
Train Deal ½m.
🚻 ◻ 🏠 🍽 🎧 (also available for the visually impaired, those with learning difficulties, and in French and German) ♿ (courtyards and ground floor only, parking available)

⚙ Deddington Castle

Oxfordshire
(p. 232/236/239, 7K)

Extensive earthworks conceal the remains of a 12th-century castle.

Open Any reasonable time. (Property managed by Deddington Parish Council.)
Entry Free.
Access S of B4031 on E side of Deddington, 17m N of Oxford on

A423. (OS Map 151; ref SP 471316.)
Bus Stagecoach Midland Red X59 Oxford–Banbury to within ½m. Tel 01788 535555.
Train King's Sutton 5m.
🐕

⚙ Donnington Castle

Berkshire (p. 232, 5K)

Built in the late 14th century, the twin-towered gatehouse of this castle survives amidst some impressive earthworks.

Open Any reasonable time (exterior viewing only).
Entry Free.
Access 1m N of Newbury off B4494. (OS Map 174; ref SU 461694.)
Bus Bennetts 130/4 from Newbury (Tel 01635 248423).
Train Newbury 1¼m.
🅿 ♿ (steep slopes within grounds) 🐕

⊙ Dover Castle
Ø *Kent (p. 233, 4P)*

See p. 52–55 for full details.

⊙ Down House
⊛ *Downe, Greater London (p. 233, 5N)*

See p. 26–27 for full details.

⊙ Dymchurch Martello Tower
Kent (p. 233, 40)
One of many artillery towers
which formed part of a chain of
strongholds intended to resist
invasion by Napoleon.

Open Telephone **01304 211 067** for
opening details.
Entry £1/80p/50p.
Access from High Street only.
(OS Map 189; ref TR 102294.)
Bus Stagecoach East Kent 11, 12/A,
Stagecoach South Coast 711

Folkestone–Hastings
(pass close ⇌ Folkestone Central).
Tel 0845 769 6996.
Train Sandling 7m; Dymchurch
(R H & D Railway), adjacent.
🐕

⊙ Eynsford Castle
Kent (p. 233, 5N)
One of the first stone castles built
by the Normans. The moat and
remains of the curtain wall and
hall can still be seen.

Open 1 March–30 Sep: 10am–6pm
daily. 1 Oct–28 Feb 2001: 10am–4pm
daily.
Entry Free.
Access In Eynsford off A225.
(OS Map 177; ref TQ 542658.)

Bus Arriva Kent Thameside G2,
413/15 ⇌ Eynsford–Dartford.
Tel 0845 769 6996.
Train Eynsford 1m.
P ♿ 🐕

⊙ Farnham Castle Keep
Surrey (p. 233, 5L)
A motte and bailey castle, once
one of the seats of the Bishop of
Winchester, which has been in
continuous occupation since the
12th century.
Open 1 April–30 Sep: 10am–6pm
daily. 1–31 Oct: 10am–5pm daily.
Entry £2/£1.50/£1.

Tel 01252 713393
Access ½ m N of Farnham town
centre on A287. (OS Map 186;
ref SU 839474.)
Bus from surrounding areas.
Tel 01737 223000.
Train Farnham ¼ m.
P ⏸ 🐕 📷

✚ Faversham: Stone Chapel
Kent (p. 233, 50)
The remains of a small medieval
church incorporating part of a 4th-
century Romano-British pagan
mausoleum.

Open Any reasonable time.
(Property managed by the
Faversham Society.)
Entry Free.
Access 1¼ m W of Faversham on A2.
(OS Map 178; ref TQ 992614.)

Bus Arriva Kent & Sussex 333
Maidstone–Faversham (pass
⇌ Faversham). Tel 0845 769 6996.
Train Faversham 1½ m.
🐕

⊙ Flowerdown Barrows
Hampshire (p. 232, 4K)
Round barrows of a Bronze Age
burial site which were once part
of a larger group.

Open Any reasonable time.
Entry Free.
Access In Littleton, 2½ m NW
of Winchester off A272.
(OS Map 185; ref SU 459320.)

Bus Stagecoach Hampshire bus
68/A/C from Winchester (pass
⇌ Winchester) Tel 01256 464501.
Train Winchester 2m. 🐕

Dover

No fortress in England can boast a longer history than Dover Castle. Commanding the shortest sea crossing between England and the Continent it has served from the Iron Age onwards as a vital strategic centre.

Henry II's keep

There has been a castle in Dover since the defences of an Anglo-Saxon fortress were strengthened in 1066 by William of Normandy, who built the first earthwork castle before moving on to London. Under Henry II, the castle was totally rebuilt, and the walls of the Inner Bailey and the eastern part of the outer curtain wall erected. Most impressive is the monumental keep, built by Henry II's great architect, Maurice the Engineer, in the 1180s, which stands at the heart of a concentric ring of defences.

Throughout, the internal arrangement of the keep is ingeniously designed. Its three-towered forebuilding, carrying the entry staircase and two chapels, is an elaborate and magnificent approach to the main apartments. The upper chapel, richly decorated and reserved for the royal family's use, is especially fine. The former royal apartments are still most impressive in their monumental scale, despite having lost most of their original decoration.

Dover, the Key to England

Unlock Dover and you unlock England. Two exhibitions highlight the important role Dover played when the country was threatened with invasion.

The first is a presentation involving the latest technology of light, film and sound retracing how, in 1216, a group of rebel barons

invited the French Dauphin to invade England and seize the throne from King John, whom they regarded as a tyrant. The future Louis XVIII eagerly accepted the invitation and it was not long before the whole of the south east from Lincoln to the Channel (including London and the Tower) was under his control. In this crisis, only two castles in the area, Windsor and Dover, defied the French. The capture of Dover, one of the greatest royal castles in England, was of vital importance to the success of the invasion and a great siege was begun under the direction of Prince Louis himself. But Louis had not bargained for Hubert de Burgh's resolute defence of Dover. The castle held for months, threatening his cross-

Channel supply routes, while the tide turned against him throughout the country. He was obliged to raise the siege and return to London. It was de Burgh's ship which led the English fleet to a decisive victory off the coast in August 1217. No little thanks to Dover, Louis's enterprise had collapsed.

The second new and exciting exhibition offers a tableau of the preparations for Henry VIII's visit to Dover. After his divorce from Catherine of Aragon in 1529 Henry felt himself to be isolated in Europe. Two former rivals, the Holy Roman Emperor Charles V and Francis I of France were threatening to cement an alliance with the Pope and invade England. All trade had been suspended with the Continent and ambassadors were leaving the country, fearing for their lives. War seemed inevitable, and Henry was keen to build up England's defences in preparation. Coastal forts were being erected at Deal and Walmer, and a large harbour was already under way at Dover.

In 1539 Henry came to Dover to oversee the work. The exhibition invites visitors into the King's chambers to see all that was involved in preparing for Henry's arrival. The famous monarch did not travel light, and hundreds of locked strong-boxes preceded him, containing everything that the King of England could possibly need – from provisions to hunting equipment, from chests full of plans and documents to desks, furniture and decorations.

Opposite page, far left, Henry II. Above him, Henry VIII. This page, above, part of the exhibition retracing the visit of Henry VIII to Dover in 1539. Below, general view of Dover Castle.

Dover's secret tunnels

The White Cliffs of Dover are among England's most celebrated sights, yet hidden inside them is a fascinating and secret world: below, deep underground, are miles of tunnels.

The first tunnels under Dover Castle were constructed in the Middle Ages to provide a protected line of communication for the soldiers manning the northern outworks and to allow the garrison to gather unseen before launching a surprise attack. During the Napoleonic Wars, this system of tunnels was greatly expanded to fortify the castle in readiness for a French invasion. Seven tunnels (running with damp and prone to collapse) were dug as barracks for the soldiers and officers who were filling both castle and town to overflowing. These were capable of accommodating up to 2,000 troops. They are the only underground barracks ever built in Britain.

Operation Dynamo: Dunkirk evacuation 26 May–3 June 1940

At 1857 hours on 26 May 1940 the signal was received to commence Operation Dynamo – the evacuation of the British Expeditionary Force (BEF) and French troops from Dunkirk's beaches.

As France fell before the German advance, and with less than a week to prepare, it was the awesome responsibility of Vice-Admiral Ramsay to plan the evacuation of up to 40,000 troops under constant attack from German forces. For nine days Admiral Ramsay and his staff worked round the clock, with the cliff tunnels becoming the nerve centre of the operation. From here an endless stream of phone calls were made in what one naval staff-officer called 'organised chaos' - calls for more destroyers, more merchant ships, calls to the Admiralty for weapons, tugs, medical supplies, and most importantly, for trained personnel.

The best estimate had been that only 45,000 of the troops could be brought back, yet this number was far surpassed. The ferocious air attacks and continuous bombardment of ships made the task ever more perilous, but although the price was heavy, Winston Churchill was able to report to a packed House of Commons that the operation had been a success; by 4 June, over 338,000 men had been brought back – the whole of the BEF and 139,000 French soldiers.

Today you can experience life as it was for the 700 personnel in the worst days of the war. Relive the drama as a wounded Battle of Britain pilot is taken into the underground hospital to fight for his life in the operating theatre, or see the Command Centre in which Churchill formulated the plans which would eventually lead to Allied victory. Today, wartime secrets are revealed for all to see.

▲ Zeffirelli's *Hamlet,* starring Mel Gibson, was filmed here.
- **New for 2000** This spring, see a new interpretation of Sir Admiral Ramsay's casemate in the Secret Wartime tunnels.
- Special World War II event to commemorate the anniversary of the evacuation of Dunkirk, 28 & 29 May 2000. Call 01304 211067 for details.
- Exciting reconstruction and exhibition retracing Henry VIII's visit to Dover in March 1539.
- Come and see a dramatic interpretation of life at Dover in 1216 under siege from the French.
- For easy access around the castle take a free ride on the land train.
- Princess of Wales' Royal Regiment Museum.
- Themed function area (in the Keep) available for hire; phone 01304 205830 for details.
- Superb Gift Shops.

Open 1 April–30 Sep: 10am–6pm daily. 1–31 Oct: 10am–5pm daily. 1 Nov–31 March 2001: 10am–4pm daily. Closed 24–26 Dec and 1 Jan 2001.

Entry £6.90/£5.20/£3.50. Family ticket (2 adults & 3 children) £17.30. (includes admission to the tours of the Secret Wartime tunnels – last tour begins at 5pm (summer) and 3pm (winter).

Tel 01304 201628

Access On E side of Dover. (OS Map 179; ref TR 326416.)

Local Tourist Information
Dover (Tel 01304 205108).
Bus Stagecoach East Kent 90 from ⇌ Dover Priory (not available Sun or Bank Hol Mon). Tel 0845 7696996.
Train Dover Priory 1½ m.
🅿 🏭 ♿ 🍴 (The Keep Restaurant, open all year; The Tunnel Café, open April–Oct and throughout most of the winter; for private functions phone 01304 205830.)
🎧 *small charge* (separate tour for battlement walk – available in French, German and Japanese.)
🎧 E 🖼 🛍 ♿ (courtyard & grounds – some very steep slopes)
🐕 (restricted areas)

Above, the reconstructed telephone and telex exchange.
Opposite page, top, one of the underground hospital's ward rooms .
Below, the Anti-Aircraft Operations Room. The position of enemy aircraft was charted on the illuminated screens and coordinated on the plotting tables.
Bottom left, Admiral Ramsay and Winston Churchill plotting in the tunnels.

◎ Fort Brockhurst

Hampshire (p. 232, 3K)

This was a new type of fort, built in the 19th century to protect Portsmouth with formidable firepower. Largely unaltered, the parade ground, gun ramps and moated keep can all be viewed.

• Fort available for private hire.

• See nesting birds, and look out for ghostly activity in Prisoner Cell No. 3!

• View the RAF Gosport Aviation Heritage Exhibition.

Open 1 April–30 Sep: 10am–6pm Sat–Sun. 1–31 Oct: 10am–5pm Sat–Sun.

Entry £2/£1.50/£1.

Tel 02380 581059

Access Off A32, in Gunner's Way, Elson, on N side of Gosport. (OS Map 196; ref SU 596020.)

Bus First Provincial 81–7 Fareham–Gosport Ferry (pass ⇌ Fareham, also Gosport Ferry Links with ⇌ Portsmouth & Southsea) Tel 01329 232208.

Train Fareham 3m.

🚻 (grounds & ground floor only; toilets) ♿ (restricted areas)

◎ Fort Cumberland

Hampshire (p. 232, 3K)

Constructed in the shape of a wide pentagon by the Duke of Cumberland in 1746, this fort is perhaps the most impressive piece of 18th-century defensive architecture in England.

Open 24 June, 9 and 10 Sep, by guided tour only. Advance booking is required for tours; please call **01732 778028**.

Entry £2/£1.

Access In the Eastney district of Portsmouth on the estuary approach via Henderson Road, a turning off Eastney Road, or from the Esplanade. (OS Map 196; ref SZ 682992.)

Bus First Provincial 16/A ⇌ Portsmouth & Southsea-Hayling Ferry. Tel 02392 650967.

Train Fratton 2m.

✪ Horne's Place Chapel

Kent (p. 233, 4O)

This 14th-century domestic chapel was once attached to the manor house. The house and chapel are privately owned.

Open By arrangement. Please telephone **01304 211067**.

Entry Free.

Access 1½ m N of Appledore. (OS Map 189; ref TQ 957307.)

Train Appledore 2½ m.

🅿 (nearby) ♿

◎ Hurst Castle

Hampshire (p. 232/235, 3I)

One of the most sophisticated fortresses built by Henry VIII, and later strengthened in the 19th and 20th centuries, to command the narrow entrance to the Solent.

Open 1 April–31 Oct: 10am–5.30pm or dusk daily. (Property managed by Hurst Castle Services.)

Entry £2.50/£2/£1.50.

Tel 01590 642344

Access On Pebble Spit S of Keyhaven. Best approached by ferry from Keyhaven, call 01590 642500 (June–Sep, 9am–2pm) or answerphone 01425 610784, for ferry details. (OS Map 196; ref SZ 319898.)

Bus Wilts & Dorset 123/4 Bournemouth–Lymington (pass ⇌ New Milton) to within 2½ m, or 1m to ferry. Tel 01202 673555.

Train Lymington Town 4½ m to Keyhaven, 6½ m to Fort.

🍴 🛈 (Castle Café, not managed by English Heritage; weekends only April and May, daily June–Sep)

♿ (restricted areas)

⊙ King James's and Landport Gates

Hampshire (p. 232, 3K)

These gates were once part of Portsmouth's 17th-century defences.

Open Any reasonable time. Exterior viewing only.

Entry Free.

Access King James's Gate: forms entrance to United Services Recreation Ground (officers) on Park Rd; Landport Gate: as above, men's entrance on St George's Rd. (OS Map 196; King James's Gate ref SU 638000, Landport Gate ref SU 634998.)

Bus From surrounding areas. Tel 01962 868944.

Train Portsmouth Harbour ⅓m.

🔾

▲ Kit's Coty House and Little Kit's Coty House

Kent (p. 233, 5N)

Ruins of two prehistoric burial chambers.

Open Any reasonable time.

Entry Free.

Access W of A229 2m N of Maidstone. (OS Map 188; ref TQ 745608 & TQ 745604.)

Bus Arriva Kent & East Sussex 101

⇌ Maidstone East–Gillingham. Tel 0845 769 6996.

Train Aylesford 2½m.

🔾

✚ Knights Templar Church

Kent (p. 233, 4P)

The foundations of a small circular 12th-century church.

Open Any reasonable time.

Entry Free.

Access On the Western Heights above Dover.

(OS Map 179; ref TR 313408.)

Train Dover Priory ¾m.

🔾 (restricted areas)

⊙ Lullingstone Roman Villa

ⓘ *Kent (p. 233, 5N)*

The villa, built c. AD100 and discovered in 1939, was one of the finds of the 20th century.

• See the new reconstruction drawings of this amazing archaeological find.

Open 1 April–30 Sep: 10am–6pm daily. 1–31 Oct: 10am–5pm daily. 1 Nov–31 March 2001: 10am–4pm daily. Closed 24–26 Dec and 1 Jan 2001.

Entry £2.50/£1.90/£1.30.

Tel 01322 863467

Access ½m SW of Eynsford off A225, off junction 3 of M25.

Follow A20 towards Brands Hatch.(OS Map 177; ref TQ 529651.)

Local Tourist Information

Clacketts Lane (Tel 01959 565063)

Train Eynsford ¾m.

🅿 🚻 🎧 (also available for the visually impaired and those with learning difficulties and in French and German) 🛍 📷 🔾

Above, a detail of the mosaic floor in the Audience Room of Lullingstone Roman Villa; the figure is of "Summer" wearing a garland of corn. Left, display of Roman pottery.

Medieval Merchant's House

The medieval timber framed house at 58 French Street is one of the earliest surviving merchant's houses in England. It was built in about AD 1290 by John Fortin, a wealthy merchant who traded with

Throughout the medieval period, Southampton was one of the busiest ports in England trading with merchants from Bordeaux, Genoa and Venice in such goods as wine, spices, silks and dyestuffs and exporting English wool and cloth.

furnishings of the period. Each piece is copied from a surviving example or a manuscript illustration, and is of a quality that might be expected in a wealthy merchant's house of the period.

merchants from Bordeaux. It was both a residence and a place of buisness located on one of the busiest streets in medieval Southampton just inland from the port.

It has a cellar and a shop at the front, with living accommodation comprising a hall and private room on the ground floor and two bedrooms on the upper floor. The house has been returned to its mid-14th century appearance by the removal of later floors, partitions and fireplaces.

Life in a medieval merchant's house is vividly evoked by the introduction of replica

Open 1 April–30 Sep: 10am–6pm daily. 1–31 Oct: 10am–5pm daily.
Entry £2.10/£1.60/£1.10.
Tel 02380 221503
Access 58 French Street, ¼ m S of city centre just off Castle Way (between High St and Bugle St). (OS Map 196; ref SU 419112.)
Bus First Southampton 17A from ⇌ Southampton.
Tel 02380 224854.
Train Southampton ¾ m.
🚻 🎧 (also available for the visually impaired and those with learning difficulties) ♿ (one step) 📷 📖 ❌

Top left, the shop interior. Left, the exterior view of house. Above, and above left, interior of the house.

◉ Maison Dieu

Kent (p. 233, 5O)

Part of a medieval complex of royal lodge, almshouses and hospital, this is much as it was 400 years ago.

Open 3 April–31 Oct: 2–5pm Sat–Sun and Bank Holiday Mon. For further details call **01795 534542**. (Property managed by The Faversham Society.)

Entry £1/80p.

Access In Ospringe on A2,

½ m W of Faversham. (OS Map 178; ref TR 002608.)

Bus Arriva Kent & East Sussex 333/5 Maidstone–Faversham (pass ⇌ Faversham) Tel 0845 769 6996.

Train Faversham ¾ m.

🛉🛉 ✖

◉ Medieval Merchant's House

Hampshire (p. 232, 4K)

See opposite page for full details.

Right, interior of Medieval Merchant's House. Far right, canopied bed.

⊕ Milton Chantry

Kent (p. 233, 5N)

A small 14th-century building which housed the chapel of a leper hospital and a family chantry. It later became a tavern and, in 1780, part of a fort.

Open 1 March–23 Dec: 10am–4pm Wed–Sun and Bank Holiday Mon. Closed Jan–Feb 2001. (Property managed by Gravesend Borough Council.)

Entry £1.50/75p/75p.

Tel 01474 321520

Access In New Tavern Fort Gardens E of central Gravesend off A226. (OS Map 177; ref TQ 652743.)

Bus From surrounding areas. Tel 0845 769 6996.

Train Gravesend ¾ m.

✖

◯ Minster Lovell Hall and Dovecote

Oxfordshire (p. 232, 6J)

The handsome ruins of Lord Lovell's 15th-century manor house.

Open Any reasonable time. Dovecote – exterior only.

Entry Free.

Access Adjacent to Minster Lovell church, 3m W of Witney off A40. (OS Map 164; ref SP 324114.)

Bus: Stagecoach Oxford 102 Witney–Carterton with connections from ⇌ Oxford. Tel 01865 772250.

Train Charlbury 7m.

✖

⊕ ◯ Netley Abbey

Hampshire (p. 232, 4K)

A 13th-century Cistercian abbey converted in Tudor times for use as a house.

Open Any reasonable time.

Entry Free.

Tel 02380 453076

Access In Netley, 4m SE of Southampton, facing Southampton Water. (OS Map 196; ref SU 453089.)

Bus First Southampton 16/C ⇌ Southampton–Hamble. Tel 02380 224854.

Train Netley 1m.

P ♿ 🛉🛉 (nearby, across road near estuary) ✖

Gardens

Gardens, parks and other designed landscapes play an important role in creating the rich pattern of the English landscape. Many of these were designed and planted hundreds of years ago, ornamented with fine buildings, and influenced by celebrated designers like 'Capability' Brown, Humphry Repton, William Nesfield, Joseph Paxton and Gertrude Jekyll. Urban parks, squares, cemeteries, grand country estates, suburban villas, and new

towns, all reflect the social aspirations and creative talents of their owners.

Over 1,200 gardens and designed landscapes have already been identified as of national importance and included on our Register of Parks and Gardens of special historic interest. Amongst these are a number managed and cared for by English Heritage. These range from the sumptuous royal gardens and park at Osborne House, family home of Queen Victoria, to the quiet little gardens surrounding the modest timber-framed Boscobel House in Shropshire.

Many of English Heritage's 400 properties have landscapes of great scenic beauty. Some of our castles and abbeys form picturesque ruins in larger park landscapes designed and created in the 18th or 19th centuries; examples are Sherborne, Old Wardour, Roche Abbey and the National Trust's Fountains Abbey. Gardens are now recognised as an important part of our cultural heritage; our recent acquisitions, Brodsworth Hall, Down House and Eltham Palace have significant and attractive historic gardens.

Since its formation English Heritage has been carrying out a systematic programme of surveys, research, management and restoration of its gardens and landscapes. Many of our properties provide ideal havens for wildlife, including endangered species like bats, fungi, birds and veteran trees. Restoration of the Quarry Garden at Belsay Hall, the 1832 parterre at Audley End House and new garden at Walmer Castle have been followed recently by the painstaking consolidation of Wigmore Castle in Herefordshire, where ground-

breaking work has shown that protection of both the built and natural environments can, with care, be achieved in harmony. The first fruits of our Contemporary Heritage Garden Competition will be ripe in the Summer of 2000. At Eltham Palace you will be able to see the South Moat Border and White Wood by Isabelle Van Groeningen and in the Walled Garden at Osborne House, a fruit and flower garden in celebration of Queen Victoria and Prince Albert by Rupert Golby. From manicured gardens to monuments set in breathtaking scenery, English Heritage offers much to enjoy.

Below, the gardens at Belsay Hall, Northumberland. Left, Down House, Greater London. Top, summer seat in the gardens of Walmer Castle, Kent.

⊖ North Hinksey Conduit House

Oxfordshire (p. 239, 6K)
Roofed reservoir for Oxford's first
water mains, built in the early 1600s.
Open Any reasonable time. Exterior
viewing only.

Entry Free.
Access In North Hinksey off A34,
2½ m W of Oxford. Located off
track leading from Harcourt Hill;
use footpath from Ferry Hinksey
Lane (near railway station).

(OS Map 164; ref SP 494049.)
Train Oxford 1½m located off track
leading from Harcourt Hill; use
footpath from Ferry Hinksey Lane
(near railway station).

⊖ North Leigh Roman Villa

Oxfordshire (p. 232/236/239, 7J)
The remains of a large and well-built
Roman courtyard villa. The most
important feature is an almost
complete mosaic tile floor, intricately
patterned in reds and browns.

Open Grounds – any reasonable
time. Viewing window for mosaic.
Pedestrian access only from main
road (550 metres – 600 yards).
Entry Free.
Access 2m N of North Leigh, 10m
W of Oxford off A4095.

(OS Map 164; ref SP 397154.)
Bus Stagecoach Oxford 11
Oxford–Witney to within 1 ½m.
Tel 01865 772250.
Train Handborough 3½m.
P (in layby, not in access lane)

○ Northington Grange

Hampshire (p. 232, 4K)
See p. 62 for full details.

⊖ Old Soar Manor

Kent (p. 233, 5N)
Remains of a late 13th-century
knight's manor house.
Open 1 April–30 Sep: 10am–6pm
daily. Keykeeper. (Property
maintained, managed and owned
by the National Trust.)

Entry Free.
Tel 01732 810378
Access 1m E of Plaxtol.
(OS Map 188; ref TQ 619541.)
Bus Arriva Kent & East Sussex/JRS
Traveline 222 (⇌ Borough Green–
⇌ Tunbridge Wells); JRS Traveline
404 Sevenoaks–Shipbourne

(passing ⇌ Sevenoaks); on both
alight E end of Plaxtol, thence ¼m
by footpath. Tel 0845 769 6996.
Train Borough Green and
Wrotham 2½m.
P (limited) (National Trust Kent
& East Sussex office)

⊕ Osborne House

Isle of Wight (p. 232, 3K)
See p. 64–67 for full details.

Northington Grange

Northington Grange and its landscaped park, as you see it today, formed the core of the house as designed by William Wilkins in 1809, and was one of the earliest Greek Revival houses in Europe. The story of the Grange is however rather more complex and evidence of other phases of building can be seen as you walk round the site.

The first house on the site was built by William Samwell between 1664 and 1673. The remains of this house survived largely intact behind all the subsequent modifications. It was this house which was leased to the Prince of Wales in 1795, and for which an inventory of the furniture survives, so that we know how each room was used.

In 1807 the owner Henry Drummond returned home from a Grand Tour of Europe, and influenced by buildings he had seen, determined to convert his house into the Greek style. The young architect William Wilkins was employed to do this, and changed the external appearance of the Grange into that of a Greek temple by rendering the brick walls and adding porticoes. Drummond and Wilkins however argued, and the house was sold before the work was completed. The new owner, Alexander Baring, used the house for large scale entertainment and found that it was too small. Accommodation was added, and a magnificent dining room based on the Temple of Apollo at Bassae and a conservatory were built.

Of Baring's alterations only the conservatory remains today, which was later used to house the art collection of the subsequent American owners.

The house had a formal garden in the Italian Revival style which was surrounded by a naturalistic landscape park with a lake, and extensive walled gardens where vegetables and fruit were grown to support the household. The conservatory contained rare tender plants such as oranges.

Open Any reasonable time (exterior viewing only).

🎬 *Eugene Onegin*, with Ralph Fiennes, was filmed here.

Entry Free.

Access 4m N of New Alresford off B3046 along farm track (450 metres – 493 yards). (OS Map 185; ref SU 562362.)

Bus Oakley buses 309 Basingstoke–Alresford to within ½m (passes close ≋ Basingstoke) Tel 01962 846924.

Train Winchester 8m.

🅿 ♿ (with assistance) 🐕

Victorian England

We can't escape the products of the Victorian age. From the beginning of Queen Victoria's reign until her death at Osborne in 1901, England the peaceful rural home of Charles Darwin; and of course the Royal villa by the sea at Osborne on the Isle of Wight.

English Heritage celebrates the achievements of the Victorian age in other ways with, amongst many other things, our Listing Team

saw a period of unprecedented population growth and urban spread. Iron railway tracks criss-crossed the length and breadth of the country, mills and factories sprang up in towns and countryside alike. Commerce, banking, public institutions, police and fire services emerged and their buildings, along with schools, pubs and theatres, and also a vast number of churches and chapels, feature prominently in our high streets and city centres. Some of these fine structures are now in the care of English Heritage and open to the public.

Jewels in our crown include the Albert Memorial, the glittering testament to Queen Victoria's love of Albert; Down House in Bromley,

The Victorian passion for elaborate gardens and inventive landscaping can be seen at Osborne, Brodsworth and Audley End, all winners of National Heritage awards in 1999, and in the landscaped grounds at Witley Court. Victorian mill working conditions can be understood at Stott Park Bobbin Mill, Cumbria; the intensity of ecclesiastical Gothic Revival decoration can be admired at St Mary's Church, Studley Royal; the Victorian passion for collecting can be seen at Audley End in the assembly of paintings, stuffed birds and animals acquired by the third and for fourth Barons Braybrooke.

which advises the Department of Culture, Media and Sport on the specialness of the Victorian legacy of buildings and grant-in-aid programmes which help to repair and restore Victorian structures from towers to tombstones.

School children and teachers studying the Victorians as part of the curriculum will find their studies illuminated by our Victorian sites: visit and enjoy!

Above, clockwise from far left, the Albert Memorial, London; St Mary's Church, Studley Royal, North Yorkshire; Audley End, in Essex; and Osborne House, on the Isle of Wight. Above, Queen Victoria, a replica by Sir George Hayter, 1863.

Osborne House

Osborne House was 'a place of one's own, quiet and retired', for Queen Victoria and Prince Albert. They found tranquillity on the Isle of Wight, far from the formality of court life at Buckingham Palace and Windsor Castle.

When visitors see Osborne for the first time, knowing that the young Victoria and Albert had wanted a modest country home, they are surprised by its scale and magnificence. The house is set on rising ground overlooking the Solent, where the ships that helped Britannia rule the waves sailed to and fro. Two tall towers in an Italian style dominate, above fountains set on terraces and rolling wooded parkland.

Victoria married Albert in 1840 and they bought Osborne, then a relatively small house, five years later. Its ambitious replacement was the work of Thomas Cubitt, best known for his buildings in London, and the result was a house Italianate in style rather than in the Gothic

idiom one often associates with the Victorians.

The interiors at Osborne abound with opulence and grandeur – the Indian room, marbled pillars, gilding, statuary, and magnificent paintings remind us that this family had links with all the crowned heads of Europe. Despite the idea of cosy domesticity at Osborne, the formality of monarchy was never far away. The royal household was organised according to a strict regime, the formality of which extended to the preparation of the Queen's table and her meals. Situated directly below the Dining Room is the newly open Table Deckers' Room and the Servery, where one can see how these preparations were carried out. The role of the Table Decker (a post which has now disappeared), is described in a book of 1848, as 'to superintend the arrangement of

Her Majesty's table, placing everything in perfect order previously to the dinner being served'. This would have included responsibility for ornate table decorations.

Like the house, the gardens at Osborne were in formal Italianate style, and were designed by both Cubitt and the Prince. The Walled Garden produced fruit and flowers for the House and is being restored as part of the Contemporary Heritage Gardens scheme launched by English Heritage. It is with a view to recapturing the spirit of the garden as it was *then*, that Rupert Golby has been chosen to re-design it. Triumphal arches of Victoria plum festooned with climbing roses, honeysuckle, and clematis will be one of

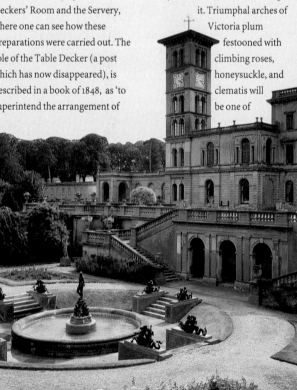

the features of the new garden, and the cold frame will be filled with Parma violets, Queen Victoria's favourite flower.

The completion of Osborne, in 1851, coincided with the Great Exhibition – Albert's greatest achievement – held in the Crystal Palace in Hyde Park. Victoria and Albert with their many children embodied the family ideal and helped restore respect for the monarchy after the low esteem in which it was held under George IV and William IV. Although of necessity State affairs took place at Osborne, it was essentially a family holiday home. The Queen had her first experience of sea bathing there – she liked it until she put her head under the water. Victoria and Albert's nine children played freely

Top, the Queen's Sitting Room.
Above, the Royal Family on the terrace of Osborne House in 1857.
Opposite page, general views of the house.

Left, the Dining Room as it is today. Below, the Billiard Room and the table for which Prince Albert himself designed the frieze panels and light fitting.
Right, Queen Victoria and Princess Beatrice by an unknown artist, c. late 1860s. Right, main picture, the stairwell with Amazons and an Argonaut *by Joseph Engel.*

in their own little home, Swiss Cottage, which was given to them on Victoria's birthday in 1854. As a memento of their youth, Victoria commissioned marble sculptures of their infant arms, which still lie in ghostly display in the Nursery Sitting Room.

A new routine helped ease painful memories after Albert died, and Victoria took great comfort in the company of her youngest daughter. Princess Beatrice lived at Osborne in the Durbar Wing which was built in 1890-91 by craftsmen from India.

Queen Victoria died on 22 January 1901 on a couch bed in the Queen's Bedroom, surrounded by her children. A newspaper report on the day of her death described the people of Cowes as 'stunned by the calamity, which affects them peculiarly', an indication of the special relationship that had grown up between this community and their monarch. The extent to which Victoria herself had come to find a sense of freedom and repose at the Isle of Wight is made equally clear. The report goes on to state that she would often drive through the streets there: 'The country generally did not know of these drives. [...]

they were taken as a mark of the Queen's confidence in the townsfolk. She went about unattended.'

Shortly after her death Edward VII gave Osborne House to the nation, and with recent restoration, it has become one of the most evocative memorials to Britain's longest reigning monarch.

Access 1m SE of East Cowes.
(Map 196; ref SZ 516948.)
Local Tourist Information
Cowes (Tel 01983 291914) and
Newport (Tel 01983 525450).
Bus Southern Vectis 4 Ryde–
E Cowes, 5 Newport–E Cowes.
Tel 01983 827005.
Train Ryde Esplanade 7m;
Wootton (IoW SteamRailway) 3m.
Ferry East Cowes 1½ m (Red
Funnel. Tel 02380 334010);
Fishbourne 4m; Ryde 7m (both
Wightlink. Tel 0870 582744).
🅿 🚻 🍴 (The Café, open
April–Oct. Also Swiss Cottage
Tearoom for quality lunches
and teas) ♿ (exterior and ground
floor only; vehicles with disabled
passengers may set them down
at the house entrance before
returning to car park)
🄴 🖾 🄾 🖾 🖾

🎥 *Mrs Brown*, starring Dame
Judi Dench and Billy Connolly,
was filmed here.
★ Voted third best property in the
1999 NPI Awards for the South
East.
• **New for 2000** Opening of the
Table Deckers' Room and
Walled Garden.
• The Wightlink Summer concerts:
telephone 01983 200022 for details.
• Isle of Wight Garden Show at
Osborne House 13 & 14 May 2000.
Inclusive ferry and garden show
entry tickets available from Red
Funnel, tel 02380 304010.
• Children's play area.
• Free Children's Activity Sheet.
Open House: 1 April–31 Oct: 10am–
5pm daily. Gardens: 1 April–31 Oct:
10am–6pm daily (last admission to
house 4pm).
1 Nov–17 Dec & 31 Jan–31 March
2001: 10am–2.30pm on Sun, Mon,
Wed, Thur, by pre-booked guided
tour only.

Bookings: **01983 200022** or
01983 281784.
Note: Major refurbishment will be
undertaken in the Durbar Wing in
Spring 2000. The Durbar Room
will be closed from 3 November
2000 until Spring 2001. During that
period, access to other parts of the
house may also be limited.
Entry 1 April–31 Oct: House &
Gardens: £6.90/£5.20/£3.50. Family
ticket (2 adults & 3 children) £17.30.
Gardens only: £3.50/£2.60/£1.80.
1 Nov–12 Dec & 6 Feb–19 March
2001: House only: £5/£4/£3.
Tel 01983 200022

☯ Pevensey Castle

East Sussex (p. 233, 3N)

William the Conqueror landed at Pevensey on 28 Sep 1066 and may have used the Saxon Shore Fort as a shelter for his troops. Look out for the remains of an unusual keep enclosed within the castle's walls.

Open 1 April–30 Sep: 10am–6pm daily. 1–31 Oct: 10am–5pm daily. 1 Nov–31 March 2001: 10am–4pm Wed–Sun. Closed 24–26 Dec and 1 Jan 2001.

Entry £2.50/£1.90/£1.30.

Tel 01323 762604

Access In Pevensey off A259. (OS Map 199; ref TQ 645048.)

Bus Eastbourne Buses 19, Stagecoach South Coast 400, 711 from Eastbourne. Tel 01273 474747.

Train Pevensey & Westham or Pevensey Bay, both ½m.

P (charge payable) ⚐📶 (nearby) 🎧 (also available for the visually impaired and those with learning difficulties) 🍴 (Castle Cottage Tearoom and Restaurant, open all year in the evenings Thu–Sat except Jan. Tel 01323 460382) 📷 🔲 🐕 (restricted areas)

☯ Portchester Castle
🄍

Hampshire (p. 232, 3K)

A residence for kings, this castle has a history stretching back nearly 2,000 years. There are Roman walls – the most complete in Europe– substantial remains of the castle, and an exhibition telling the story of Portchester.

• Free Children's Activity Sheet and CD-Rom showing details of English castles.

Open 1 April–30 Sep: 10am–6pm daily. 1–31 Oct: 10am–5pm daily. 1 Nov–31 March 2001: 10am–4pm daily. Closed 24–26 Dec and 1 Jan 2001.

Entry £2.70/£2/£1.40.

Tel 02392 378291

Access On S side of Portchester off A27, Junction 11 on M27. (OS Map 196; ref SU 625046.)

Bus First Provincial 1/A/C, 5 Fareham–Southsea to within ½m. Tel 02392 650967.

Train Portchester 1m.

P ⚐ (grounds & lower levels only) 📶 (in car park) 📷 🔲 🐕 (restricted areas)

☯ Reculver Towers and Roman Fort

Kent (p. 233, 5P)

Standing in a country park, a 12th-century landmark of twin towers and the walls of a Roman fort.

Open Any reasonable time. External viewing only.

Entry Free.

Tel 01227 740676

Access At Reculver 3m E of Herne Bay. (OS Map 179; ref TR 228694.)

Bus Stagecoach East Kent 655 from Herne Bay. Tel 0845 769 6996.

Train Herne Bay 4m.

P 📶 🐕 ⚐ (ground floor only – long slope up from car park)

◷ Richborough Roman Fort

Kent (p. 233, 5P)

This fort and township date back to the Roman landing in AD43. The fortified walls and the massive foundations of a triumphal arch which stood 25 metres (80 feet) high still survive. The museum shows aspects of Roman life and artefacts from this busy Roman township.

• Roman Handling Collection.

• Children's club – phone property for details.

• Beautiful picnic spot.

Open 1 April–30 Sep: 10am–6pm daily. 1–31 Oct: 10am–5pm daily. 1 Nov–30 Nov : 10am–4pm

Wed–Sun. 1 Dec–28 Feb 2001: 10am–4pm Sat–Sun. 1 March–31 March 2001: 10am–4pm Wed–Sun. Closed 24–26 Dec and 1 Jan 2001.

Entry £2.50/£1.90/£1.30.

Tel 01304 612013

Access 1½m N of Sandwich off A257. (OS Map 179; ref TR 324602.)

Train Sandwich 2m.

P ♿ 🎧 ⚹ 📷

🚻 (restricted areas)

◷ Richborough Roman ⊖ Amphitheatre

Kent (p. 233, 5P)

Ditch associated with the nearby 3rd-century castle.

Open Any reasonable time, but difficult access through farmed field. Please telephone Richborough Roman Fort on **01304 612013** for details.

Entry Free.

Access 1¼m N of Sandwich off A257, Junction 7 of M2, onto A2. (OS Map 179; ref TR 321598.)

Train Sandwich 1¾m.

◷ Rochester Castle

Kent (p. 233, 5N)

Built on the Roman city wall, this Norman bishop's castle was a vital royal stronghold.

Open 1 April–30 Sep: 10am–6pm daily. 1–31 Oct: 10am–5pm daily. 1 Nov–31 March 2001: 10am–4pm daily. Closed 24–26 Dec and 1 Jan 2001. (Property managed by Rochester upon Medway City Council.)

Entry Please call for details

Tel 01634 402276

Access By Rochester Bridge (A2), Junction 1 of M2 and Junction 2 of M25. (OS Map 178; ref TQ 742686.)

Bus From surrounding areas. Tel 0845 769 6996.

Train Rochester ½m.

🚻 (in castle grounds) ⚹ ▭

🎧 *small charge* 🚻

⊕ Rollright Stones

Oxfordshire (p. 232/236/239,71)
Three groups of stones, known as 'The King's Men', 'The Whispering Knights' and 'The King Stone', spanning nearly 2,000 years of the Neolithic and Bronze Ages.

Open The King's Men any reasonable time by courtesy of the owner, who may levy a charge. The King Stone & The Whispering Knights any reasonable time, by footpath.
Entry Free.

Access Off unclassified road between A44 and A3400, 2m NW of Chipping Norton near villages of Little Rollright and Long Compton. (OS Map 185; ref SP 297308.)
P (in layby) 🍽

⊕ Royal Garrison Church

Hampshire (p. 233, 3K)
Originally a hospice for pilgrims, this 16th-century chapel became the Garrison Church after the dissolution.

Open 1 April–30 Sep: 11am–4pm Mon–Fri. Keykeeper in winter (Tel 02392 378291).
Entry Free.
Tel 02392 378291
Access On Grand Parade S of

Portsmouth High St. (OS Map 196; ref SU 633992.)
Bus From surrounding areas. Tel 01962 868944.
Train Portsmouth Harbour ¾m.
P (nearby) 🦽 🍽

⊕ Rycote Chapel

Oxfordshire (p. 232/239, 6K)
A 15th-century chapel, with exquisitely carved and painted woodwork and many intriguing features, such as two roofed pews and a musicians' gallery.

📽 The wedding scene from LWT's *Jane Eyre* was filmed here.
Open 1 April–30 Sep: 2–6pm Fri–Sun and Bank Holidays.
Entry £1.60/£1.20/80p.
Access 3m SW of Thame off A329. (OS Map 165; ref SP 667046.)

Bus Arriva The Shires 260, 280, Oxford–Aylesbury (pass ⇌ Haddenham and Thame Parkway) to within ¼m. Tel 0345 788788.
Train Haddenham & Thame - Parkway 5m.
P 🏠 🍽 🦽 (assistance required)

⊕ St Augustine's Abbey

Kent (p. 233, 50)
This great shrine, founded by St Augustine in 597, the year he arrived in England from Rome, marks the birthplace of Christianity in this country. St Augustine himself is buried here. Along with the Cathedral, the Abbey is part of the Canterbury World Heritage Site – Christian monuments representing the most important change in English life since Roman times.

• Enjoy the museum and free interactive audio tour.

Open 1 April–30 Sep: 10am–6pm daily. 1–31 Oct: 10am–5pm daily. 1 Nov–31 March 2001: 10am–4pm daily. Closed 24–26 Dec and 1 Jan 2001.

Entry £2.50/£1.90/£1.30.
Tel 01227 767345
Access In Longport ¼m E of Cathedral Close. (OS Map 179; ref TR 154578.)
Local Tourist Information Canterbury (Tel 01227 766567)

Bus From surrounding areas. Tel 0845 769 6996.
Train Canterbury East & West, both ¾m.
P (nearby)
🦽 (some steps)
🎧 *interactive*
E 🚻 🏠 🍽

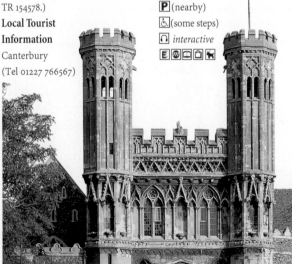

✛ St Augustine's Cross

Kent (p. 233, 5P)
19th-century cross, in Celtic design,
marking the traditional site of
St Augustine's landing in 597.
Open Any reasonable time.

St Augustine's Cross

Entry Free.
Access 2m E of Minster off B29048.
(OS Map 179; ref TR 340641.)
Bus Thanet Bus 01 Ramsgate –
Canterbury. Tel 0845 769 6996.
Train Minster 2m. 🦽 ⊞

◓ St Catherine's Oratory

⊖ *Isle of Wight (p. 232, 3K)*
Affectionately known as the
Pepperpot, this 14th-century
lighthouse stands on the highest
point of the island.
Open Any reasonable time.
External viewing only.
(Property maintained and
managed by the National Trust.)
Entry Free.

Access ¼m NW of Niton.
(OS Map 196; ref SZ 494773.)
Bus Southern Vectis 6/A Ventnor-
Newport, 7/A Yarmouth–Ryde, to
within ½ or 1m depending on route.
Tel 01983 827005.
Train Shanklin 9m.
Ferry West Cowes 14m;
East Cowes 14m (Red Funnel. Tel
02380 334010); Yarmouth 15m
(Wightlink. Tel 0870 582744).
🅿 ⊞

✛ St John's Commandery

Kent (p. 233, 4P)
A medieval chapel, converted into
a farmhouse in the 16th century. It
has a fine moulded plaster ceiling
and a remarkable timber roof.

Open Any reasonable time
for exterior viewing. Internal
viewing by appointment only,
call **01304 211067** for details.
Entry Free.

Access 2m NE of Densole off A260.
(OS Map 179; ref TR 232440.)
Bus Stagecoach East Kent 16
⇌ Folkestone Central–Canterbury
to within 1m. Tel 0845 769 6996.
Train Kearsney 4m. ⊞

✛ St Leonard's Tower

Kent (p. 233, 5N)
An early and particularly fine
example of a Norman tower keep,
built c.1080 by Gundulf, Bishop
of Rochester.
Open Any reasonable time for
exterior viewing.
To view interior, contact West
Malling Parish Council, Mon–Fri,
9am–noon, tel **01732 870872**.
Entry Free.
Access On unclassified road
W of A228. (OS Map 188;
ref TQ 675570.)

Bus Arriva Kent & East Sussex 70
from Maidstone, 151 from Chatham.
Tel 0345 696 996.

Train West Malling 1m.
🦽 (grounds only) ⊞

❂ Silchester Roman City
❂ Walls and Amphitheatre
Hampshire (p. 232, 5K)
The best-preserved Roman town walls in Britain, with an impressive, recently restored amphitheatre.

Open Any reasonable time.
Entry Free.
Access On minor road 1m E of Silchester. (OS Map 175; ref SU 643624.)

Bus Stagecoach Hampshire Bus 44A from Basingstoke (passes ≷Bramley) to within 1m. Tel 01962 846924.
Train Bramley or Mortimer, 2 ¾m.
🅿 ⛺

⊕ Stone Chapel
See Faversham: Stone Chapel, p. 51.

♡ Sutton Valence Castle
Kent (p. 233, 5O)
The ruins of a 12th-century stone keep.

Open Any reasonable time.
Entry Free.
Access 5m SE of Maidstone in Sutton Valence village on A274. (OS Map 188; ref TR 815491.)

Bus Arriva Kent & East Sussex 12 Maidstone–Tenterden (pass ≷Headcorn) Tel 0845 769 6996.
Train Headcorn 4m, and Hollingbourne 5m. ⛺

◉ Temple Manor
Kent (p. 233, 5N)
The 13th-century manor house of the Knights Templar.

Open 1 April–30 Sep: 10am–6pm Sat–Sun and Bank Holidays. Please telephone **01634 827980** for details. (Property managed by Rochester upon Medway City Council.)
Entry Free.

Access In Strood (Rochester) off A228. (OS Map 178; ref TQ 733686.)
Bus From surrounding areas. Tel 0845 769 6996.
Train Strood ¼m.
🅿 ♿ (grounds only)

⊕ Titchfield Abbey
Hampshire (p. 232, 4K)
Remains of a 13th-century abbey overshadowed by a grand Tudor gatehouse.

Open 1 April–30 Sep: 10am–6pm daily. 1–31 Oct: 10am–5pm daily. 1 Nov–31 March 2001: 10am– 4pm daily. (Property managed by The Titchfield Abbey Association.)
Entry Free.

Access ½m N of Titchfield off A27. (OS Map 196; ref SU 541067.)
Bus Solent Blue Line 26 Fareham–Southampton. Tel 02380 226235.
Train Fareham 2m.
🅿 ♿ ⛺

⬤ Uffington Castle, White Horse and Dragon Hill

Oxfordshire

(p. 232/235/239, 6J)

A group of sites lying along the Ridegway, an old prehistoric route. There is a large Iron Age camp enclosed within ramparts, a natural mound known as Dragon Hill and the spectacular White Horse, cut from turf to reveal the chalk.

Open Any reasonable time. (Property owned and managed by the National Trust.)

Entry Free.

Access S of B4507, 7m W of Wantage.

(OS Map 174; ref SU 301866.) P 🐾

⬤ Upnor Castle

Kent (p. 233, 5N)

Well-preserved 16th-century gun fort, built to protect Queen Elizabeth I's warships.

Open 1 April–30 Sep: 10am–6pm daily. Telephone 01634 827980 for further details.

(Site managed by Rochester-upon-Medway City Council.)

Entry Please call for details.

Tel 01634 718742

Access At Upnor, on unclassified road off A228.

(OS Map 178; ref TQ 758706.)

Bus Arriva Kent & East Sussex 197

from 🚃Chatham, otherwise 191/ 4 Chatham–Hoo, alight Wainscott, thence 1m. Tel 0845 769 6996.

Train Strood 2m.

P (at a slight distance from castle – park before village)

🚻 🎧 ♿ (grounds only)

🐾 (restricted areas)

⬤ Walmer Castle and Gardens

Kent (p. 233, 5P)

See p. 74-75 for full details.

⬤ Waverley Abbey

Surrey (p. 232, 4L)

See p. 76 for full details.

Walmer Castle and Gardens

Built to withstand the wrath of the French and Spanish following Henry VIII's break with the Roman Catholic Church, the defences of Walmer Castle have in fact never been put to the test. Early 1539 saw England under the threat of invasion and Henry built a series of castles from Cornwall to Kent, which ended with the linked fortresses of Deal, Walmer and Sandown. The expected attack never materialized and, although the castles of the Downs were brought to readiness again in 1588 to repel the Spanish Armada, no fighting took place.

Walmer was transformed when it became the official residence of the Lords Warden of the Cinque Ports, an ancient title that originally involved control of the five most important medieval ports on the south coast. Past Wardens include William Pitt the Younger, the Duke of Wellington and Sir Winston Churchill. By the 18th century, however, the position was largely ceremonial, although it retained immense prestige and a substantial salary. The Duke of Dorset was the first Lord Warden to use Walmer, turning the fort into a stately home, increasing the number of first-floor rooms by extending the living quarters out over the bastions. Further additions were made by Earl Granville, Lord Warden from 1865, who commissioned the extension of the gatehouse bastion.

The magnificent gardens surrounding the castle owe much to the enthusiasm of Pitt the Younger, and much of his early landscaping remains.

The castle is full of memories of former Lords Warden, including two rooms that are now dedicated to the Duke of Wellington.

Today's Lord Warden, Queen Elizabeth the Queen Mother, still visits Walmer and some rooms used by her are open to visitors. Another treat is the recently completed magnificent Queen Mother's Garden.

- Superb Gift Shop.
- Free audio tour available.
- Visit the Lord Wardens' Tea Rooms for homemade lunches and afternoon tea.
- Plants on sale.

Open 1 April–30 Sep: 10am–6pm daily. 1–31 Oct: 10am–5pm daily. 1 Nov–31 Dec & 1–31 March 2001: 10am–4pm Wed–Sun. Closed 24–26 Dec, Jan–Feb 2001 and when Lord Warden is in residence.
Entry £4.50/£3.40/£2.30.
Tel 01304 364288
Access On coast S of Walmer on A258. Junction 13 off M20 or from M2 to Deal. (OS Map 179; ref TR 378501.)
Local Tourist Information
Deal (Tel 01304 369576) and Dover (Tel 01304 205108).
Bus From surrounding areas. Tel 0845 769 6996.
Train Walmer 1m.
🚻🛍 **P** (nearby approach to castle) 🎧 (also available for the visually impaired, those with learning difficulties, and in French and German) ♿ (courtyard & garden only, parking available) 🍴 (Lord Wardens' Tea Rooms: open daily April–Oct, Sun only Nov–March) 📷✗

Opposite page, bottom, Walmer gardens. Top left and right, aerial and general views of Walmer Castle. This page, top, the gatehouse bastion; right, the Corridor and Lantern. Above, the original 'Wellington boots'.

Waverley Abbey

THE NORTH-WEST VIEW OF WAVERLEY-ABBY, IN THE COUNTY OF SURR.

Waverley was the first Cistercian abbey to be established in England. It was founded in 1128 by William Gifford, the Bishop of Winchester, with monks from L'Aumone in France.

The Cistercians were an order of monks who took their name from the abbey of Citeaux in Burgundy. They developed a simple and austere form of monasticism in the early 12th century which looked back to the 6th century teachings of St Benedict. Their abbeys were sited in remote locations to avoid the distractions of everyday life, and the monks devoted their lives to regular prayer, study and manual labour. Cistercian monks became known as 'white monks' from their simple undyed habits.

The surviving buildings at Waverley date from the 13th century when the abbey church was rebuilt on a much grander scale than the original construction.

The buildings are typical of the Cistercian Order and are arranged around a courtyard or cloister with the church on the north side. The surviving buildings include the chapter house where the main business of the abbey would take place, and the domestic quarters of both the choir monks and the lay brothers who would have performed much of the manual labour to support the abbey estates.

Like other monastic foundations Waverley was suppressed by

Above, an engraving of Waverley Abbey by Buck, 1737.

Henry VIII in 1536, and the buildings were largely demolished for their valuable building materials. A history of the abbey was published in the 18th century which provided the inspiration for Sir Walter Scott's first novel, *Waverley*.

Open Any reasonable time.

Entry Free.

Access 2m SE of Farnham off B3001 and off Junction 10 of M25. (OS Map 186; ref SU 868453.)

Train Farnham 2m.

P (limited) 🚻 ♿

⬤ Wayland's Smithy

Oxfordshire
(p. 232/235/239, 6J)
Near to the Uffington White Horse
lies this evocative Neolithic burial
site, surrounded by a small circle of
trees.
Open Any reasonable time.
(Property managed by the National
Trust.)
Entry Free.
Access On the Ridgeway ¼m NE of
B4000 Ashbury- Lambourn road.
(OS Map 174; ref SU 281854.)

◐ Western Heights

Dover, Kent (p. 232, 4P)
Parts of the moat of a 19th-century
fort built to fend off French attacks.
Now part of the White Cliffs
Countryside Project.
Open Any reasonable time.
Entry free
Tel 01304 241806
Access Above Dover town on
W side of harbour.
(OS Map 179; ref TR 312408.)
Train Dover Priory ¼m.

✛ Wolvesey Castle (Old Bishop's Palace)

Hampshire (p. 232, 4K)
One of the greatest medieval
buildings in England, the palace
was the chief residence of the
Bishops of Winchester. Its
extensive ruins still reflect their
importance and wealth. The last
great occasion at Wolvesey was on
25 July 1554 when Queen Mary and
Philip of Spain held their wedding
breakfast in the East Hall.
Open 1 April–30 Sep: 10am–6pm
daily. 1–31 Oct: 10am–5pm daily.
Closed 1 Nov–31 March 2001. Please
call 01732 778028 to arrange out of
season visits.
Entry £1.80/£1.40/90p.
Tel 01962 854766

Access ¼m SE of Winchester
Cathedral, next to the Bishop's
Palace; access from College St.
(OS Map 185; ref SU 484291.)

Bus From surrounding areas.
Tel 01962 846924.
Train Winchester ¾m.

◑ Yarmouth Castle

Isle of Wight (p. 232, 3J)
This last addition to Henry VIII's
coastal defences was completed in
1547. It houses exhibitions of
paintings of the Isle of Wight and
photographs of old Yarmouth.
• Magnificent picnic spot with
  views over the Solent.
Open 1 April–30 Sep: 10am–6pm
daily. 1–31 Oct: 10am–5pm daily.
Entry £2.10/£1.60/£1.10.
Tel 01983 760678
Access In Yarmouth adjacent to
car ferry terminal.
(OS Map 196; ref SZ 354898.)
Ferry Yarmouth adjacent
(Wightlink. Tel 0870 582 744).
P (coach & car park 200 yards,
limited roadside of 1hr)
(ground floor only)

South West

Left, and in the background, one of the wonders of the world, Stonehenge, in Wiltshire; below, a Tudor Special Event at Mulcheney Abbey, in Somerset; right, King Doniert's Stone, in Cornwall.

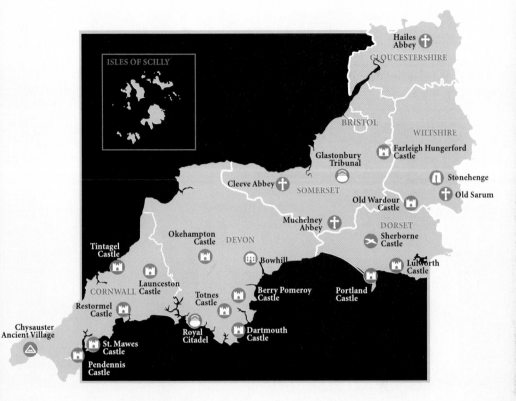

ISLES OF SCILLY

Hailes
Abbey

GLOUCESTERSHIRE

BRISTOL

WILTSHIRE

Farleigh Hungerford
Castle

Glastonbury
Tribunal

Cleeve Abbey

SOMERSET

Stonehenge

Old Sarum

Old Wardour
Castle

Muchelney
Abbey

DORSET

Okehampton
Castle

DEVON

Sherborne
Castle

Tintagel
Castle

Bowhill

Lulworth
Castle

Launceston
Castle

CORNWALL

Berry Pomeroy
Castle

Portland
Castle

Totnes
Castle

Restormel
Castle

Chysauster
Ancient Village

Royal
Citadel

Dartmouth
Castle

St. Mawes
Castle

Pendennis
Castle

⊙ Abbotsbury Abbey Remains

Dorset (p. 235, 3G)

The remains of a cloister building of this Benedictine abbey.

Open Any reasonable time. (Property managed by the Ilchester Estates.)

Entry Free.

Access In Abbotsbury, off B3157, near churchyard.

(OS Map 194; ref SY 578852.)

Bus First Southern National 210 ⇌ Weymouth–Bridport.

Tel 01305 783645.

Train Upwey 7 ½ m.

P ⊞

---

⑰ Alexander Keiller Museum

Wiltshire (p. 232/235, 5I)

The investigation of Avebury Stone Circles was largely the work of Alexander Keiller in the 1930s. He put together one of the most important prehistoric archaeological collections in Britain, which can be seen here.

Open 1 April–31 Oct: 10am–6pm daily. 1 Nov–31 March 2001: 10am–4pm daily. Closed 24–26 Dec and 1 Jan 2001.

Entry £1.80/80p. (Collection on loan to the National Trust.)

Tel 01672 539250

Access In Avebury 7m W of

Marlborough. (OS Map 173; ref SU 100700.)

Bus Thamesdown 49/A Swindon–Devizes/Marlborough; Wilts & Dorset 5/6 Salisbury–Swindon (all pass close ⇌ Swindon).

Tel 0345 090 899.

Train Pewsey 10m; Swindon 11m.

P (in village) ⊞ ⊞ ⊞ ⊞ ⊞

Avebury

Wiltshire

See also Silbury Hill, The Sanctuary, West Kennet Avenue, West Kennet Long Barrow and Windmill Hill.

Right, Avebury Stone Circles.

---

① Avebury Stone Circles

Wiltshire (p. 232/235, 5I)

Complex, gigantic and mysterious, the Circles were constructed 4,500 years ago. The remains of the Circles still surround the later village of Avebury.

Open Any reasonable time. (Property owned and managed by the National Trust.)

Entry Free.

Access In Avebury 7m W of Marlborough. (OS Map 173; ref SU 103700.)

Bus Thamesdown 49/A Swindon–Devizes/Marlborough; Wilts & Dorset 5/6 Salisbury–Swindon (all pass close ⇌ Swindon).

Tel 0845 709 0899.

Train Pewsey 10m; Swindon 11m.

P ⊞ ⊞ (in village) ⊞

⊛ Ballowall Barrow

Cornwall (p.234, 1A)

In a spectacular position, this is an unusual Bronze Age chambered tomb with a complex layout.

Open Any reasonable time. (Property managed by the National Trust.)

Entry Free.

Access 1m W of St Just, near Carn

Gloose. (OS Map 203; ref SW 354313.)

Bus First Western National 11/A Penzance–St Just thence 1m.

Tel 01209 719988.

Train Penzance 8m. ⊞

⊜ Bant's Carn Burial Chamber & Halangy Down Ancient Village

St Mary's, Isles of Scilly (p. 234, 4A)

In a wonderful scenic location, on a

hill above the site of the ancient Iron Age village, lies this Bronze Age burial mound with entrance passage and chamber.

Open Any reasonable time.

Entry Free.

Access 1m N of Hugh Town. (OS Map 203; ref SV 911124.) ⊞

☯ Bayard's Cove Fort

Devon (p. 235, 2E)

A small artillery fort built before 1534 to defend the harbour entrance.

Open Any reasonable time. (Property managed by South Hams District Council.)

Entry Free.

Access In Dartmouth, on riverfront. (OS Map 202; ref SX 879510.)

Bus Stagecoach Devon 200

Paignton–Kingswear, thence ferry to Dartmouth; First Western National 89 Totnes–Dartmouth. Tel 01392 382800.

Train Paignton, 7m via vehicle ferry.

⬢ Belas Knap Long Barrow

Gloucestershire (p. 232/239, 7H)

A good example of a Neolithic long barrow, with the mound still intact and surrounded by a stone wall. The chamber tombs, where the remains of 31 people were found, have been opened up so that visitors can see inside.

Open Any reasonable time. (Property managed by Gloucestershire County Council.)

Entry Free.

Access 2m S of Winchcombe, near Charlton Abbots, ½ m on Cotswold Way. (OS Map 163; ref SP 021254.)

Bus Castleways from Cheltenham to within 1 ¾m. Tel 01242 602949.

Train Cheltenham 9m.

☯ Berry Pomeroy Castle

♡
6
Devon (p. 235, 2E)

A romantic castle, unusual in combining the remains of a large castle with a flamboyant courtier's mansion.

• Picnic spot of exceptional beauty.

Open 1 April–30 Sep: 10am–6pm daily. 1–31 Oct: 10am–5pm daily.

Entry £2.20/£1.70/£1.10.

Tel 01803 866618

Access 2 ½m E of Totnes off A385. (OS Map 202; ref SX 839623.)

Train Totnes 3 ½m.

▢ ⴕ P (no coach access)

⌧ ⴰ ⬢ (grounds & ground floor only) ⬛ (not managed by English Heritage)

Right, Berry Pomeroy Castle.

⬢ Blackbury Camp

Devon (p. 235, 3F)

An Iron Age hill fort, defended by a bank and ditch.

Open Any reasonable time.

Entry Free.

Access 1½m SW of Southleigh off B3174/A3052.

(OS Map 192; ref SY 188924.)

Train Honiton 6 ½m.

✛ Blackfriars

6
Gloucestershire (p. 232/239, 7H)

A small Dominican priory church. Most of the original 13th-century church remains, including a rare scissor-braced roof.

Open Access restricted. Please telephone **0117 975 0700** for further information.

Entry Free.

Access In Ladybellegate St off Southgate St and Blackfriars Walk. (OS Map 162; ref SO 830186.)

Bus From surrounding areas. Tel 01452 425543.

Train Gloucester ½ m.

81

⊕ Bowhill

Devon (p. 235, 3E)

A mansion of considerable status built c.1500 by a member of the Holland family. The impressive Great Hall has been carefully restored by English Heritage craftsmen using traditional materials and techniques.

Open Good Friday to Easter Monday inclusive, Bank Holidays and the 2nd and 4th Thursday of each month until end Oct 2000. Tours 2–4pm. Access at other times by prior arrangement with the administrator. (Property managed by the Devonshire Association.) **Tel 01392 252461**

Entry £1.50.
Access 1½m SW of Exeter on B3212. (OS Map 192; ref SX 906916.)
Bus From surrounding areas. Tel 01392 382800.
Train Exeter, St Thomas ½m.
P ✖

⊙ Bradford-on-Avon Tithe Barn

Wiltshire (p. 232/235, 5H)

A medieval barn with slate roof and wooden beamed interior.

Open 10.30am–4pm daily. Closed 25 Dec. Keykeeper.
Entry Free.
Access ¼m S of town centre, off B3109.
(OS Map 173; ref ST 824604.)

Bus First Badgerline X4/5 Bath–Salisbury, 265 Bath–Frome Tel 0845 709 0899.
Train Bradford-on-Avon ¼m.
P ♿ ✖

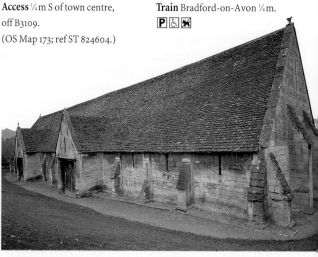

▲ Bratton Camp and White Horse

Wiltshire (p. 232/235, 5H)

A large Iron Age hill fort.

Open Any reasonable time.
Entry Free.
Access 2m E of Westbury off B3098, 1m SW of Bratton. (OS Map 184; ref ST 900516.)

Train Westbury 3m.
P ✖

✠ Butter Cross

Somerset (p. 235, 4E)

A medieval stone cross.

Open Any reasonable time. (Property managed by the National Trust.)
Entry Free.
Access Beside minor road to Alcombe, 350 metres (400 yards) NW of Dunster parish church.

(OS Map 181; ref SS 988439.)
Bus First Southern National 28, 928 Taunton–Minehead, also 38/9 from Minehead to within ½m. Tel 01823 272033.
Train Dunster (W Somerset Railway) 1m.

● Carn Euny Ancient Village

● *Cornwall (p. 234, 1A)*

The remains of an Iron Age settlement, with foundations of stone huts and an intriguing curved underground passage, or 'fogou'.

Open Any reasonable time. (Property managed by the Cornwall Heritage Trust.)

Entry Free.

Access 1¼ m SW of Sancreed off A30. (OS Map 203; ref SW 402289.)

Bus First Western National 10A/B Penzance–St Just to within 2m. Tel 01209 719988.

Train Penzance 6m.

P (600-metre walk [660 yards] to property from car park in Brane)
🐾

● Chisbury Chapel

Wiltshire (p. 232/235, 5J)

A thatched 13th-century chapel rescued from use as a farm building.

Open Any reasonable time.

Entry Free.

Access On unclassified road, ¼ m E of Chisbury off A4,

6m E of Marlborough. (OS Map 174; ref SU 280658.)

Train Bedwyn 1m.
🐾

● Christchurch Castle and Norman House

Dorset (p. 232/235, 3J)

Early 12th-century Norman keep and Constable's house.

Open Any reasonable time.

Entry Free.

Access In Christchurch, near Priory. (OS Map 195; ref SZ 160927.)

Bus From surrounding areas. Tel 01202 673555.

Train Christchurch ¾ m.
🐾

● Chysauster Ancient Village

● *Cornwall (p.234, 1A)*

The original inhabitants of this deserted ancient Romano-Cornish settlement occupied the site almost 2,000 years ago.

The 'village' consisted of eight stone-walled homesteads known as 'courtyard houses'. Each house had an open central courtyard surrounded by a number of thatched rooms. The house actually forms one of the oldest village streets in the country.

Open 1 April–30 Sep: 10am–6pm daily. 1–31 Oct: 10am–5pm daily.

Tel 07831 757934

Entry £1.60/£1.20/80p.

Access 2½ m NW of Gulval off B3311. (OS Map 203; ref SW 473350.)

Bus First Western National 16 Penzance–St Ives to within 1 ½ m. Tel 01209 719988.

Train Penzance 3 ½ m.
P 🍴 ♿ 📷 🐾

● Cirencester Amphitheatre

Gloucestershire (p. 232/235/239, 6H)

A large well-preserved Roman amphitheatre, earth covered.

Open Any reasonable time.

(Property managed by Cotswold District Council.)

Entry Free.

Access Next to bypass W of town – access from town or along Chesterton Lane from W end

of bypass on to Cotswold Avenue Park next to obelisk. (OS Map 163; ref SP 020014.)

Bus Alex Cars/Stagecoach rail-link from ⇌ Kemble (4m). Tel 01452 425543. 🐾

Cleeve Abbey

Somerset (p. 235, 4F)

One of the few 13th-century monastic sites where you can still see such a complete set of cloister buildings.

Open 1 April–30 Sep: 10am–6pm daily. 1–31 Oct: 10am–5pm daily. 1 Nov–31 March 2001: 10am–1pm, 2–4pm daily. Closed 24–26 Dec and 1 Jan 2001.

- **Year of the Artist venue**
  From June to November 2000, a digital photography/print residency will reflect the Abbey and its landscape throughout the four seasons. Events will be held during the residency leading to an exhibition in the autumn. Please call for details.

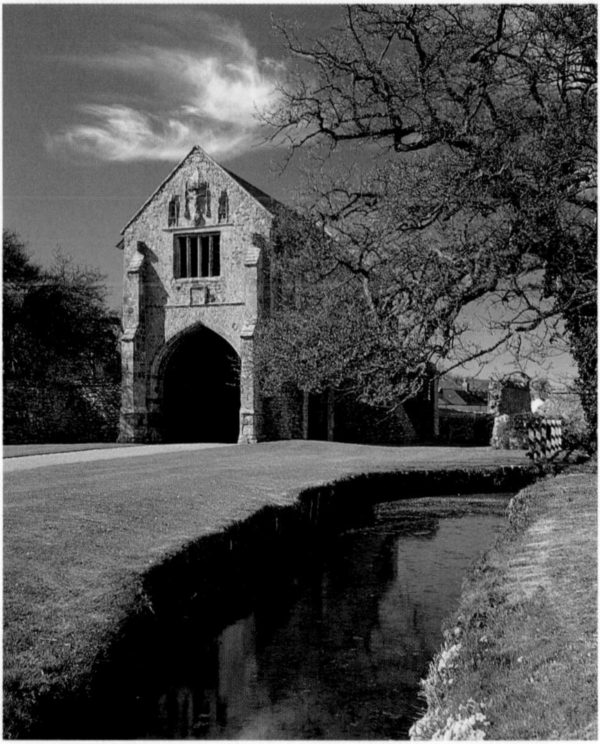

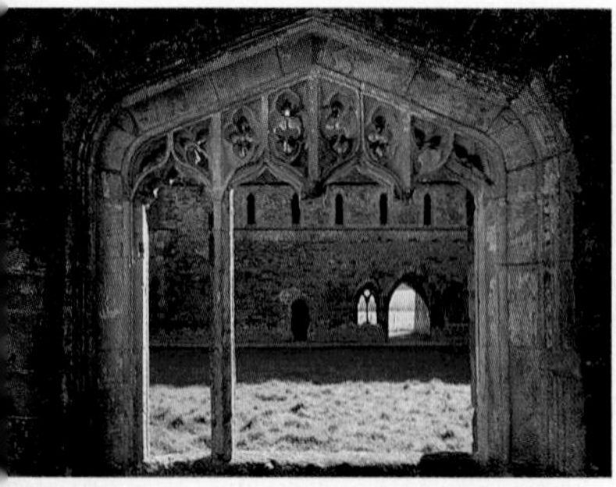

Entry £2.60/£2/£1.30.
Tel 01984 640377
Access In Washford, ¼m S of A39. (OS Map 181; ref ST 047407.)
Bus First Southern National 28, 928 ⇄Taunton–Minehead, also 38 from Minehead. Tel 01823 272033.
Train Washford (W Somerset Railway) ½m.
P E (restricted areas)
(grounds & ground floor only)

Cromwell's Castle

Tresco, Isles of Scilly (p. 234, 5A)

Standing on a promontory guarding the lovely anchorage between Bryher and Tresco, this 17th-century round tower was built to command the haven of New Grimsby.

Open Any reasonable time.
Entry Free.
Access On shoreline, ¾m NW of New Grimsby. (OS Map 203; ref SV 882159.)

Dartmouth Castle

Devon (p. 235, 2E)

See opposite page for full details.

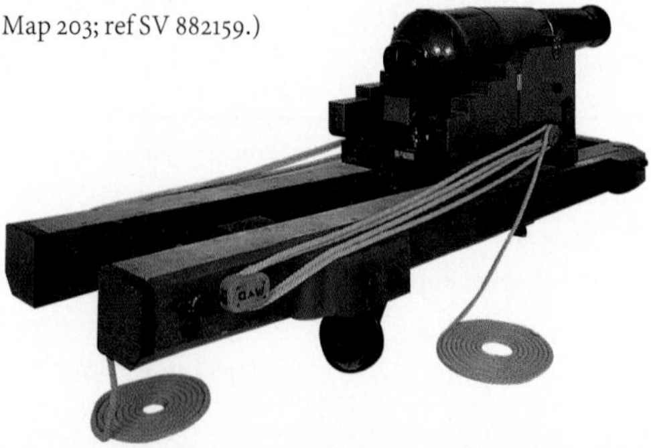

Dartmouth Castle

This brilliantly positioned defensive castle juts out into the narrow entrance to the Dart estuary, with the sea lapping at its foot.

Begun late in the 14th century, when the merchants of Dartmouth felt the need to protect their homes and warehouses from invasion, it was one of the first castles constructed with artillery in mind. It is said that Chaucer chose the colourful and powerful John Hawley, merchant and mayor of Dartmouth at that time, as a model for the Shipman in his masterpiece, *The Canterbury Tales*. Since the 14th century Dartmouth has seen 600 years of fortification and preparation for war.

The views from the castle of the town of Dartmouth, the River Dart and out to the Channel are exceptionally beautiful.

• **New for 2000** New hands-on exhibitions bring 600 years of Dartmouth Castle's history to life.

• Ride from Paignton by steam train! Contact Dart Valley Light Railway on 01803 553760.

• Picnic spot of exceptional beauty.

Open 1 April–30 Sep: 10am–6pm daily. 1–31 Oct: 10am–5pm daily. 1 Nov–31 March 2001: 10am–1pm, 2–4pm Wed–Sun. Closed 24–26 Dec and 1 Jan 2001.

Entry £2.90/£2.20/£1.50.

Tel 01803 833588

Access 1m SE of Dartmouth off B3205, narrow approach road. (OS Map 202; ref SX 887503.)

Local Tourist Information Dartmouth (Tel 01803 834224).

Bus Stagecoach Devon 200 Paignton–Kingswear, thence ferry to Dartmouth; First Western National 89 Totnes–Dartmouth. Tel 01392 382800. On both, alight Dartmouth thence 1m walk or foot ferry.

Train Paignton 8m via ferry.

P (limited) 🚻 📷 ✗ ⌂

⬟ Daws Castle

Somerset (p. 235, 4F)

The site where the people of the Saxon town of Watchet sought refuge against the threat of Viking attack.

Open Any reasonable time.
Entry Free.
Access ⅓m W of Watchet off B3191 on cliff edge.
(OS Map 181; ref ST 062434.)

Bus First Southern National 28, 928 ⇌Taunton–Minehead.
Tel 01823 272033.
Train Watchet
(W Somerset Railway) ¾m.
P (layby 200 metres) 🐕

✚ Dupath Well

Cornwall (p. 234, 2D)

A charming granite-built well house set over a holy well of c.1500 and almost complete.

Open Any reasonable time.
(Property managed by the Cornwall Heritage Trust.)
Entry Free.
Access 1m E of Callington off A388.
(OS Map 201; ref SX 374693.)

Bus First Western National 76, X76 Plymouth–Launceston, thence 1m.
Tel 01752 222666.
Train Gunnislake 4½m.
🐕

⬤ Farleigh Hungerford Castle

Somerset (p. 232/235, 5H)
See opposite page for details.

⬤ Fiddleford Manor

Dorset (p. 232/235, 4H)

Part of a medieval manor house, with a remarkable interior. The splendid roof structures in the hall and upper living room are the best in Dorset.

Open 1 April–30 Sep: 10am–6pm daily. 1 Oct–31 March 2001: 10am–4pm daily. Closed 24–26 Dec and 1 Jan 2001.
Entry Free.
Access 1m E of Sturminster Newton off A357.
(OS Map 194; ref ST 801136.)
Bus Damory 310 from Blandford.
Tel 01258 452545.
P 🐕 ♿ (ground floor only – 1 step)

⬤ Gallox Bridge

Somerset (p. 235, 4E)

A stone packhorse bridge with two ribbed arches which spans the old mill stream.

Open Any reasonable time.
(Property managed by the National Trust.)
Entry Free.
Access Off A396 at S end of Dunster.
(OS Map 181; ref SS 990432.)

Bus First Southern National 28, 928 ⇌Taunton–Minehead, also 38/9 from Minehead to within ⅛m.
Tel 01823 272033.
Train Dunster (W Somerset Railway) ¼m.
♿ 🐕

Farleigh Hungerford Castle

In the glorious rolling valley of the River Frome stand the ruins of Farleigh Hungerford Castle, home to the Hungerford Lords for three centuries.

The 'manor of Farleigh' first passed into the hands of the Hungerfords in 1370, when it was acquired and then fortified by Sir Thomas Hungerford. Sir Thomas's son added the outer court and Priest's House early in the 15th century. It was at that time that the manor became known as 'Farleigh Hungerford'.

Although there is little trace today of the the domestic ranges where the family actually lived (the inner court), the courtyard, with its distinctive form of cobbling, is still identifiable. By the beginning of the 18th century Farleigh had fallen into a state of ruin, and of the original Castle only the two southern towers and parts of the curtain wall still survive.

For three centuries the Castle was the setting for colourful and often gruesome events: one Lady Hungerford was made a prisoner in her own castle, in the so-called Lady Tower, another is said to have killed her husband and then burnt his remains in the kitchen furnace.

But the Castle also houses many unique treasures. In the 14th-century chapel of St Leonard are rare medieval wall paintings and the crypt contains one of the most important collections of lead coffins in the country.

Open 1 April–30 Sep: 10am–6pm daily. 1–31 Oct: 10am–5pm daily. 1 Nov–31 March 2001: 10am–1pm, 2–4pm Wed–Sun.
Closed 24–26 Dec and 1 Jan 2001.
Entry £2.30/£1.70/£1.20.
Tel 01225 754026

Access In Farleigh Hungerford, 9m SE of Bath, 3 ½m W of Trowbridge on A366.
(OS Map 173; ref ST 801577.)
Bus First Badgerline X3 Bristol–Frome (passes ⇌ Bath Spa & close ⇌ Frome) to within 1m. Tel 0117 955 3231.
Train Avoncliff 2m; Trowbridge 3 ½m.
🅿 🚻 📷 🎧 ♿ (exterior only) ✈

⚫ Garrison Walls

St Mary's, Isles of Scilly (p. 234, 4A)
You can take a pleasant walk along the ramparts of these well-preserved walls and earthworks, built as part of the island's defences.
Open Any reasonable time.
Entry Free.
Access Around the headland W of Hugh Town.
(OS Map 203; ref SV 898104.)

⊙ Glastonbury Tribunal

⊕ *Somerset (p. 235, 4G)*
A well-preserved medieval town house, probably used by a merchant for commercial purposes.
Open 1 April–30 Sep: 10am–5pm Sun–Thur, 10am–5.30pm Fri–Sat. 1 Oct–31 March 2001: 10am–4pm Sun–Thur, 10am–4.30pm Fri–Sat. Closed 25–26 Dec and 1–2 Jan 2001 (Property managed by Glastonbury Tribunal Ltd.)
Entry Tourist Information Centre: free.
Display areas: £2/£1.
Tel 01458 832954
Email *glastonbury.tic@ukonline.co.uk*
Access In Glastonbury High St. (OS Map 182; ref ST 499390.)
Bus First Badgerline 376, 929, 976
⇌ Bristol Temple Meads–Street. Tel 0117 955 3231.
🅿 ⑩
♿ (ground floor only - 2 steps)

⊘ Great Witcombe Roman Villa

Gloucestershire (p. 232/235/239, 6H)
The remains of a large villa. Built around three sides of a courtyard, it had a luxurious bath-house complex.
Open Exterior: any reasonable time. Guided tours arranged by The Cotswold AONB Partnership: 29 May, 25 June, 13 Aug, 10 Sep, 10am–4pm (last tour 3.30pm).
Entry Free.
Access 5m SE of Gloucester, off A417, ½m S of reservoir in Witcombe Park, 440 yards from Cotswold Way National Trail. (OS Map 163; ref SO 899144.)
Bus Stagecoach City of Gloucester 50 ⇌ Gloucester–Cheltenham to within 1½m. Tel 01452 527516.
Train Gloucester 6m.
♿ 🅿 (no access for coaches)
No parking permitted in lane past car park.

⊕ Greyfriars

∅ *Gloucestershire (p. 239, 7H)*
Remains of a late 15th- and early 16th-century Franciscan friary church.
Open Any reasonable time. (Property managed by Gloucester City Council.)
Entry Free.
Access On Greyfriars Walk, behind Eastgate Market off Southgate St. (OS Map 162; ref SO 830186.)
Bus From surrounding areas. Tel 01452 425543.
Train Gloucester ½m.
♿ ♿

⚫ Grimspound

Devon (p. 234, 3E)
Late Bronze Age settlement with the remains of 24 huts in an area of 4 acres enclosed by a stone wall.
Open Any reasonable time. (Property managed by Dartmoor National Park Authority.)
Entry Free.
Access 6m SW of Moretonhampstead off B3212.
(OS Map 191; ref SX 701809.)
Bus First Western National 82
⇌ Exeter St David's–Plymouth to within 2m. Tel 01392 382800.

✪ Hailes Abbey

Gloucestershire (p. 232/236/239, 7H)
This Cistercian abbey was built by
Richard, Earl of Cornwall in the 13th
century, in gratitude for surviving
a perilous sea journey.

When Edmund, second son
of Earl Richard, presented the
community with a phial said to
contain the blood of Christ, the
abbey became a magnet for pilgrims
right up to the Dissolution, after
which time the abbey church was
demolished and the other buildings
sold.

- **Year of the Artist Venue**
Sculpture residency from June to
August leading to an exhibition in
the autumn. Please call for details.
Open 1 April–30 Sep: 10am–6pm
daily. 1–31 Oct: 10am–5pm daily.
1 Nov–31 March 2001: 10am– 4pm
Sat–Sun. Closed 24–26 Dec and
1 Jan 2001. (Property owned by the

National Trust but maintained and
managed by English Heritage).
Entry £2.60/£2/£1.30. National
Trust members admitted free but
small charge for special events.
Tel 01242 602398
Access 2m NE of Winchcombe off
B4632. (OS Map 150; ref SP 050300.)
Bus Castleways from Cheltenham
to within 1½m. Tel 01242 602949.
Train Cheltenham 10m.

🅿 🚻 ⓪ 🛆 🎧 (also available for

the visually impaired, those with
learning difficulties and wheelchair
users) ♿ (general access, 1 step to
museum)

◗ Halligye Fogou

Cornwall (p. 234, 1B)
One of several strange underground
tunnels, associated with Iron Age
villages, which are unique to
Cornwall.
Open Any reasonable time, but

completely blocked between
31 Oct and 31 March 2001. A torch
is advisable. (Property managed
by the Trelowarren Estate.)
Entry Free to the monument. An
estate entry and car parking charge
will be made by the Estate.

Access 5m SE of Helston off B3293
E of Garras on Trelowarren Estate.
(OS Map 203; ref SW 714239.)
Bus Trurorian T2/3 from Truro.
Tel 01872 273453.
Train Penryn 10m.

◑ Harry's Walls

St Mary's, Isles of Scilly (p. 234, 4B)
An uncompleted 16th-century fort
intended to command the harbour
of St Mary's Pool.

Open Any reasonable time.
Entry Free.
Access ¼m NE of Hugh Town.
(OS Map 203; ref SV 910110.)
🐕

◕ Hatfield Earthworks

Wiltshire (p. 232/235, 5J)
Part of a 3,500-year-old Neolithic
enclosure complex, formerly with
a Bronze Age barrow in its centre.

Open Any reasonable time.
Entry Free.
Access 5 ½m SE of Devizes off A342
NE of village of Marden.

(OS Map 173; ref SU 091583
or SU 092583.)
Train Pewsey 5m.
🐕

⊘ Hound Tor Deserted
Medieval Village
Devon (p. 234, 3E)
Remains of three or four medieval
farmsteads, first occupied in the
Bronze Age.

Open Any reasonable time.
(Property managed by Dartmoor
National Park Authority.)
Entry Free.

Access 1½ m S of Manaton off
the Ashburton road. Park in Hound
Tor car park, ½ m walk.
(OS Map 191; ref SX 746788.)
🐕

⊙ Hurlers Stone Circles
Cornwall (p. 234, 2C)
These three Bronze Age stone
circles in a line are some of the best
examples of ceremonial standing
stones in the South West.

Open Any reasonable time.
(Property managed by the
Cornwall Heritage Trust.)
Entry Free.
Access ½ m NW of Minions off
B3254.(OS Map 201; ref SX 258714.)

Bus First Western National
73 Liskeard–Pensilva to within 2m.
Tel 01209 719988.
Train Liskeard 7m.
🅿️🐕

⊙ Innisidgen Lower and
Upper Burial Chambers
St Mary's, Isles of Scilly (p. 234, 4B)
Two Bronze Age cairns, about

30 metres (200 feet) apart, with
stunning views towards St Martin's.
Open Any reasonable time.
Entry Free.

Access 1¼ m NE of Hugh Town.
(OS Map 203; ref SV 921127.)
🅿️

⊙ Jordan Hill Roman Temple
⊙
Dorset (p. 232/235, 3H)
Foundations of a Romano-Celtic
temple enclosing an area of about
22 square metres (240 square feet).

Open Any reasonable time.
Entry Free.
Access 2m NE of Weymouth off
A353. (OS Map 194; ref SY 698821.)

Bus First Southern National A from
Weymouth. Tel 01305 783645.
Train Upwey or Weymouth,
both 2m.
🐕

⊙ King Charles's Castle
Tresco, Isles of Scilly (p. 234, 5A)
At the end of a bracing coastal walk
to the northern end of Tresco

you will find the remains
of this castle built for coastal
defence.
Open Any reasonable time.

Entry Free.
Access ¼ m NW of New Grimsby.
(OS Map 203; ref SV 882161.)
🐕

⊙ King Doniert's Stone
Cornwall (p. 234, 2C)
Two decorated pieces of a 9th-
century cross with an inscription
believed to commemorate
Durngarth, King of Cornwall,
who drowned c. 875.

Open Any reasonable time.
(Property managed by the
Cornwall Heritage Trust.)
Entry Free.
Access 1m NW of St Cleer off B3254.
(OS Map 201; ref SX 236688.)

Bus First Western National 73
Liskeard–Pensilva to within ½ m.
Tel 01209 719988.
Train Liskeard 4m.
🅿️ (layby) 🐕

⬤ Kingston Russell Stone Circle

Dorset (p. 235, 3G)

A Bronze Age stone circle of 18 stones.
Open Any reasonable time.
Entry Free.

Access 2m N of Abbotsbury, 1m along footpath off minor road to Hardy Monument.
(OS Map 194; ref SY 577878.)

Train Dorchester West or South, both 8m.
P (on verge near entrance to Gorwell Farm) 🐎

✚ Kingswood Abbey Gatehouse

Gloucestershire (p. 232/235/239, 6H)

This gatehouse, with a richly carved mullioned window, is all that remains of the Cistercian abbey.
Open Exterior: any reasonable time. Key for interior obtainable from shop nearby during opening hours.

Entry Free.
Access In Kingswood off B4060 1m SW of Wotton-under-Edge.
(OS Map 162; ref ST 748919.)
Bus First Badgerline 309 Bristol–Dursley. Tel 0117 955 3231.
Train Yate 8m.
🚻 (adjacent to monument) 🐎

🌐 Kirkham House

Devon (p. 235, 2E)

This well-preserved, medieval stone house, much restored and repaired, gives a fascinating insight into life in a town residence in the 15th century.

Open 19 Apr, 17 May, 21 June, 19 July, 16 Aug, 20 Sep: 10am–5pm. Also 21 and 24 April, 1 and 29 May and Sun in July and Aug: 2–5pm in association with the Paignton Preservation & Local History Society.

Entry Free.
Access In Kirkham St, off Cecil Rd, Paignton.
(OS Map 202; ref SX 885610.)
Bus From surrounding areas. Tel 01392 382 800.
Train Paignton ½ m. 🐎

✚ Knowlton Church
⓪ and Earthworks

Dorset (p. 232/235, 4J)

The ruins of this Norman church stand in the middle of Neolithic earthworks, symbolizing the transition from pagan to Christian worship.

Open Any reasonable time.
Entry Free.
Access 3m SW of Cranborne on B3078. (OS Map 195; ref SU 024100.) 🐎

⊕ Launceston Castle

Dorset (p. 232/235, 3H)
See opposite page for details.

⊕ Ludgershall Castle and Cross

⊕ *Wiltshire (p. 234/235, 5J)*
Ruins of an early 12th-century
royal hunting palace and a late-
medieval cross.

Open Any reasonable time.
Entry Free.
Access On N side of Ludgershall off
A342. (OS Map 184; ref SU 264513.)
Bus Stagecoach Hampshire
Bus/Wilts & Dorset 7–9

⇌ Andover–Salisbury.
Tel 0845 709 0899.
Train Andover 7m.
P (limited) ♿ (part of site
only & village cross) ⛺

⊕ Lulworth Castle

Dorset (p. 232/235, 3H)
An early 17th-century romantic
hunting lodge, Lulworth Castle
became a fashionable country house
set in beautiful parkland during the

18th century. Gutted by fire in 1929,
the exterior has been restored by
English Heritage. Interior displays
trace and recreate its history.
Open 26 March–29 Oct: 10am–6pm
Sun–Fri. Last admission to castle
4.30pm. 30 Oct–25 March 2001:
10am–4pm Sun–Fri. Last admission
to castle 3pm. Closed 24-25 Dec.
Open 1 Jan 2001. (Property owned
and managed by the Lulworth Estate.)

Tel 01929 400352
Entry £4/£3.50/£3 until 31 March
2000. £4.50/£3.50/ £3 from 1 April
2000.
English Heritage members wishing
to see the castle only will be
admitted free on presentation of
their membership card. Access to
the Chapel, Woodland Walk, Play
Area, Children's Summer Farm and
Park will be half price. Members
will be charged full admission price
for special events. On occasions, the
Castle may be closed.

Access In east Lulworth off
B3070, 3m NE of Lulworth Cove.
(OS Map 194; ref SY 853822.)
Bus Weaverbus 30 from
Weymouth (passing ⇌ Moreton).
Tel 01305 834 730.
Train Wool 4m.
🚻 P ⛺ ♿ (limited) 🎁🖼🎨🍴
(not managed by English Heritage)

*Above, Lulworth castle, interior.
Above left, painting of the Lulworth
Castle as it was in the early 18th
century, by Bruyn 1731.*

Launceston Castle

Set on the high motte of a stronghold built soon after the Norman Conquest, Launceston Castle – Castel Lanstefan – still dominates the main route into Cornwall. Affording magnificent views of the town and surrounding countryside, the now peaceful location of this medieval castle belies its turbulent history as the fortress used by the powerful Earls of Cornwall.

In addition to its role as fortress, the castle served a number of other purposes. As a grand country house, Launceston was the ideal setting for the lavish entertainment of the various earls and their guests. In grim contrast, as the venue for the County Assizes and Jail, the castle witnessed the trials and

hangings of numerous criminals, with the last execution recorded in 1821. George Fox, founder of the Society of Friends, was imprisoned here in the reign of Charles II, and was able to sample firsthand the cramped and unhygienic conditions for which the jail became infamous.

When, in the late 13th century, the administrative centre for Cornwall was moved from Launceston to Lostwithiel, the castle's status and fortunes declined, although it was still regarded with fear as the location for the courthouse and jail.

After the demolition of the Assizes in 1840, the Duke of Northumberland converted the Castle into a park and so it

remained until the next phase in its colourful history, when it was used as a hospital by the US Army, in 1944.

· **New for 2000** A hands-on exhibition and displays featuring finds from excavations at the castle.

Open 1 April–30 Sep: 10am–6pm daily. 1–31 Oct: 10am–5pm daily. 1 Nov–31 March 2001: 10am–1pm, 2–4pm Fri–Sun. Closed 24–26 Dec and 1 Jan 2001.

Entry £1.80/£1.40/90p.

Tel 01566 772365

Access In Launceston.
(OS Map 201; ref SX 330846.)

Bus First Western National 76, X76 Plymouth–Launceston, X10
⇌Exeter St David's–Boscastle.
Tel 01392 382800.
♿(outer bailey) ⬛ 📷 🐴

⓪ Lydford Castles and Saxon Town

Devon (p. 234, 3D)

Standing above the gorge of the River Lyd, this 12th-century tower was notorious as a prison. The earthworks of the original Norman fort are to the south.

Open Any reasonable time. (Property managed by the National Trust.)
Entry Free.
Access In Lydford off A386, 8m S of Okehampton. (OS Map 191; Castle ref SX 510848, Fort ref SX 509847.)

Bus First Western National 86 Plymouth–Barnstaple.
Tel 01392 382800.

P 🐾

⓪ Maiden Castle

Dorset (p. 235, 3G)

See opposite page for full details.

⊖ Meare Fish House

Somerset (p. 235, 4G)

A simple, well-preserved stone dwelling.

Open Any reasonable time. Key from Manor House farm.
Entry Free.

Access In Meare village on B3151. (OS Map 182; ref ST 458418.)

🐾

⬤ Merrivale Prehistoric Settlement

Devon (p. 234, 3D)

The remains of an early Bronze Age village with two rows of standing stones stretching up to 263 metres (288 yards) across the moors.

Open Any reasonable time. (Property managed by Dartmoor National Park Authority.)
Entry Free.
Access 1m E of Merrivale. (OS Map 191; ref SX 553746.)

Bus First Western National 98 Yelverton–Tavistock (with connections from Plymouth).
Tel 01392 382800.
Train Gunnislake 10m.

🐾

⊕ Muchelney Abbey

Somerset (p. 235, 4G)

See p. 96 for full details.

Maiden Castle

This is the finest and largest Iron Age hill fort in Europe. Its massive banks enclose an area equivalent to 50 football pitches, which would have been home to about 200 families. When the site was excavated in the 1930s and 1980s it provided important information about the way of life of these communities, as well as dramatic proof of British resistance to the Roman invasion in AD43 .

Despite its impressive size, Maiden Castle, with its enormous earthworks and series of ramparts and complicated entrances, was not able to withstand capture by the Romans. Writing about 50 years after the invasion, the Roman historian Tacitus suggested why this may have been so: 'nothing has helped us more in fighting against this powerful nation than their inability to co-operate.' Supporting this idea is that defended enclosures similar to Maiden Castle are known to have been constructed on almost every hilltop in the South West – 31 in Dorset alone – suggesting that long term tribal rivalries prevented the Britons from uniting in their own defence.

It is clear from the thousands of pebbles found in piles within the ramparts that the normal weapon of these Iron Age defenders was the sling, although this primitive form of defence was no match for the superior equipment and professionalism of the Roman Army. A cemetery of about 30 graves near the eastern gateway is thought to be linked to the battle for the castle.

Open Any reasonable time.

Entry Free.

Access 2m S of Dorchester. Access off A354, N of bypass. (OS Map 194; ref SY 670885.)

Train Dorchester South or West, both 2m.

Muchelney Abbey

Outlined in the grass of the quiet island village of Muchelney are the foundations of this Benedictine abbey, said to be the second oldest religious foundation in Somerset (only Glastonbury is older). Tradition has it that monks were first established at Muchelney by Ine, a 7th-century King of Wessex. This first monastery did not survive the Viking invasions but the abbey was refounded about 950 and lasted for nearly six centuries.

Muchelney Abbey underwent alteration when it came under Norman influence. It was rebuilt in the Romanesque style, although a small Saxon crypt was preserved within the foundations of the new abbey church, perhaps as a safe place for relics. The present remains date largely from the 12th century.

The most conspicuous feature of the site today is the Abbot's Lodging which had only just been completed when the abbey was surrendered to Henry VIII in 1539. Built of blue lias, a local stone used for walling, with fine details worked in golden Ham stone from the quarries near Montacute, the Abbot's Lodging survived the Dissolution largely because it served as an attractive and convenient home for its new owners. The Abbot's Parlour houses a splendid fireplace with carved stone lions above it, and fragments of blue and crimson glass showing the initials of the 16th-century Abbot Broke.

Open 1 April–30 Sep: 10am–6pm daily. 1–31 Oct: 10am–5pm daily.
Entry £1.70/£1.30/90p.
Tel 01458 250664
Access In Muchelney 2m S of Langport.
(OS Map 193; ref ST 428248.)
Bus First Southern National 54 Taunton–Yeovil (passes close ≥Taunton) to within 1m.
Tel 01823 272033.
🅿 🚻 🄾 ⊠ 🔄 ♿ (grounds & part of ground floor only)

Top left, aerial view of the abbey church foundations. Top, interior of the Abbot's Parlour. This page, interior of the cloister.

National Monuments Record Centre

Wiltshire (p. 232/235/6J)

The NMR Centre holds 12 million historic and modern photographs, texts and documents – the national record of England's heritage. Visit the public search room, or pop into the Gallery, where a programme of exhibitions, publications, tours and events introduce the wealth of the services the NMR has to offer.

- **New for 2000** New Study Programme. Call 01793 414 735 for bookings and information.
- Special Events for Heritage Open Days.

Open NMR: 9.30am–5pm Tue–Fri and one Saturday a month.

Tel 01793 414 600

The Gallery: 11am–5pm Wed–Sun.

Tel 01793 414 797

A tour of the NMR Centre leaves the Gallery at 2.15pm on the third Sat of most months. Please call for details.

Entry Free.

Access Great Western Village, Kemble Drive, Swindon town centre. (OS map 173; SU 145849.)

Train Swindon ¼m.

Below, May Day garlands near Didcot, Oxford, 1904.

For information and historic photographs of buildings in **London**, visit the London office at 55 Blandford St, W1H 3AF.

Tel 0207 208 8200

Open 10am–5pm Tue–Fri.

ENGLISH HERITAGE

NATIONAL MONUMENTS RECORD

⊙ Netheravon Dovecote

Wiltshire (p. 232/235, 5J)

A charming 18th-century brick dovecote, standing in a pleasant orchard, with most of its 700 or more nesting boxes still present.

Open Exterior viewing only.

Entry Free.

Access In Netheravon, 4 ½m N of Amesbury on A345. (OS Map 184; ref SU 146485.)

Bus Wilts & Dorset 5/6 Salisbury–Swindon (pass close ⇌Salisbury and Swindon). Tel 01722 336855.

Train Pewsey 9m, Grateley 11m.

◉ The Nine Stones

Dorset (p. 235, 3G)

Remains of a prehistoric circle of nine standing stones constructed about 4,000 years ago.

Open Any reasonable time.

Entry Free.

Access ½m W of Winterbourne Abbas, on A35. (OS Map 194; ref SY 611904.)

Bus First Southern National 31 Weymouth– ⇌Axminster

(passing ⇌ Dorchester South). Tel 01305 783645.

Train Dorchester West or South, both 5m.

P (small layby opposite, next to barn; cross road with care)

⬔ Notgrove Long Barrow

Gloucestershire
(p. 232/236/239, 7J)
A Neolithic burial mound with
chambers for human remains
opening from a stone-built
central passage.

Open Any reasonable time.
(Property managed by
Gloucestershire County Council.)
Entry Free.
Access 1½m NW of Notgrove on
A436. (OS Map 163; ref SP 096211.)

Bus Pulham's Moreton-in-
Marsh–Cheltenham (passes
close ⇌Moreton-in-Marsh).
Tel 01451 20369.
🅿 🍽

⬤ Nunney Castle

○ *Somerset (p. 232/235, 5H)*
A small 14th-century moated castle
which is distinctly French in style.
Open Any reasonable time.
Entry Free.
Access In Nunney 3½m SW of
Frome, off A361 (no coach access).
(OS Map 183; ref ST 737457.)
Bus First Badgerline 161/2, 926
Frome–Wells. Tel 01749 673084.
Train Frome 3½m.
♿(exterior only) 🍽

⬔ Nympsfield Long Barrow

Gloucestershire
(p. 232/235/239, 6H)
A chambered Neolithic long barrow
30 metres (90 feet) in length.

Open Any reasonable time.
Entry Free.
(Property managed by
Gloucestershire County Council.)
Access 1m NW of Nympsfield
on B4066. (OS Map 162;
ref SO 795014.)

Bus Stagecoach Stroud Valley 15
Stroud–Dursley (passes close
⇌Stroud). Tel 01452 425543.
Train Stroud 5m.
🅿 🚻(public; 50 metres [55 yards])
🍽

✛ Odda's Chapel

Gloucestershire
(p. 232/239, 7H)
A rare Anglo-Saxon chapel
attached, unusually, to a half-
timbered farmhouse.

Open 1 April–30 Sep: 10am–6pm
daily. 1 Oct–31 March 2001: 10am–
4pm daily. Closed 24–26 Dec and
1 Jan 2001. (Property managed by
Deerhurst Parish Council.)
Entry Free.

Access In Deerhurst (off B4213) at
Abbots Court SW of parish church.
(OS Map 150; ref SO 869298.)
Bus Swanbrook Coaches
⇌ Gloucester–Tewkesbury.
Tel 01452 425543.
Train Cheltenham 8m. 🅿 🍽

Offa's Dyke

Gloucestershire (p. 235/239, 6G)
Three-mile section of the great earthwork built by Offa, King of Mercia 757–96, from the Severn estuary to the Welsh coast as a defensive boundary to his kingdom.

Open Any reasonable time. (Property managed by Forest Enterprise.)
Entry Free.
Access 3m NE of Chepstow off B4228. Access via Forest Enterprise Tidenham car park. 1m walk (waymarked) down to Devil's Pulpit on Offa's Dyke. (Access suitable only for those wearing proper walking shoes; not suitable for very young, old or infirm.) (OS Map 162; ref SO 546009–548977.)
Bus Stagecoach Red & White 69 Chepstow–Monmouth to within ½m. Tel 01633 266336.
Train Chepstow 7m.

Okehampton Castle

Devon (p. 234, 3D)
The ruins of the largest castle in Devon include the Norman motte and the keep's jagged remains. There is a picnic area of exceptional beauty and there are also lovely woodland walks.
Open 1 April–30 Sep: 10am–6pm daily. 1–31 Oct: 10am–5pm daily.
Entry £2.30/£1.70/£1.20.
Tel 01837 52844
Access 1m SW of Okehampton town centre.
(OS Map 191; ref SX 584942.)
Bus First Western National X9/10 Exeter–Bude/Boscastle, 86 Plymouth–Barnstaple.
Tel 01392 382800.

(picnic tables available) (also available for the visually impaired and those with learning difficulties)

Old Blockhouse

Tresco, Isles of Scilly (p. 234, 5A)
The remains of a small 16th-century gun tower overlooking the white sandy bay at Old Grimsby.

Open Any reasonable time.
Entry Free.
Access On Blockhouse Point, at S end of Old Grimsby harbour. (OS Map 203; ref SV 898155.)

Old Sarum

Wiltshire (p. 232/235, 4J)
See p. 100 for full details.

Old Sarum

This great earthwork with its huge banks and ditch lies near Salisbury, on the edge of the Wiltshire chalk plains. Originally built by Iron Age peoples around 500BC, Romans, Saxons and, most importantly, the Normans were all occupants of what is now known as Old Sarum. It was here in 1070 that William the Conqueror paid off his army, and, in 1085, demanded loyalty from his nobles. A castle, a sumptuous palace and a great cathedral were built within the earthwork. However, disputes between soldiers and priests, and inadequate water supplies were huge hindrances.

In 1226 with the founding of New Sarum, the city we know as Salisbury, the settlement faded away. Although the old cathedral was abandoned and a magnificent new one built in the valley with plentiful water, the castle at Old Sarum remained in use until Tudor times.

Today the remains – of the prehistoric fortress, of the Norman palace, castle and cathedral – evoke powerful memories of the people who have ruled England over the millennia. In addition, the chalk downland, with its many wild flowers, makes it a magical spot.

• **Major Special Events** will include jousting spectacular and battles re-enactments.

Open 1 April–30 Sep: 10am–6pm daily (7pm in July & Aug). 1–31 Oct: 10am–5pm daily. 1 Nov–31 March 2001: 10am–4pm daily. Closed 24–26 Dec and 1 Jan 2001.
Entry £2/£1.50/£1.
Tel 01722 335398
Access 2m N of Salisbury, Wiltshire off A345. (OS Map 184; ref SU 138327.)
Local Tourist Information
Salisbury (Tel 01722 334956).
Bus Wilts & Dorset/Stagecoach Hampshire Bus 3, 5–9 from Salisbury. Tel 01722 336855.
Train Salisbury 2m.
🅿 ♿ (outer bailey and grounds only)

◐ Old Wardour Castle

Wiltshire (p. 232/235, 4H)

Built in the late 14th century for John, 5th Lord Lovel, the six-sided castle with its many rooms for guests was designed in the French style of the period which Lord Lovel greatly admired. Not only was it a secure house but, above all, a luxurious residence intended to impress everyone with its builder's wealth, taste and power.

Badly damaged during the English Civil War the old castle survived and is today one of the most attractive and 'romantic ruins' in England.

• Interpretation depicting the history of the castle.

Robin Hood, Prince of Thieves, with Kevin Costner, was filmed here.

Open 1 April–30 Sep: 10am–6pm daily. 1–31 Oct: 10am–5pm daily. 1 Nov–31 March 2001: 10am–1pm, 2–4pm Wed–Sun. Closed 24–26 Dec and 1 Jan 2001. **Entry** £2/£1.50/£1.

Tel 01747 870487

Access Off A30 2m SW of Tisbury. (OS Map 184; ref ST 939263.)

Bus Wilts & Dorset 26 Salisbury–Shaftesbury (passes ⇌ Tisbury). Tel 01722 336855.

Train Tisbury 2½m.

Ⓟ ♿ 🏠 (grounds only) 🐴

◐ Over Bridge

Gloucestershire (p. 232/239, 7H)

A single-arch masonry bridge spanning the River Severn, built by Thomas Telford 1825–27.

Open Any reasonable time.

(Property managed by Gloucester City Council.)

Entry Free.

Access 1m NW of Gloucester city centre at junction of A40 (Ross) & A417 (Ledbury). (OS Map 162;

ref SO 817196.)

Bus Frequent services by different operators from ⇌ Gloucester. Tel 01452 425543.

Train Gloucester 2m.

Ⓟ (in layby) 🐴

◐ Pendennis Castle

Cornwall (p. 234, 1B)

See p. 102–103 for full details.

◐ Penhallam

Cornwall (p. 234, 3C)

Ruins of a medieval manor house surrounded by a protective moat.

Open Any reasonable time.

Entry Free.

Access 1m NW of Week St Mary, off minor road off A39 from

Treskinnick Cross (10 mins' walk from car park on forest track). (OS Map 190; ref SX 224974.)

Ⓟ (limited) 🐴

◐ Porth Hellick Down
◐ Burial Chamber

St Mary's, Isles of Scilly (p. 234, 4B)

Probably the best-preserved Bronze

Age burial mound on the Islands, with an entrance passage and chamber.

Open Any reasonable time.

Entry Free.

Access 1½m E of Hugh Town. (OS Map 203; ref SV 929108.)

🐴

◐ Portland Castle

Dorset (p. 232/235, 3H)
See p. 105 for full details.

Pendennis Castle

Pendennis and its neighbour St Mawes Castle face each other across the mouth of the River Fal. They are the Cornish end of a chain of castles built by Henry VIII along the south coast as protection against the threat of attack from France. Few have seen active service but Pendennis was adapted over 400 years to meet new enemies, from the French and Spanish in the 16th century, through to World War II.

The land on which the castle stands was originally owned by the Killigrew family, governors of Pendennis for many years. The lodgings fronting the keep were built around 1550 to provide them with more comfortable accommodation.

In the later years of Elizabeth I's reign, a new type of defensive wall with bastions was added around the original fort. Strengthened again prior to the Civil War, Pendennis was host to the future Charles II in 1646, who sailed from there to the

Isles of Scilly. It withstood five months of siege before becoming the penultimate Royalist garrison to surrender on the mainland. Pendennis was rearmed in the late 19th and early 20th centuries, seeing action in World War II.

This page.
Left, the keep, as seen from the north. Below, aerial view of Pendennis and the coastline. Bottom, the World War I Guardroom.

Opposite page.
Right, visitors at the Half Moon Battery. Main picture, a historical special event at Pendennis.

· **New for 2000** 'The Noon Day Gun' Everyday at noon in July and August, one of the castle's guns will fire to mark mid-day.

· The excellent site facilities include the Discovery Centre and the Guardhouse, which has been returned to its World War I appearance.

· Visit the secret defences, including the World War II Half Moon Battery.

· 16th-century keep, complete with Tudor gun deck.

· Underground magazines and tunnels.

Open 1 April–30 June: 10am–6pm daily. 1 July–31 Aug: 9am–6pm daily (8pm, grounds only). 1 Sep–30 Sep: 10am–6pm daily. 1–31 Oct: 10am–5pm daily. 1 Nov–31 March 2001: 10am–4pm daily. Closed 24–26 Dec and 1 Jan 2001.

Entry £3.80/£2.90/£1.90.

Tel 01326 316594

Access On Pendennis Head, Cornwall, 1m SE of Falmouth. The Falmouth 'Land Train' stops in Castle Car Park (summer only). (OS Map 204; ref SW 824318.)

Local Tourist Information Falmouth (Tel 01326 312300).

Train Falmouth Docks ½m.

P ⊞ ⅏ ♿ (grounds, parts of keep) ⊡ E ⊞ (Pendennis Castle Tearoom: open April–Oct) ⊡ ⊠ 🐕 (restricted areas)

Restormel Castle

Cornwall (p. 234, 2C)

Surrounded by a deep moat and perched on a high mound, the huge circular keep of this Norman castle survives in remarkably good condition.

Built as a symbol of wealth and status, and home to Edward, the Black Prince, it offers splendid views over the surrounding countryside.

• A marvellous picnic spot.

Open 1 April–30 Sep: 10am–6pm daily. 1–31 Oct: 10am–5pm daily.
Entry £1.60/£1.20/80p.
Tel 01208 872687

Access 1½ m N of Lostwithiel off A390. (OS Map 200; ref SX 104614.)

Train Lostwithiel 1½ m.

Royal Citadel

Devon (p. 234, 2D)

A dramatic 17th-century fortress, with walls up to 21 metres (69 feet) high, built to defend the coastline from the Dutch, and still in use today.

Open By guided tour only (each lasts 1 ¼ hours) 1 May–30 Sep: 2.30pm. Tickets from Plymouth Dome below Smeaton's Tower on Hoe. For security reasons tours may be suspended at short notice.
Entry £3/£2.50/£2
Tel 01752 775841

Access At E end of Plymouth Hoe. (OS Map 201; ref SX 480538.)
Bus From surrounding areas. Tel 01752 222666. Plymouth City Bus. Tel 01752 222221.
Train Plymouth 1¼ m.

St Breock Downs Monolith

Cornwall (p. 234, 2C)

A prehistoric standing stone, originally about 5 metres (16 feet) high, set in beautiful countryside.

Open Any reasonable time. (Property managed by the Cornwall Heritage Trust.)
Entry Free.

Access On St Breock Downs, 3¾ m SW of Wadebridge off unclassified road to Rosenannon. (OS Map 200; ref SW 968683)
Train Roche 5½ m.

St Briavel's Castle

Gloucestershire (p. 235/239, 6G)

A splendid 12th-century castle now used as a youth hostel, which is appropriate for a building set in such marvellous walking country.

Open Exterior: any reasonable time. Bailey: 1 April–30 Sep: 1pm–4pm daily.
Entry Free.

Access In St Briavel's, 7m NE of Chepstow off B4228. (OS Map 162; ref SO 559046.)
Train Chepstow 8m.

St Catherine's Castle

Cornwall (p. 234, 2C)

A small fort built by Henry VIII to defend Fowey Harbour.

Open Any reasonable time.
Entry Free.
Access ¼ m SW of Fowey along footpath off A3082. (OS Map 200; ref SX 118508.)

Bus First Western National 24 St Austell–Fowey to within ½ m. Tel 01209 719988.
Train Par 4m.
P (in Fowey; ½ m walk)

Portland Castle

This coastal fortress, overlooking Portland harbour, has enjoyed a diverse and fascinating history. Built to defend Weymouth Harbour against potential French and Spanish invasion, it survives largely unaltered to this day.

Its squat fan appearance is typical of the castles built by Henry VIII in the early 1540s, and the castle's guns and emplacements reflect the developments in weaponry occurring at the time, with new types of heavy gun made possible by better casting techniques perfected in the king's own foundries.

But it was not until the Civil War that the castle witnessed serious fighting, when it was seized by both Royalists and Parliamentarians at various intervals.

In Victorian times the castle became the private residence of one

Captain Charles Manning, builder of the great Portland breakwater, but the government resumed control of it in 1870. From then Portland Castle has continued to play an important part in the defence of the country; in the First World War it was a Seaplane Station and during the Second World War it was at the forefront of the preparations to recapture northern Europe – D-Day.

- **New for 2000** Opening of the Captain's House and Garden for the first time to the public.
- **New for 2000** Hands-on displays in the castle: come face to face with Henry VIII in the Great Hall!
- New tearoom.

Open 1 April–30 Sep: 10am–6pm daily. 1–31 Oct: 10am–5pm daily.
Entry £2.80/£2.10/£1.40.
Tel 01305 820539
Access Overlooking Portland Harbour in Castleton, Isle of Portland, follow brown and white tourism signs.
(OS Map 194; ref SY 684743.)
Bus Dorset Transit 1, 10 from Weymouth. Tel 01305 783645.
(Waterbus from Brewer's Quay.)
Train Weymouth 4½ m.

(ground floor only – 1 deep step)

✛ St Catherine's Chapel

Dorset (p. 235, 3G)

A small stone chapel, set on a hilltop, with an unusual roof and small turret used as a lighthouse.

Open Any reasonable time. (Property managed by the Ilchester Estates.)
Entry Free.
Access ½ m S of Abbotsbury by pedestrian track from village off B3157. (OS Map 194; ref SY 572848.)
Bus First Southern National 210 ⇌Weymouth–Bridport. Tel 01305 783645.
Train Upwey 7 ½ m.

✛ St Mary's Church

Gloucestershire (p. 239, 7G)

A Norman church with superb wall paintings from the 12th–14th centuries.

Open 1 April–30 Sep: 10am–6pm daily. 1 Oct–31 March 2001: 10am–4pm daily. Closed 24–26 Dec. (Property managed by the Friends of Kempley Church.)

Entry Free.
Access 1m N of Kempley off B4024, 6m NE of Ross-on-Wye. (OS Map 149; ref SO 670313.)
Train Ledbury 8m.

◎ St Mawes Castle

Cornwall (p. 234, 1B)

With magnificent architecture and a breathtaking waterside setting, St Mawes Castle is the most perfectly preserved of Henry VIII's coastal fortresses. It has not undergone any internal alterations, and is unique in that respect.

St Mawes was built to counter the invasion threat from Europe, working in partnership with its twin castle, Pendennis, across the other side of the Fal estuary. However it quickly fell to landward attack from Parliamentarian forces in 1646 and was not properly refortified until the later 19th and 20th centuries.

· **New for 2000** Summer Wednesday guided tours.
Open 1 April–30 Sep: 10am–6pm daily. 1–31 Oct: 10am–5pm daily. 1 Nov–31 March 2001: 10am–1pm, 2–4pm Fri–Tue. Closed 24–26 Dec and 1 Jan 2001.
Entry £2.50/£1.90/£1.30.

Tel 01326 270 526
Access In St Mawes on A3078. (OS Map 204; ref SW 842328.)
Bus First Western National 51 Truro–St Mawes. Tel 01209 719988.
Train Penmere, 4m via Prince of Wales Pier and ferry.

▲ The Sanctuary

Wiltshire (p. 232/235, 5J)

Possibly 5,000 years old, The Sanctuary consists of two concentric circles of stones and six of timber uprights indicated by concrete posts. The Sanctuary is connected to Avebury by the West Kennet Avenue of standing stones.
Open Any reasonable time. (Property managed by the National Trust.)

Entry Free.
Bus Wilts & Dorset 5/6 Salisbury–Swindon (pass close ⇌Swindon). Tel 0845 709 0899.
Train Pewsey 9m, Bedwyn 12m.
P (in layby) 🖼

Sherborne Old Castle

Dorset (p. 232/235, 4G)

Cromwell said of Sherborne that it was a 'malicious and mischievous castle'. But he would: it had taken him 16 days to capture this early 12th-century castle during the Civil War. It was then abandoned.

Open 1 April–30 Sep: 10am–6pm daily. 1–31 Oct: 10am–1pm, 2–5pm daily. 1 Nov–31 March 2001: 10am–1pm, 2–4pm Wed–Sun. Closed 24–26 Dec and 1 Jan 2001.
Entry £1.60/£1.20/80p.
Tel 01935 812730
Access ½m E of Sherborne off B3145. (OS Map 183; ref ST 647167.)
Train Sherborne ¼m.

Silbury Hill

Wiltshire (p. 232/235, 5I)

An extraordinary artificial prehistoric mound, the largest Neolithic construction of its type in Europe.

Open Viewing area at any reasonable time – no access to hill itself. (Property managed by the National Trust.)
Entry Free.
Access 1m W of West Kennet on A4. (OS Map 173; ref SU 100685.)

Bus Thamesdown 49/A Swindon –Devizes/Marlborough; Wilts & Dorset 5/6 Salisbury– Swindon (all pass within ¼m and pass close Swindon).Tel 0845 709 0899
Train Pewsey 9m, Swindon 13m.
(viewing area)

Sir Bevil Grenville's Monument

Somerset (p. 232/235, 5H)

Commemorates the heroism of a Royalist commander and his Cornish pikemen at the Battle of Lansdown.

Open Any reasonable time.
Entry Free.
Access 4m NW of Bath, on N edge of Lansdown Hill,

near road to Wick. (OS Map 172; ref ST 721703.)
Train Bath Spa 4½m.
(in layby)

Stanton Drew Circles and Cove

Somerset (p. 235, 5G)

Recent research at this assembly of stone circles, avenues and a 'Cove' of three standing stones has shown that there was once also a huge timber structure within the Great Circle. The ritual complex dates from about 3000BC.

Open Cove – any reasonable time. Two main stone circles: access at discretion of land owner who may levy a charge.
Entry Cove: free.
Stone Circle: see above.

Access Circles: E of Stanton Drew village; Cove: in garden of Druid's Arms. (OS Map 172; Circles ref ST 601634, Cove ref ST 598633.)
Train Bristol Temple Meads 7m.

❶ Stonehenge

Wiltshire (p. 232/235, 5J)
See p. 110-113 for full details.

❸ Stoney Littleton Long Barrow

Somerset (p. 232/235, 5H)
This Neolithic burial mound is about 30 metres (100 feet) long and has chambers where human remains once lay.

Open Exterior only – any reasonable time.
Entry Free.

Access 1m S of Wellow off A367. (OS Map 172; ref ST 735573.)
Train Bath Spa 6m.
Ⓟ(limited)🐾

❹ Temple Church

Bristol (p. 235, 5G)
The handsome tower and walls of this 15th-century church defied the bombs of World War II. The graveyard is now a pleasant public garden.

Open Exterior only– any reasonable time.
Entry Free.
Access In Temple St off Victoria St. (OS Map 172; ref ST 593727.)

Bus From surrounding areas. Tel 0117 955 3231.
Train Bristol Temple Meads ¼m.
🐾

❺ Tintagel Castle

🗝 *Cornwall (p. 234, 3C)*
See p. 114-115 for full details.

❻ Totnes Castle

🗝 *Devon (p. 234, 2E)*
A superb motte and bailey castle, with splendid views across the rooftops and down to the River Dart – a fine example of Norman fortification.

Built at the very heart of a Saxon town, the once great surrounding ditch is today filled with cottages and gardens.

• Family Discovery Pack available.
Open 1 April–30 Sep: 10am–6pm daily. 1–31 Oct: 10am–5pm daily. 1 Nov–31 March 2001: 10am–1pm, 2–4pm Wed–Sun. Closed 24–26 Dec and 1 Jan 2001.
Entry £1.60/£1.20/80p.
Tel 01803 864406
Access In Totnes, on hill overlooking the town.

(OS Map 202; ref SX 800605.)
Train Totnes ¼m.
Ⓟ (64 metres [70 yards]), cars only, narrow approach roads.
🏠🐾🎪

Above, Totnes Castle.

❸ Tregiffian Burial Chamber

Cornwall (p. 234, 1A)
A Neolithic or early Bronze Age chambered tomb by the side of a country road.

Open Any reasonable time. (Property managed by the Cornwall Heritage Trust.)
Entry Free.

Access 2m SE of St Buryan on B3315. (OS Map 203; ref SW 430245.)
Train Penzance 5 ½m.
🐾

osts and legends

Much of the work carried out by English Heritage consists of archaeological and architectural investigation, conservation and historical research. But we are acutely aware that the appeal of our sites lies in other factors too: the awe and fascination evoked by stories of the people who once lived in the properties, the sense of atmosphere which allows us to conjure up our own images of the often dramatic events which once took place in them.

At what point history gives way to legend and myth, and to what extent the truth becomes embellished and eventually altered by the telling of stories from one generation to the next, is difficult to say. Sometimes the shift is from fiction to fact: part of the story of Tintagel is that it was the legendary birthplace of King Arthur, now acknowledged as a historical figure and not just a heroic legend; and while we would treat with suitable cynicism the story that Merlin transported the stones to build Stonehenge from Ireland, we recognise that this tale reflects the awe and mystery which have always surrounded our great stone circle.

Almost all English Heritage sites have stories attached to them. Did you know that there have been sightings at Bolsover of a woman putting a wrapped bundle, thought to be a baby, into the kitchen fire? And that visitors have reported being slapped and pinched by unseen hands? Okehampton Castle has the grim ghost of Lady Howard whose eternal fate it is to drive round the castle in a coach made from the bones of her four dead husbands, removing the grass from the castle mound one blade at a time. The Nine Ladies who make up the stone circle in Derbyshire are said to have been turned to stone for the sin of dancing on the Sabbath to the music of a fiddle played by the Devil himself. We have the great Mary, Queen of Scots at Wingfield Manor, where she was imprisoned; a headless Sir Walter Raleigh at Sherborne Old Castle, and a ghostly drummer boy at Richmond Castle!

You don't have to believe the tales of ghosts, mysterious presences or unexplained noises,

but you do have to acknowledge that this aspect of our properties adds to their appeal. With the lives of those who once occupied these ancient places long over, it is through the stories associated with them that they are kept alive for us; all those people – nobles and servants, villains and saints, cowards and heroes, who lived and died in English Heritage's marvellous properties.

Main picture Peveril Castle in Derbyshire. Left, Clifford's Tower in North Yorkshire. Above Okehampton Castle in Devon.

Stonehenge

The great and ancient stone circle of Stonehenge is one of the wonders of the world.

What visitors see today are the substantial remnants of the last in a sequence of monuments erected between c.3000 and 1600BC. Each was a circular structure, aligned along the rising of the sun at the midsummer solstice. The first 'Stonehenge' consisted of a circular bank and ditch with a ring of 56 wooden posts, now known as Aubrey Holes. Later monuments all used, and reused, the great stones we see today, which were brought from some distance away. The final phase comprised an outer circle of huge standing stones – super-hard

sarsens, from the Marlborough Downs – topped by lintels making a continuous ring. Inside this stood a horseshoe of still larger stones, five pairs of uprights with a lintel across each pair, known as trilithons. Stones were connected using mortice and tenon and tongue and groove joints, possibly copying previous wood construction techniques. Smaller bluestones, from the Preseli Mountains in South Wales, were arranged in a circle and a horseshoe, within the great sarsen stone circle and horseshoe. In an earlier phase these bluestones had been erected in a different arrangement.

There has always been intense debate over quite what purpose Stonehenge served. Certainly it was the focal point in a landscape filled with prehistoric ceremonial structures. It also represented an enormous investment of labour and time. Huge efforts were needed to carry the stones tens, sometimes hundreds of miles by land and water, and then to shape and raise them. Only a sophisticated society could have organised so large a workforce and possessed the design and construction skills necessary to produce Stonehenge and its surrounding monuments.

Stonehenge's orientation on the rising and setting sun has always

been one of its most remarkable features. Whether this was simply because the builders came from a sun-worshipping culture, or because – as some scholars have believed – the circle and its banks were part of a huge astronomical calendar, remains a mystery.

What cannot be denied is the ingenuity of the builders of Stonehenge. With just very basic tools at their disposal, they shaped the stones and formed the mortices and tenons that linked uprights to lintels. Using antlers and bones, they dug the pits to hold the stones and made the banks and ditches that enclosed them.There are direct links with the people who built

Stonehenge in their artefacts: tools, pottery and even the contents of their graves. Some of these are displayed in the museums at Salisbury and Devizes.

Burial mounds, which possibly contained the graves of ruling families, are also integral to the landscape. The long barrows of the New Stone Age, and the various types of circular barrows that came after, are still visible, as are other earthworks and monuments. Some, such as the long oval earthwork to the north, the Cursus, once thought to be a chariot racecourse, remain enigmatic. The Cursus and other parts of the Stonehenge landscape may be visited. Woodhenge, two

miles to the north-east, was a wooden oval post structure aligned with the summer solstice sun and contemporary with the first phase of Stonehenge.

Now a World Heritage Site, Stonehenge and all its surroundings remain powerful witnesses to the once great civilization of the Stone and Bronze Ages, between 5,000 and 3,000 years ago.

• Superb gift shop .

Open 16 March–31 May: 9.30am–6pm daily. 1 June–31 Aug: 9am–7pm daily. 1 Sep–15 Oct: 9.30am–6pm daily. 16–23 Oct: 9.30am–5pm daily. 24 Oct–15 March 2001: 9.30am–4pm daily. Closed 24–26 Dec and 1 Jan 2001.

Recommended last admission time no later than 30 minutes before the advertised closing time. Stonehenge will close promptly 20 minutes after the advertised closing time.

Entry £4/£3/£2. Family ticket (2 adults & 3 children) £10.

National Trust members admitted free. (Under the guardianship, and managed by English Heritage. The site is surrounded by 1,500 acres of land, owned by the National Trust, with excellent walks.) When weather conditions are bad, access may be restricted and visitors may not be able to use the walkway.

Tel 01980 624715 (info line)

Access 2m W of Amesbury on junction of A303 and A344/A360. (OS Map 184; ref SU 123422.)

Private Access Line
Tel 01980 626267

Local Tourist Information
Amesbury (Tel 01980 622833), Salisbury (Tel 01722 334956).
Bus Wilts & Dorset 3

⇌ Salisbury–Stonehenge. Tel 01722 336855.

Train Salisbury 9 ½ m.

🅿 🚻 ♿ ♿ 📷

🎦 (Stonehenge Kitchen, open all year.) 🎧 (also available in French, German and Japanese; large print and braille guides in English only) 🎧 *interactive* (available in nine languages & hearing loop – subject to availability) 🦮 (Guide and Hearing dog welcome)

Tintagel Castle

With its spectacular location on one of England's most dramatic coastlines, Tintagel is one of the most awe-inspiring and romantic spots in Britain. It is also a place of legends. Joined to the mainland by a narrow neck of land, Tintagel Island faces the full force of the Atlantic. On the mainland itself, the gaunt remains of the medieval castle, thought to date from the second quarter of the 13th century, represent only one phase in a long history of occupation. Even before Richard, Earl of Cornwall, built his castle, Tintagel had come to be associated with King Arthur, as the great legendary warrior leader's birthplace. The legend, depicted in Geoffrey of Monmouth's fabulous *History* (written c. 1139), has lived on.

After a period as a Roman settlement and military outpost, Tintagel is thought to have been the stronghold of a Celtic king during the fifth and sixth centuries. Nearby an early Christian church stands on the site of what may have been a cemetery for important men.

Legend has it that one of the important men connected with Tintagel may have been King Mark, whose nephew Tristan fell in love with Isolt (or Isolde). Their doomed romance is part of Tintagel's story, as are Geoffrey of Monmouth's tales, in which Uther Pendragon, aided by Merlin, seduced Queen Igraine at Tintagel. Tintagel's Arthurian connection was later renewed by Alfred, Lord Tennyson in his *Idylls of the King*.

The remains of the 13th-century castle are breathtaking. Steep stone steps, stout walls and rugged windswept cliff edges encircle the Great Hall, where Richard, Earl of Cornwall, may once have feasted. The emphasis at Tintagel is always on the word 'may', as it has so many legends and unanswered questions as well as an amazing capacity to surprise us, even after years of investigation.

In June 1998, excavation works were undertaken under the overall direction of Professor Chris Morris of the University of Glasgow on a relatively sheltered and small site on the eastern side of the island, first excavated in the 1930s. Pottery from the 5th and 6th centuries AD was found, as well as some fine glass fragments believed to be from 6th- or 7th- century Malaga and, even more remarkably, a 1500-year-old piece of slate on which remain two Latin inscriptions. One has remnants of at least four letters, although it is impossible at the moment to say what this represents. The second reads: 'Artognou, father of a descendant of Coll, has had [this] made'. Who exactly Artognou may have been continues to be a subject for lively speculation.

Year of the Artist venue Writer in
residence from June to August
2000. Please call for details.
Late closing 9 July–26 August.
Family Discovery Pack and free
Children's Activity Sheet available.
Open 1 April–8 July: 10am–6pm
daily. 9 July–26 Aug: 10am–7pm
daily (8pm on Wed if special event).
7 Aug–30 Sep: 10am–6pm daily.
–31 Oct: 10am–5pm daily. 1 Nov–
1 March 2001: 10am–4pm daily.
Closed 24–26 Dec and 1 Jan 2001.
Entry £2.90/£2.20/£1.50.
Tel 01840 770328
Access On Tintagel Head, ½m
along uneven track from
Tintagel, no vehicles.
(OS Map 200; ref SX 048891.)
Local Tourist Information
Tintagel Visitors' Centre
(Tel 01840 779 034); Camelford
(Tel 01840 212954, summer only);
Padstow (Tel 01841 533449).
Bus First Western National X10
☎ Exeter St David's–Boscastle.
Tel 01392 382800.
P (in the village, 600 metres [660
yards]) 🚻 📷 ♿ ⛽ 🅿️ (Please note

*Left a reconstruction
drawing of the medieval
castle, c. AD 1230.
Opposite page, the 6th-
century AD inscription
stone discovered in 199*

⬢ Trethevy Quoit

Cornwall (p. 234, 2D)
An ancient Neolithic burial chamber, standing 2.7 metres (9 feet) high and consisting of five standing stones surmounted by a huge capstone.

Open Any reasonable time. (Site managed by the Cornwall Heritage Trust.)
Entry Free.

Access 1m NE of St Cleer near Darite off B3254. (OS Map 201; ref SX 259688.)
Bus First Western National 73 Liskeard–Pensilva to within ½m. Tel 01209 719988.
Train Liskeard 3½m. 🐕

⬢ Uley Long Barrow (Hetty Pegler's Tump)

Gloucestershire (p. 232/235/239, 6H)
Dating from around 3000BC, this 55 metre-long (180 foot) Neolithic chambered burial mound is unusual in that its mound is still intact.

Open Any reasonable time. (Property managed by Gloucestershire County Council.)
Entry Free.
Access 3½m NE of Dursley on B4066. (OS Map 162; ref SO 790000.)

Bus Stagecoach Stroud Valleys 15 Stroud–Dursley (pass close ⇌ Stroud). Tel 01452 425543.
Train Stroud 6m. 🐕

⬢ Upper Plym Valley

Devon (p. 234, 2D)
Scores of prehistoric and medieval sites covering six square miles of ancient landscape.

Open Any reasonable time. (Property managed by the National Trust.)
Entry Free.

Access 4m E of Yelverton. (OS Map 202.) 🐕

⬢ West Kennet Avenue

Wiltshire (p. 232/235, 5J)
An avenue of standing stones, which ran in a curve from Avebury Stone Circles to The Sanctuary, probably dating from the late Neolithic.

Open Any reasonable time. (Property owned and managed by the National Trust.)
Entry Free.
Access Runs alongside B4003. (OS Map 173; ref SU 105695.)

Bus Thamesdown 49/A Swindon–Devizes/Marlborough; Wilts & Dorset 5/6 Salisbury–Swindon (all pass close ⇌Swindon). Tel 0845 709 0899.
Train Pewsey 9m, Swindon 12m. ♿(on roadway)🐕

⏛ West Kennet Long Barrow

Wiltshire (p. 232/235, 5J)
A Neolithic chambered tomb,
consisting of a long earthen mound
containing a passage with side
chambers and with the entrance
guarded by a large stone.
Open Any reasonable time.
(Property managed by the
National Trust.)
Entry Free.
Access ¼m SW of West Kennet
along footpath off A4.
(OS Map 173; ref SU 104677.)
Bus Thamesdown 49/A

Swindon–Devizes/Marlborough;
Wilts & Dorset 5/6 Salisbury–
Swindon (all pass close ⇌ Swindon).

Tel 0845 709 0899.
Train Pewsey 9m, Swindon 13m.
P (in layby) 🐾

⏛ Windmill Hill

Wiltshire (p. 232/235, 5J)
Neolithic remains of three
concentric rings of ditches,
enclosing an area of 21 acres.

Open Any reasonable time.
(Property owned and managed by
the National Trust.)
Entry Free.
Access 1½m NW of Avebury.
(OS Map 173; ref SU 086714.)

Bus Thamesdown 49/A
Swindon–Devizes/Marlborough;
Wilts & Dorset 5/6 Salisbury–
Swindon (all pass close ⇌
Swindon). Tel 0845 709 0899.
Train Swindon 11m. 🐾

⏛ Winterbourne Poor Lot Barrows

Dorset (p. 235, 3G)
Part of an extensive 4,000-year-
old Bronze Age cemetery.
Open Any reasonable time.
Entry Free.

Access 2m W of Winterbourne
Abbas, S of junction of A35 with
minor road to Compton Valence.
Access via Wellbottom Lodge –
180 metres (200 yards) E along A35
from junction.
(OS Map 194; ref SY 590906.)

Bus First Southern National 31
Weymouth– ⇌Axminster (passes
⇌Dorchester South).
Tel 01305 783645.
Train Dorchester West or South,
both 7m.
🐾

⏛ Woodhenge

Wiltshire (p. 232/235, 5J)
Neolithic ceremonial monument of
c.2300BC, consisting of a bank and
ditch and six concentric rings of
timber posts, now shown by
concrete markers. The entrance

and long axis of the oval rings
points to the rising sun
on Midsummer Day.
Open Any reasonable time.
Entry Free.
Access 1½m N of Amesbury,
off A345 just S of Durrington.

(OS Map 184; ref SU 151434.)
Bus Wilts & Dorset 5/6
Salisbury–Swindon (pass close
⇌Salisbury & Swindon), 16 from
Amesbury. Tel 0845 709 0899.
Train Salisbury 9m.
P ♿ 🐾

⏛ Yarn Market

Somerset (p. 235, 4E)
A 17th-century octagonal market hall.
Open Any reasonable time. (Property
managed by the National Trust.)

Entry Free.
Access In Dunster High St.
(OS Map 181; ref SS 992437.)
Bus First Southern National 28,
928 ⇌Taunton–Minehead to

within ¼m; also 38/9 from
Minehead. Tel 01823 272033.
Train Dunster (W Somerset
Railway) ½m.
♿ 🐾

East of England

Left, Thomas Howard (1561–1626), first Earl of Suffolk, by Biagio Rebecca, from the sequence of family portraits in the Saloon at Audley End House, in Essex; middle, view of the parterre from the house at Wrest Park, in Bedforshire, with urns in the foreground. Thomas, Earl de Grey, who designed the house in the 1830s, bought the urns for the terrace and added the family's coat of arms to four of them; right, lead statue of William III, painted to look like stone. It dates from the 1730s and stands outside the Pavilion at Wrest Park.

Castle Rising
Castle

Castle
Acre Priory

Row 111 House, Old Merchant's
House & Greyfriars Cloisters

Longthorpe
Tower

NORFOLK

Berney Arms
Windmill

Grimes
Graves

CAMBRIDGESHIRE

Saxtead Green
Post Mill

Framlingham
Castle

Denny
Abbey

SUFFOLK

Bushmead
Priory

Orford Castle

BEDFORDSHIRE

Wrest Park
Gardens

Audley End
House & Gardens

Landguard
Fort

HERTFORDSHIRE

ESSEX

Tilbury Fort

119

Audley End House and Gardens

Audley End House and Gardens was one of the great wonders of the nation when it was built by the first Earl of Suffolk, Lord Treasurer to James I. It was on the scale of a great royal palace, and soon became one after Charles II bought it in 1668 for £50,000, using it as a base when he attended the races at Newmarket. Returned to the Suffolks in 1701, substantial parts of the house were demolished. Even so, what remains is one of the most significant Jacobean houses in England. Successive owners have since left their stylistic imprint both within the graceful exterior and on the surrounding parkland.

As we see it now, Audley End's interior, with its historic picture collection and furniture, is largely the product of its owner in the mid-19th century, the third Lord Braybrooke. The challenge for the visitor today is to piece together the many changes over time that have created such a harmonious whole.

The rooms at Audley End are a blend of many generations of taste, the differences sometimes subtly combined, sometimes dramatically exploited. The main structure has remained remarkably little-altered since the main front court was demolished in 1708 and the east wing came down in 1753. Some rooms have been changed substantially, especially the huge Hall with its powerful Jacobean screen and ceiling. In the 1760s Adam brought his individual brand of graceful neoclassical architecture to the house, as seen in the Great Apartment, while 'Capability' Brown transformed the parkland.

Sir John Griffin Griffin, later fourth Baron Howard de Walden and first Baron Braybrooke, introduced sweeping changes before he died in 1797. The third Baron Braybrooke, who inherited house and title in 1825, stamped his taste equally firmly upon it and with longer-lasting results. He

installed his huge picture collection, filled the rooms with furnishings, and reinstated something of the original Jacobean feel to the State Rooms.

The fourth Lord Braybrooke was more interested in archaeology and ornithology than redecorating. His Natural History collection is a real feature of the house. After Audley End was requisitioned in World War II, the ninth Lord Braybrooke resumed possession and in 1948 the house was sold to the Ministry of Works, English Heritage's predecessor.

Much has been done recently to restore the park and the Victorian gardens, including the magnificent parterre. A special guidebook focuses on the extensive grounds and ornamental gardens.

After 250 years, the great Kitchen Garden is now open to visitors. Hidden behind its high brick walls, much of the 19th-century structure survives, including an impressive

170ft-long vinehouse, possibly containing its original vine. The walls have been 're-clothed' with carefully trained fruit trees, and paths have been edged with 8,000 box plants. The best of Victorian traditional methods will be married with the latest organic techniques, for a harvest of vegetables, soft fruits and flowers, much of which will be sold on site.

★ Winner of the 1999 NPI Awards in Eastern Counties.

· Popular open-air concerts, craft & garden shows during the summer.

· Organic Kitchen Garden with produce for sale.

Note: Visitors are advised to contact the site for details of admission prices and opening times for special events before making their journey.

Open Grounds: 1 April–30 Sep: 11am–6pm Wed–Sun and Bank Hol. House: 1 April–30 Sep: 1–6pm Wed–Sun and Bank Hol. Last admission 5pm. House & Grounds: 1–31 Oct: 10am– 3pm Wed–Sun (site closes at 4pm). Pre-booked guided tour: 1 April–30 Sep 10am–noon Wed–Fri (extra charge).

Entry House and Grounds: £6.50/£4.90/£3.30. Family ticket (2 adults & 3 children) £16.30. Grounds only: £4.50/£3.40/£2.30, family ticket £11.30.

Tel 01799 522399 (information line)

Access 1m W of Saffron Walden on B1383 (M11 exits 8, 9, Northbound only, & 10). (OS Map 154; ref TL 525382.)

Local Tourist Information
Birchanger (Tel 01279 508656); Cambridge (Tel 01223 322640).

Bus Hedingham/Viceroy 59 from ⇌ Audley End, Myall 102 Cambridge ⇌ Audley End, First Eastern National 301, Arriva E Herts & Essex 504 Bishops Stortford–Saffron Walden. Tel 0345 000333.

Train Audley End 1¼ m.

🅿 🚍 🛒👥♿🍴 (The Parterre Restaurant) ♿ (substantial ground-floor area & gardens only)📷📷(French, Dutch, German, and Japanese information sheets available. No photography allowed within house.)

Organic garden shop.

This page, top right, the interior of the chapel. Top left, Theophilius Howard, 2nd Earl of Suffolk, by Biagio Rebecca. Above, the Great Drawing Room, designed by Robert Adam.
Opposite page, general view of Audley End.

Audley End House and Gardens *See p. 120-121 for full details.*
Essex (p. 233/236, 7N)

Baconsthorpe Castle

Norfolk (p. 237, 10O)
Remains of the gatehouses of a large
15th-century fortified manor house,
partly surrounded by a moat.
Open All year: 10am–4pm daily.
Entry Free.
Access ¼ m N of village of Bacons-
thorpe off unclassified road 3m E of
Holt. (OS Map 133; ref TG 122382.)
Train Sheringham 4 ½m.

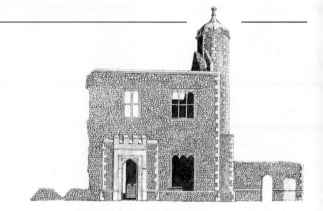

Berkhamsted Castle

Hertfordshire (p. 234, 6L)
The extensive remains of a large
11th-century motte and bailey castle.
Open All year: 10am–4pm daily.

Please contact keykeeper,
Mr Stevens, on **01442 871737**.
Entry Free.
Access By Berkhamsted station.
(OS Map 165; ref SP 996083.)

Bus From surrounding areas.
Tel 0843 924 4344.
Train Berkhamsted, adjacent.

Berney Arms Windmill

Norfolk (p. 237, 9P)
One of the best and largest
remaining marsh mills in Norfolk,
with seven floors, making it a
landmark for miles around.
Built to grind a constituent of
cement, it was in use until 1951,
ending its days pumping water
to drain surrounding marshes.
*The mill remains open in 2000 whilst
restoration of its sails takes place.*
Open 1 April–31 Oct: 9am–1pm,
2–5pm daily.
Entry £1.60/£1.20/80p.
Tel 01493 700605
Access 3 ½m NE of Reedham
on N bank of River Yare.
Accessible by hire boat, or by
footpath from Halvergate (3 ½m).
(OS Map 134; ref TG 465051.)
Train Berney Arms ¼m.

Windmills

Windmills were once everywhere in the flatter and windier counties of England. Together with watermills, they were as familiar a sight as, for example, petrol stations are today. But their image these days is usually the romantic one of beached ghostly galleons encountered in lonely marshes rather than as the

a post as the sails catch the wind. The whole structure had to be perfectly balanced to enable the two millstones to keep level and grind together. The craftsmanship of millwrights kept many ancient post mills in service for centuries.

Sibsey Trader in Lincolnshire (below) is of a later type: a brick tower mill. Here the 'tower' stays still while just the roof or cap swivels around at the top so that the sails can turn to the wind. Brick towers could be as tall as six or seven storeys. The other type of mill, common in Kent, is the smock mill, where the tower is made

of white- painted horizontal boards to look like a farm worker's smock. Once invented, the machinery of milling could be used in many different ways. Wind and water mills were used to make gunpowder, barrels, spades and bobbins.

Berney Arms Windmill in Norfolk is different again: it used to grind the ingredients of cement. Later it became a water-pumping mill, designed to drain the meadows behind the banks of the Broad it stands on near Great Yarmouth, and its sails were once connected to a large paddle wheel beside it.

workaday centre of parish life where everyone brought their corn to be milled.

Around 40 windmills still grind today, many of them manned only occasionally by enthusiasts. English Heritage looks after a good collection representing all the main types. Saxtead Green in Suffolk (top) is the earliest type of windmill: a post mill. Here, the whole wooden shed which houses the machinery turns on

✛ Binham Priory

Norfolk (p. 237, 100)

Extensive remains of a Benedictine
priory. The original nave of the
church is still in use as the parish
church.

Open Any reasonable time.
(Site managed by Binham Parochial
Church Council.)

Entry Free.

Tel 0500 626116

Access ¼ m NW of village of
Binham-on-Wells on road off
B1388. (OS Map 132; ref TF 982399.)

Bus Sanders 78 Cromer–Fakenham.
Tel 0845 300 6116.

◉ Binham Wayside Cross

Norfolk (p. 237, 100)

Medieval cross marking the site of
an annual fair held from the reign
of Henry I until the 1950s.

Open Any reasonable time.
Entry Free.
Access On village green
adjacent to Priory.
(OS Map 132; ref TF 982399.)

Bus Sanders 78
Cromer– Fakenham.
Tel 0845 300 6116.

◉ Blakeney Guildhall

Norfolk (p. 237, 100)

The surviving basement, most
likely used for storage, of a
14th-century merchant's house.

Open Any reasonable time.
Entry Free. (Property managed
by Blakeney Parish Council.)
Access In Blakeney off A149.
(OS Map 133; ref TG 030441.)

Bus Sanders 78
Cromer–Fakenham.
Tel 0845 300 6116.
Train Sheringham 9m.

◔ Burgh Castle

Norfolk (p. 237, 9P)

Impressive walls, with projecting
bastions, of a Roman fort built in
the late 3rd century to defend the
coast against Saxon raiders.

Open Any reasonable time.
(Property managed by Norfolk
Archaeological Trust.)
Entry Free.
Access At far W end of Breydon
Water, on unclassified road 3m

W of Great Yarmouth.
(OS Map 134; ref TG 475046.)
Bus First Blue Bus 6/7 from Great
Yarmouth. Tel 0845 602 0121.
Train Great Yarmouth 5m.

✛ Bury St Edmunds Abbey

Suffolk (p. 237, 80)

A Norman tower and 14th-century
gatehouse of a ruined Benedictine
abbey, church and precinct.
The visitor centre has interactive
displays.

Open Abbey: all year 7.30am–
4/5pm Mon–Sat.
9am–5pm Sun and Bank Holidays.
Visitor Centre: 1 April–31 Oct:
10am–5pm daily.
(Property managed by St
Edmundsbury Borough Council.)

Entry Free.
Tel 01284 764667
Access E end of town centre.
(OS Map 155; ref TL 858642.)
Bus From surrounding areas.
Tel 0645 583358.
Train Bury St Edmunds 1m.

✪ Bushmead Priory

Bedfordshire (p. 236, 8M)

A rare survival of the medieval refectory of an Augustinian priory whose original timber-framed roof is almost intact. The building contains interesting wall paintings and stained glass.

Open July–Aug: 10am–1pm, 2–6pm Sat–Sun and Bank Holidays.

Entry £1.95/£1.50/£1.
Tel 01234 376614
Access Off B660, 2m S of Bolnhurst.
(OS Map 153; ref TL 115607.)
Train St Neots 6m.

---

❷ Caister Roman Site

Norfolk (p. 237, 9P)

The remains of a Roman fort, including part of a defensive wall, a gateway and buildings along a main street.

Open Any reasonable time. (Property managed by Great Yarmouth Borough Council.)
Entry Free.
Access Near Caister-on-Sea, 3m N of Great Yarmouth.

(OS Map 134; ref TG 518125.)
Bus First Blue Bus 6–8, 602–5.
Tel 0845 300 6116.
Train Great Yarmouth 3m.

---

❸ Castle Acre: Bailey Gate

Norfolk (p. 237, 9N)

The north gateway to the medieval planned town of Acre, with flint towers.

Open Any reasonable time.
Entry Free.

Access In Castle Acre, at E end of Stocks Green, 5m N of Swaffham.
(OS Map 132; ref TF 819152.)

---

❹ Castle Acre Castle

Norfolk (p. 237, 9O)

The remains of a Norman manor house, which became a castle with earthworks, set by the side of the village.

Open Any reasonable time.
Entry Free.

Access At E end of Castle Acre, 5m N of Swaffham.
(OS Map 132; ref TF 819152.)

---

❺ Castle Acre Priory

Norfolk (p. 237, 9N)

Castle Acre Priory lies a short distance to the south-west of Castle Acre Castle, and the village of Castle Acre. Its ruins span seven centuries and include a 12th-century church whose elaborately decorated great west front still rises to its full height, a 15th-century gatehouse, and a porch and prior's lodging that are still fit to live in.

Do not miss the modern herb garden, recreated to grow both culinary and medicinal herbs.

Open 1 April–30 Sep: 10am–6pm daily. 1–31 Oct: 10am–5pm daily. 1 Nov–31 March 2001: 10am–4pm Wed–Sun. Closed 24–26 Dec and 1 Jan 2001.

Entry £3.20/£2.40/£1.60.

Tel 01760 755394
Access ¼m W of village of Castle Acre, 5m N of Swaffham.
(OS Map 132; ref TF 814148.)

(ground floor & grounds only) (also available for the visually impaired, those with learning difficulties and in French) (restricted areas)

Castle Rising Castle

Norfolk (p. 237, 10N)

A fine mid-12th-century domestic keep *(below right)*, set in the centre of massive defensive earthworks, once palace and prison to Isabella, the 'She-Wolf' of France, dowager Queen of England. The keep walls stand to their original height and many of the fortifications are intact. (Property owned by Mr Greville Howard.)

Open 1 April–30 Sep: 10am–6pm daily. 1–31 Oct: 10am–5pm daily. 1 Nov–31 March 2001: 10am–4pm Wed–Sun. Closed 24–26 Dec and 1 Jan 2001.

Entry £2.95. Concessions available and special winter rates.

Tel 01553 631330

Access 4m NE of King's Lynn off A149. (OS Map 132; ref TF 666246.)

Bus First Eastern Counties 410/1 King's Lynn–Hunstanton. Tel 01553 772343.

Train King's Lynn 4 ½m.

P (exterior only; toilets) (restricted areas)

Church of the Holy Sepulchre

Norfolk (p. 237, 8O)

The ruined nave of a priory church of the Canons of the Holy Sepulchre, the only surviving remains in England of a house of this order.

Open Any reasonable time.
Entry Free.
Access On W side of Thetford off B1107.(OS Map 144; ref TL 865831.)

Bus From surrounding areas. Tel 0845 300 6116.
Train Thetford ¾ m.

Cow Tower

Norfolk (p. 237, 9P)

A circular detached brick tower on the riverside. It once formed part of the 14th-century city defences.

Open Any reasonable time. (Property managed by Norwich City Council.)
Entry Free.
Tel 01603 212343

Access In Norwich, near cathedral. (OS Map 134; ref TG 240091.)
Bus From surrounding areas. Tel 0845 300 6116.
Train Norwich ½ m.

Creake Abbey

Norfolk (p. 237, 10O)

The ruins of the church of an Augustinian abbey.

Open Any reasonable time.
Entry Free.
Access 1m N of North Creake off B1355. (OS Map 132; ref TF 856395.)

Bus First Eastern Counties 424 Burham Market–Fakenham. Tel 0845 300 6116.

Denny Abbey and the Farmland Museum

What at first appears to be an attractive stone-built farmhouse is actually the remains of Denny Abbey, founded in 1159 by Benedictine Monks as a dependent priory of the great cathedral monastery of Ely. At different times over the next four centuries the abbey also housed the Knights Templars and Franciscan nuns, until it was finally closed down as a result of the Dissolution in 1538.

At the heart of Denny stand the medieval Franciscan refectory and the church, the latter being the only surviving building to have been used by all three religious communities. Begun by the Benedictines and adapated under the Templars, the church underwent its most radical alterations when Denny fell to the Countess of Pembroke in 1327. Part of it was converted into a residence and the 12th-century choir was demolished and replaced with a spacious aisled church, improvements which helped to ensure its ultimate survival.

The Farmland Museum is ideal for families, with specially designed activities for children, and contains agricultural machinery and displays on village and domestic life.

Open 1 April–31 Oct: noon–5pm daily. (Property managed by the Farmland Museum Trust).
Entry £3.40/£2.40/£1.20. Family ticket £8. Joint admission ticket with museum. Abbey free for English Heritage members but small charge for museum.
Tel 01223 860489
Access 6m N of Cambridge on A10. (OS Map 154; ref TL 495684.)
Bus Stagecoach Cambus 19, 109 Cambridge–Ely. Tel 01223 423554.
Train Waterbeach 3m.
P ⅃ (grounds & ground floor only) ⬜ ⅋ (weekends only) ⬛ (restricted areas)

Above left, the scissor-truss roof of Denny Abbey. Below, general view showing the north transept, nave and west doorway.

✪ De Grey Mausoleum

Bedfordshire (p. 232/236, 7L)

A remarkable treasure-house of
sculpted tombs and monuments from
the 16th to 19th centuries, dedicated
to the de Grey family of Wrest Park.
Open Weekends only.
Access through Flitton Church.
Contact keykeeper, Mrs Stimson,
3 Highfield Road, Flitton
(Tel **01525 860094**).
Entry Free.

Access Flitton, attached to church,
on unclassified road 1 ½ m W of A6
at Silsoe.
(OS Map 153; ref TL 059359.)
Train Flitwick 2m.

*Interior view of de Grey Mausoleum,
with detail of tombs.*

✪ Denny Abbey and The Farmland Museum

See page 127 for full details.
Cambridgeshire (p. 236, 10N)

✪ Duxford Chapel

Cambridgeshire (p. 233/236, 8N)
A medieval chapel, once part of
the Hospital of St John.

Open Phone **01223 443000** for
details. (Property managed by
South Cambridgeshire District
Council.)
Entry Free.

Access Adjacent to Whittlesford
station off A505.
(OS Map 154; ref TL 486472.)
Train Whittlesford, adjacent.

✪ Framlingham Castle

Suffolk (p. 237, 8P)
See opposite page for full details.

⬢ Grimes Graves

⊜ *Norfolk (p. 237, 9O)*
ⓘ *See p. 130 for full details.*

Framlingham Castle

A superb 12th-century castle which, from the outside, looks almost the same as when it was built. From the continuous curtain wall, linking 13 towers, there are excellent views over Framlingham and the charming reed-fringed mere. At different times, the castle has been a fortress, an Elizabethan prison, a poor house and a school. The many alterations over the years have led to a pleasing mixture of historical styles. The Lanman Museum, containing a local history collection, can be seen for a small extra charge.

• Walk along the full length of the towering castle walls.

• **New for 2000** Mary Tudor Events on 1 & 2 July.

Open 1 April–30 Sep: 10am–6pm daily. 1–31 Oct: 10am–5pm daily. 1 Nov–31 March 2001: 10am–4pm daily. Closed 24–26 Dec and 1 Jan 2001.
Entry £3.20/£2.40/£1.60.
Tel 01728 724189
Access In Framlingham on B1116. (OS Map 156; ref TM 287637.)

Local Tourist Information Woodbridge (Tel 01394 382240).
Bus First Eastern Counties/Ipswich Buses 82 from Ipswich (pass close ⇌ Woodbridge). Tel 0645 583358.
Train Wickham Market 6½ m; Saxmundham 7m.
🅿 🚻 🎦 🅴 🚾 🎧 *interactive* ♿ 🚻 (grounds & ground floor only) 🐕

Grimes Graves

The area of heathland known as Grimes Graves lies in the Norfolk Breckland, surrounded by conifer plantations. Here are the remarkable flint mines dug by prehistoric men some 4000 years ago to provide them with the materials needed to make axes and other tools and weapons. The visitor can descend some 10 metres (30 feet) by ladder into one excavated shaft, and look along the radiating galleries, where the flint, which was mined using picks made of red deer antler, was extracted.

From the air the site resembles the surface of the moon, the mines comprising over 300 of the saucer-shaped hollows which gave the area its name. These mysterious depressions in the landscape were once believed to be the devil's holes

of the pagan god Grim, and were thus named 'Grim's Graves' by the Anglo-Saxons. Despite attempts, over the centuries, to explain the origin of these curious hollows, it was not until 1870, when the first one was excavated and found to be an infilled mine-shaft, that the mystery was solved and the myth dispelled that this incredible landscape had been created by the gods.

• Enjoy the special flint-knapping demonstration days on 30 April, 4 June, 23 July, and 26 August.

• Free Children's Activity Sheet available.

Open 1 April–30 Sep: 10am–6pm daily. 1–31 Oct: 10am–5pm daily. 1 Nov–31 March 2001: 10am–4pm Wed–Sun. Last visit to pit 20 mins before closing.

Closed 1–2pm through the year. Closed 24–26 Dec and 1 Jan 2001. (Entry to the mines for children under 5 years will be at discretion of custodian.)

Entry £2/£1.50/£1.

Tel 01842 810656

Access 7m NW of Thetford off A134. (OS Map 144; ref TL 818898.)

Bus First Eastern Counties 200 Thetford–Newmarket, alight Santon Dowham, thence 2m. Tel 0645 583358.

Train Brandon 3½ m.

🅿 📷 🚻 ♿ (exhibition area only; access track rough) ⛔ (restricted areas)

Above left, Neolithic miners performing a ceremony after clearing a pit. In this speculative drawing by Peter Dunn, the men are shown perhaps engaging in a ritual. Above right, aerial view of Grimes Grave.

◎ Hadleigh Castle

Essex (p. 233, 6N)

The curtain wall and two towers of this 13th-century castle survive almost to their full height and overlook the Essex marshes.

Open Any reasonable time.

Entry Free.

Tel 01760 755161

Access ¾m S of A13 at Hadleigh.
(OS Map 178; ref TQ 810860.)

Bus First Thamesway and Arriva Southend services from surrounding areas to within ½m. Tel 0345 000333.

Train Leigh-on-Sea 1½m by footpath.
♿ (hilly)

◐ Houghton House

Bedfordshire (p. 232/236, 7L)

Reputedly the inspiration for 'House Beautiful' in Bunyan's *Pilgrim's Progress*, the remains of this early 17th-century mansion still contain elements that justify the description, including work attributed to Inigo Jones.

Open Any reasonable time.

Entry Free.

Access 1m NE of Ampthill off A421, 8m S of Bedford.
(OS Map 153; ref TL 039394.)

Bus Stagecoach United Counties 142/3, Arriva the Shires 223 Bedford

⇌ Flitwick. Tel 01234 228337.

Train Flitwick or Stewartby, both 3m.

P ♿

✚ Isleham Priory Church

Cambridgeshire (p. 237, 8N)

Rare example of an early Norman church. It has survived little altered despite being later converted to a barn.

Open Any reasonable time. Keykeeper (please follow instructions shown at property or telephone 01604 730320 for details).

Entry Free.

Access In Isleham, 16m NE of Cambridge on B1104.
(OS Map 143; ref TL 642744.)

Bus Stagecoach Cambus 122 from Cambridge. Tel 01223 423554.

Train Newmarket 8½m; Ely 9m.

◎ Landguard Fort

Suffolk (p. 233/237, 7P)

Overlooking the Orwell Estuary, this is an 18th-century fort with major 19th-century alterations and 20th-century additions. Considerable renovations were completed in 1998. There is a museum featuring displays of local history. Please check opening times.

• Come to Darell's Day, 2 July.
• Come to the Essex Rifles Sundays (14 May and 10 September).

Open 23 April–29 Oct: 10.30am–5pm Sun and Bank Hol. 6 June–16 Sep: 1–5pm Tue, Wed, Sat. Small groups at other times (guided tours) by arrangement. (Site managed by Landguard Fort Trust.)

Entry £2/£1.50/£1 (no unaccompanied children).

Tel 01394 277767

Access 1m S of Felixstowe near docks.
(OS Map 169; ref TM 284318.)

Bus First Eastern Counties 75/7 Ipswich–Felixstowe Dock to within ¾m. Tel 01473 253734.

Train Felixstowe 2½m.

P 🅿 ⬤ ✕ 🔲

✚ Leiston Abbey

Suffolk (p. 237, 8P)

Remains of an abbey for
Premonstratensian canons, which
include a restored chapel.

Open Any reasonable time. (Site
managed by Procorda College).
Entry Free.
Access 1m N of Leiston off B1069.
(OS Map 156; ref TM 445642.)

Bus First Eastern Counties/ First
Eastern National 80 Ipswich
Aldeburgh (pass close
⇌Saxmundham).
Tel 01645 583358.
Train Saxmundham 5m.

◓ Lexden Earthworks and Bluebottle Grove

Essex (p. 233/237, 70)

Part of a series of earthworks,
once encompassing 12 square miles,
which protected Iron Age Colchester
and were subsequently added to by
the conquering Romans.

Open Any reasonable time.
(Property managed by
Colchester Borough Council.)
Entry Free.
Access 2m W of Colchester off
A604. (OS Map 168; ref TL 965246
[Lexden Earthworks] and TL
975245 [Bluebottle Grove].)

Bus Arriva Colchester 5 from
⇌ Colchester. Tel 01206 544449.
Train Colchester or Colchester
Town, both 2½ m.

✚ Lindsay Chapel

Suffolk (p. 233/237, 70)

A little 13th-century chapel with
thatched roof and lancet windows.

Open All year: 10am–4pm daily.
Entry Free.
Access On unclassified road ½m E
of Rose Green, 8m E of Sudbury.
(OS Map 155; ref TL 978443.)

Bus Suffolk Bus 156 ⇌ Ipswich–Ely,
Sun only. Tel 0645 583358.
Train Sudbury 8m.

⊙ Longthorpe Tower

Cambridgeshire (p. 236, 9M)

The tower contains the finest example of 14th-century domestic wall paintings in northern Europe. They show many secular and spiritual objects, including the Wheel of Life, the Labours of the Months, the Nativity and King David.

Open 1 April–31 Oct: noon–5pm Sat–Sun and Bank Holidays only.

Entry £1.50/£1.10/80p.

Tel 01733 268482

Access 2m W of Peterborough on A47.(OS Map 142; ref TL 163983.)

Bus Stagecoach Viscount 14 from City Centre (passing ≠Peterborough). Tel 01733 554571.

Train Peterborough 1½ m. P (close by) ⬚ ⬚ ⬚

⊕ Mistley Towers

Essex (p. 233/237, 7O)

The remains of a church designed by Robert Adam and built in 1776. It was unusual in having towers at both the east and west ends.

Open Key available from Mistley Quay Workshops, Tel 01206 393884. (Property managed by Mistley Thorn Residents Association.)

Entry Free.

Access On B1352, 1½ m E of A137 at Lawford, 9m E of Colchester. (OS Map 169; ref TM 116320.)

Bus First Eastern National 102–4 Colchester–Harwich. Tel 0345 000333.

Train Mistley ¼m. 🔽 (exterior only) 🔽 (restricted areas)

⊙ Moulton Packhorse Bridge

Suffolk (p. 237, 8N)

Medieval four-arched bridge spanning the River Kennett.

Open Any reasonable time.

Entry Free.

Access In Moulton off B1085, 4m E of Newmarket.

(OS Map 154; ref TL 698645.)

Train Kennett 2m. P 🔽 🔽

⊕ North Elmham Chapel

Norfolk (p. 237, 10O)

Remains of an 11th-century chapel possibly built on the site of the cathedral for the Anglo-Saxon bishops of East Anglia. The chapel was converted into a fortified manor house and enclosed by earthworks in the late 14th century by the notorious Bishop of Norwich, Hugh le Despencer.

Open Any reasonable time.

(Property managed by North Elmham Parish Council.)

Entry Free.

Access 6m N of East Dereham on B1110. (OS Map 132; ref TF 988217.) 🔽

◉ Old Gorhambury House

Hertfordshire (p. 232, 6M)

The remains of this Elizabethan mansion illustrate the impact of the Renaissance on English architecture.

Open May–Sep: 2–5pm Thursday only, or at other times by appointment. Call 01727 843675 for more information.

Entry Free.

Access ¼ m W of Gorhambury House and accessible only through private drive from A4147 at St Albans (2m).

(OS Map 166; ref TL 110077.)

Bus Arriva the Shires 300 St Albans–Hemel Hempstead to start of drive. Tel 0345 788788.

Train St Albans Abbey 3m, St Albans 3½m. 🔽

Archaeology

Archaeology is the study of past societies from their physical remains. The variety of evidence archaeologists use is enormous, from the skeletal fragments of Boxgrove Man, who died 400,000 years ago, to the factories of the industrial revolution or the air raid shelters of World War Two. All can tell us where we have come from and help us to think about where we are going.

English Heritage's archaeologists, often working with others, survey our towns and countryside so that we can identify important sites, buildings and landscapes. With aerial photography we can map not only the upstanding remains of ancient fields on Dartmoor or burial mounds on the Wessex Downs, but also the thousands of sites which appear as crop marks – buried remains reflected in the growing fields.

English Heritage's geophysicists also reveal the hidden patterns of

settlements inside hillforts or discover new prehistoric ceremonial sites, such as Stanton Drew in Somerset. Only by identifying and mapping these sites can we protect and manage our archaeological heritage and develop strategies for investigating it.

The most important of these places are Scheduled – recognised as monuments of national

significance. Many others are logged in the National Monuments Record in Swindon and in local Sites and Monuments Records, where they are available to everyone – from planners to school children. Other important features such as battlefields and historic parks and gardens are logged in National Registers.

English Heritage supports projects by local archaeologists, sometimes with funding and often with advice from its archaeological scientists based in the regions. The National Centre for Archaeology in Fort Cumberland, Portsmouth, also has experts in the conservation and analysis of artefacts, the study of human and animal bones and dating techniques.

Recently English Heritage's archaeo-scientists produced a world's first when they dated the timber circle at Holme to the spring of 2049 BC.

cottages and churches or factories and shops, are a vital part of the fabric of our communities and the most visible evidence of our past. By recording and studying them we can advise on their conservation and re-use to promote a sustainable future and enhance the character of our environment. Archaeology brings together the local and the universal, the unusual and the everyday. It helps to make life interesting for everyone.

Opposite page, top, work on the measuring stage in the dendro lab of the archaeology research school. Dendrochronology is the science of dating events and variations in the environment by the study of growth rings in trees and aged wood. Below, a dry pine sample. Bottom, Boxgrove Quarry, West Sussex, general view of the site where the Boxgrove Man was found.

This page, top, the cascade at Chiswick House with archaeologists at work.

Left, Stanton Drew Circles and Cove. Below, the Boxgrove Quarry site director holding a jawbone found there.

At the Centre for Archaeology research excavations are organised. We also map complex landscapes such as the World Heritage Sites of Stonehenge and Avebury, so that we can properly care for them, often in partnership with others such as the National Trust and local authorities.

Not all archaeology is buried under the ground. The buildings of England – whether thatched

❂ Orford Castle

Suffolk (p. 237, 8p)

Originally a keep-and-bailey castle, Orford was characteristic of the Norman Conquest, with a walled enclosure and a great tower, which stood as a self-contained lordly residence and an independent, defendable strong-point.

The building we see today was a royal castle built by Henry II in the 12th century as a coastal defence. The comprehensive building records are the earliest in the kingdom. The uniquely designed polygon keep survives almost intact with three immense towers. Inside each, a spiral stair leads to a maze of rooms and passageways. Look out for the Merman!

From the top of the keep there are splendid views of Orford Ness and the surrounding countryside.
• Free Children's Activity Sheet.
• CD-Rom unit with information on English castles.
• Special events every weekend from 1 July to 28 August.

Open 1 April–30 Sep: 10am–6pm daily. 1–31 Oct: 10am–5pm daily. 1 Nov–31 March 2001: 10am–1pm, 2–4pm Wed–Sun. Closed 24–26 Dec and 1 Jan 2001.
Entry £2.60/£2/£1.30.
Tel 01394 450472
Access In Orford on B1084 20m NE of Ipswich.

(OS Map 169; ref TM 419499.)
Bus Belle 160, First Eastern Counties 122, Suffolk Country Villager Woodbridge–Orford (passes close ⇌ Woodbridge). Tel 0645 583358.
Train Wickham Market 8m.

❸ Prior's Hall Barn

Essex (p. 233/236, 7N)

One of the finest surviving medieval barns in south-east England and representative of the aisled barns of north-west Essex.

Open 1 April–30 Sep: 10am–6pm Sat–Sun. Call 01799 522842 (Audley End House) for further details.
Entry Free.
Access In Widdington, on unclassified road 2m SE of

Newport, off B1383.
(OS Map 167; ref TL 538319.)
Bus First Eastern National 301, Bishop's-Stortford–Saffron Walden. Tel 0345 000333.
Train Newport 2m.

❹ Roman Wall

Hertfordshire (p. 232, 6M)

Several hundred yards of the wall, built c. AD200, which enclosed the Roman city of Verulamium. The remains of towers and foundations of a gateway can still be seen.

Open Any reasonable time.
Entry Free.
Access On S side of St Albans, ½ m from centre off A4147. (OS Map 166; ref TL 135067.)
Bus From surrounding areas Tel 0845 724 4344.

Train St Albans Abbey ½m, St Albans 1¼ m.

Saxtead Green Post Mill

A mill has stood at the same site at Saxtead for more than 700 years, when it served the needs of the thriving farming community of Framlingham. This corn mill, the whole body of which revolves on its base, produced flour and was one of many built in Suffolk in the late 13th century, a time when agricultural output was at a peak.

It is recognised that the post mills of East Suffolk were the finest of their type, not only in England but in the world, and this impressive example is still in working order.

Originally the mill had four 'common sails', on which sailcloths were spread individually by hand; a wooden windshaft; probably a single pair of stones in the breast and a 'tailpole' at the rear to push her round instead of an automatic fantail.

Saxtead Green Post Mill, which ceased production in 1947, is still in working order and you can climb the wooden stairs to the various floors, which are full of fascinating mill machinery.

Open 1 April–30 Sep: 10am–1pm, 2–6pm Mon–Sat. 1–31 Oct: 10am–1pm, 2–5pm Mon–Sat.
Entry £2.10/£1.60/£1.10.
Tel 01728 685789
Access 2 ½ m NW of Framlingham on A1120. (OS Map 156; ref TM 253645.)
Train Wickham Market 9m.
P (in nearby layby)

⊕ Row 111 House, Old Merchant's ⊘ House and Greyfriars' Cloisters

Norfolk (p. 237, 9P)

Two 17th-century Row Houses, typical of Great Yarmouth, redisplayed to illustrate the lives of ordinary Yarmouth people of the 1870s and 1940s. Also containing architectural fittings salvaged following World War Two bombing. Nearby are the remains of a Franciscan friary, with rare early wall paintings.

• **New for 2000** Sites re-displayed throughout.

Open 1 April–31 Oct: 10am–5pm daily. Closed 1–2pm and 1 Nov–31 March 2001. Guided tours hourly: depart Row 111 House at 10am, 11am, noon, 2pm, 3pm & 4pm. **Access arrangements and opening times may be subject to change following launch of new displays mid-summer 2000. Please call for details.**
Tel 01493 857900
Entry £1.85/£1.40/90p.

Complementary displays can be visited at the nearby Elizabethan House, 100 yards along South Quay.
Tel 01493 745526
Access Great Yarmouth, make for South Quay along riverside and dock, ½ m inland from beach. Follow signs to dock and south quay. (OS Map 134; ref TG 525072 [Houses] and TG 525073 [Cloisters].)
Bus From surrounding areas. Tel 0845 300 6116.
Train Great Yarmouth ½ m.

⊕ St Botolph's Priory

Essex(p. 233/237, 70)

The nave, with an impressive arcaded west end, of the first Augustinian priory in England.
• **New for 2000** 900th Anniversary Event 10am–5pm on 22 July.

Open Any reasonable time. (Property managed by Colchester Borough Council.)
Entry Free.
Access Colchester, near

Colchester Town station. (OS Map 168; ref TL 999249.)
Bus From surrounding areas. Tel 0345 000333.
Train Colchester Town, adjacent.

⊕ St John's Abbey Gate

Essex (p. 233/237, 70)

This fine abbey gatehouse, in East Anglian flintwork, survives from the Benedictine abbey of St John.

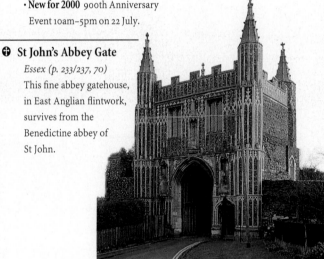

Open Any reasonable time. (Property managed by Colchester Borough Council.)
Entry Free.
Access On S side of central Colchester. (OS Map 168; ref TL 998248.)
Bus From surrounding areas. Tel 0345 000333.
Train Colchester Town ¼ m.

⊕ St Olave's Priory

Norfolk (p. 237, 9P)

Remains of an Augustinian priory founded nearly 200 years after the death in 1030 of the patron saint of Norway, after whom it is named.

Open Any reasonable time.
Entry Free.
Access 5 ½ m SW of Great Yarmouth on A143. (OS Map 134; ref TM 459996.)

Train Haddiscoe 1¼ m.
(restricted areas)

Tilbury Fort is the finest and best preserved example of 17th-century military engineering in England, remaining largely unaltered even after the latest reconstructions carried out in the 1860s.

Designed by Sir Bernard Gomme, Charles II's Chief Designer, Tilbury replaced a smaller fort dating back to the reign of Henry VIII. It was built as a low lying and largely earthen construction, designed to withstand bombardment at a time when artillery was the dominant weapon. The fortifications served both an offensive and defensive purpose, its heaviest guns mounted along the river bank protecting the approaches to the Thames from hostile shipping, and complicated outworks based on the bastion system defending it from landward attack.

Throughout the 18th and early 19th centuries Tilbury and the batteries at Gravesend formed the first line of defence for the Thames and London, although its strategic importance declined after this

Right, the Water Gate.

time, with the building of larger and more efficient forts. It is largely thanks to the fact that it was superseded in this way, however, that Tilbury has retained the dominant design features of de Gomme and thus its uniqueness.

Today, exhibitions, the powder magazine and bunker-like 'casemates' demonstrate how the fort protected the city. There's even a chance to fire an anti-aircraft gun!

Sharpe, the TV drama, was filmed here.
- Visit the 'Military Vehicle Rally' on 23–25 Aug.
- Free Children's Activity Sheet available.

Open 1 April–30 Sep: 10am–6pm daily. 1–31 Oct: 10am–5pm daily. 1 Nov–31 March 2001: 10am–4pm Wed–Sun. Closed 24–26 Dec and 1 Jan 2001.
Entry £2.60/£2/£1.30. £1 to fire anti-aircraft gun.
Tel 01375 858489
Access ½ m E of Tilbury off A126.(OS Map 177; ref TQ 651754.)
Bus Town & County 380
⇌ Tilbury–Tilbury Ferry. Tel 01375 403357.
Train Tilbury Town 1 ½ m.
🚻 🅴 🚻 ♿ (exterior, magazines & fort square) 🎧 ♿ (restricted areas)

✛ Thetford Priory

Norfolk (p. 237, 8N)

The 14th-century gatehouse is the best-preserved part of this Cluniac priory built in 1103. The extensive remains include the plan of the cloisters.

Open Any reasonable time.
Entry Free.
Access On W side of Thetford near station. (OS Map 144; ref TL 865836.)
Bus From surrounding areas. Tel 0845 300 6116.
Train Thetford ¼ m.

⊙ Thetford Warren Lodge

Norfolk (p. 237, 9O)

The ruins of a small, two-storeyed medieval house, set in pleasant woods, which was probably the home of the priory's gamekeeper.

Open Any reasonable time.
Entry Free.
Access 2m W of Thetford off B1107. (OS Map 144; ref TL 839841.)
Bus First Eastern Counties 131/2 Bury St Edmunds–Brandon (pass close ⮂ Thetford). Tel 0845 300 6116.
Train Thetford 2 ½ m.

⊙ Tilbury Fort

⊘ *Essex (p. 233, 5N)*
See p. 139 for full details.

Left, the Parade, looking north towards the Landport Gate, Tilbury Fort.

✛ Waltham Abbey Gatehouse and Bridge

Essex (p. 233, 6M)

A late 14th-century abbey gatehouse, part of the cloister and 'Harold's Bridge'.

Open Any reasonable time. (Properties managed by Lee Valley Park.)
Entry Free.
Tel 01992 702200
Access In Waltham Abbey off A112.
(OS Map 166; ref TL 381008.)
Bus Frequent services by different operators from ⮂ Waltham Cross. Tel 0345 000333.
Train Waltham Cross 1 ¼ m. ⛒ (sensory trail guide)

⊘ Weeting Castle

⊙ *Norfolk (p. 237, 9N)*

The ruins of a substantial early medieval manor house within a shallow rectangular moat.

Open Any reasonable time.
Entry Free.
Access 2m N of Brandon off B1106. (OS Map 144; ref TL 778891.)
Train Brandon 1 ½ m.

⊕ Wrest Park Gardens

⊛ *Bedfordshire (p. 232/236, 7M)*
∅ *See opposite page for full details.*

Right, the Marble Fountain and view towards the Archer Pavilion.

Wrest Park Gardens

Over 90 acres of wonderful gardens were originally laid out in the early 18th century, including the Great Garden and the exquisite, intricate French Garden, with statues and fountains. The present house, built in the 1830s, was home to the de Grey family. It was inspired by 18th-century French chateaux and forms an elegant backdrop to the gardens.

As you wander through the woods and along the canals you will come across charming garden buildings and follies, including the Orangery, the Mithraic Altar, Bowling Green House and the Chinese Temple and Bridge. The jewel at Wrest Park has to be the Archer Pavilion, with its delightful chambers and wall paintings.

At Wrest you walk, and rest you will need, so why not relax by the Long Water, Leg O'Mutton Lake or Atlas Pond? All are beautiful picnic spots.

• Visit the 'St George's Day Festival' on 23–24 April.

Open 1 April–30 Sep: 10am–6pm Sat–Sun and Bank Holidays. 1–31 Oct: 10am–5pm Sat–Sun. Last admission one hour before closing time.

Entry £3.40/£2.60/£1.70.

Tel 01525 860152

Access ¼ m E of Silsoe off A6, 10m S of Bedford. (OS Map 153; ref TL 093356.)

Bus Stagecoach United Counties /52 Bedford–Luton. Tel 01234 228337.

General view of the New House built between 1834 and 1839 with the Long Water in the foreground.

East Midlands

Below, view through the forecourt entrance towards the inner court gateway at Kirby Hall, where peacocks wander freely; middle, a detail of 'History in Action' which takes place at Kirby Hall, in Northamptonshire. It is the most spectacular historical event of its kind in Europe; right, Eleanor Cross, in Geddington, Northamptonshire; far right, the Venus Fountain at Bolsover Castle, in Derbyshire.

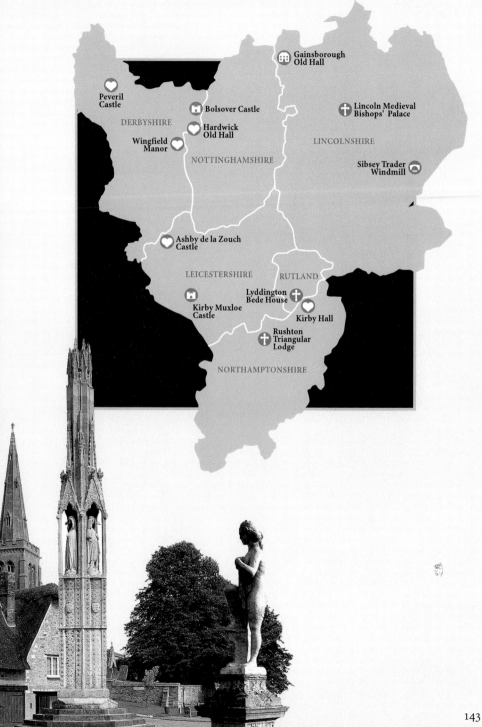

Gainsborough
Old Hall

Peveril
Castle

Bolsover Castle

Lincoln Medieval
Bishops' Palace

DERBYSHIRE

Hardwick
Old Hall

Wingfield
Manor

LINCOLNSHIRE

NOTTINGHAMSHIRE

Sibsey Trader
Windmill

Ashby de la Zouch
Castle

LEICESTERSHIRE

RUTLAND

Lyddington
Bede House

Kirby Muxloe
Castle

Kirby Hall

Rushton
Triangular
Lodge

NORTHAMPTONSHIRE

Bolsover Castle

Bolsover Castle has dominated the landscape and caught the imagination of its visitors for four centuries. Part of the attraction for visitors today is finding the castle in such an unlikely position: towering over a motorway, in a former coal-mining area, and off the beaten track. Part of it is the surprise of going through the layers of architecture: the Outer Court, the Great Court, the secret garden, the winding passages of the Little Castle. But most of it is the way that Bolsover appears to have been untouched by time. Mark Girouard, historian and champion of the castle, wrote that 'by an unlikely miracle the keep at Bolsover has survived into this century as an almost untouched expression in stone of the lost world of Elizabethan chivalry and romance.'

The house you see today stands on the site of a medieval castle built shortly after the Norman Conquest by the Peveril family. Sir Charles Cavendish bought the old castle and began the project of building the present 'Little Castle' in 1612, which, despite its embattled appearance, was designed for elegant living rather than for defence.

Sir Charles Cavendish intended the house for retiring from the world to an imaginary golden age of chivalry and pleasure. His son William, who later became a Duke, inherited in 1616 and completed the Little Castle, assisted by the designer John Smithson. William then added the stately rooms of the Terrace Range, and invited the Stuart court to a specially-written masque in 1634. Finally, he built another whole range for his horses. In the enormous Riding House he trained them in the continental art of *manège*, a kind of ballet for horses.

Summer 2000 sees the completion of a project intended to recreate the excitement of the 17th

Opposite page, top left, a 19th-century watercolour by Hibbert, featuring Bolsover. Main picture, aerial view of Bolsover. This page, top right, the Terrace Range – doorway and staircase by John Smithson. Above and right, general views.

Top, wall painting of Hercules subduing the Cretan Bull. Above, wall painting of Hercules subduing the Wild Board of Erymanthus. Below, detail of the gate pier, leading to the South Drive.

century at Bolsover. Conservation work has stabilised the fabric, replaced missing parts of the castle and it has been presented freshly through an innovative and interesting interpretation scheme.

The symbolic and erotic wall-paintings in the Little Castle, some of which were restored in the 1970s, have been conserved, and exciting discoveries have been made of original painted decoration beneath later work. The castle battlements and the Venus garden have been restored, and the fountain, with 23 new statues, will play again for the first time in centuries. The stables have been made into a new Discovery Centre.

The important part of a visit to Bolsover is that, with a bit of help from the state-of-the-art audio-tour, you can imagine the lives of the creative family who built such an unusual house. As one 17th-

century writer put it, a man's country house is 'the Theatre of his Hospitality, the Seate of Self-Fruition, the Comfortablest part of his own Life, a kind of private Princedom... an Epitomy of the whole World.'

- **New for 2000** Restored interiors of Little Castle.
- Restored and working Venus Fountain & new statuary in Summer.
- **New for 2000** New site interpretation includes new audio tour, audiovisual displays and interactive scale model of Little Castle in Summer.
- New guidebook.
- **New for 2000** Art exhibition in Little Castle 5–30 July.
- Free Children's Activity Sheet available.

English Heritage Hospitality: Bolsover is now available for civil weddings, receptions, corporate hospitality. For more information all 01246 856 456.

Open 1 April–30 Sep: 10am–6pm,
daily. 1–31 Oct: 10am–5pm, daily.
1 Nov–31 March 2001: 10am–4pm
Wed–Sun. Closed 24–26 Dec and
1 Jan 2001. May close earlier for
evening events.

Entry £4.20/£3.20/£2.10.

Tel 01246 822844

Access Off M1 at junction 29 or 30,
6m from Mansfield. In Bolsover,
6m E of Chesterfield on A632.
(OS Map 120; ref SK 471707.)

Local Tourist Information
Chesterfield (Tel 01246 207777).

Bus Stagecoach East Midlands
81–3, Chesterfield–Bolsover.
Tel 01332 292200.

Train Chesterfield 6m.

Bolsover Heritage Services offers
a unique opportunity to travel in
style to Bolsover Castle, Hardwick
Old Hall and other attractions in
the area, on a 1948 vintage coach.
Operates 30 May–30 Aug: Sun and
Bank Holiday Mon. Contact Cosy
Coach Tours on 0114 2489139 or the
District of Bolsover Leisure and
Tourism Services on 01246 242324.
🅿 (in Castle car park off main gate,
also coach drop off point) 🅿 ⬚ ⌂
♿ (disabled) 🍴 (Café open daily
April–Oct and weekends in winter)
♿ (grounds only) ✗ ⎕ 🅴
(school room, to be pre-booked)

*Above right, the Pillar Parlour. Right,
the Hall showing pillars and fireplace.*

⚇ Arbor Low Stone Circle and Gib Hill Barrow

Derbyshire (p. 236, 11J)

A fine Neolithic monument, this 'Stonehenge of Derbyshire' comprises many slabs of limestone, surrounded by an unusually large ditch.

Open 10am–5/6pm.

(Site managed by the Peak District National Park Authority.)

Entry Farmer who owns right of way to property may levy a charge.

Access ½m W of A515 2m S of Monyash. (OS Map 119; ref SK 161636.)

Bus Mainline 181 from Sheffield, 202 from Derby, both to Parsley Hay, thence 1m. Tel 01332 292200.

Train Buxton 10m.

○ Ashby de la Zouch Castle

Leicestershire (p. 236/239, 10J)

The present impressive ruins of this late-medieval castle contain certain sections of the walls of the hall, the buttery, pantry, kitchen and solar but are above all dominated by a magnificent 24-metre (80-foot) high tower, built by William, Lord Hastings, between 1474 and 1483.

Hastings Tower was slighted (split in two) during the Civil War, but still offers the visitor panoramic views of the surrounding countryside. Ashby was used by Sir Walter Scott for the famous jousting scene in his classic romance *Ivanhoe*.

• Free Children's Activity Sheet.

• Attractive picnic spot.

Open 1 April–30 Sep: 10am–6pm daily. 1–31 Oct: 10am–5pm daily. 1 Nov–31 March 2001: 10am–4pm Wed–Sun. Closed 24–26 Dec and 1 Jan 2001.

Entry £2.60/£2/£1.30.

Tel 01530 413343

Access In Ashby de la Zouch, 12m S of Derby on A511. (OS Map 128; ref SK 363167.)

Bus Arriva North Midlands 9, 27 Burton on Trent–Ashby de la Zouch; Arriva Fox County 118, 218 Leicester–Swadlincote. Tel 01332 292200.

Train Burton-on-Trent 9m.

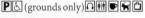 (grounds only)

⊖ Bolingbroke Castle

Lincolnshire (p. 236, 11M)

Remains of a 13th-century hexagonal castle, birthplace of Henry IV in 1367 and besieged by Parliamentary forces in 1643.

Open 1 April–30 Sep: 9am–9pm daily. 1 Oct–31 March 2001: 9am–7pm daily. (Site managed by Heritage Lincolnshire.)

Entry Free.

Access In Old Bolingbroke, 16m N of Boston off A16. (OS Map 122; ref TF 349649.)

Train Thorpe Culvert 10m.

⊙ Bolsover Castle

Derbyshire (p. 236/239, 11K)

⊘ *See p. 144–147 for full details.*

⊕ Chichele College

Northamptonshire (p. 236, 8L)

Parts of a quadrangle remain of this college for secular canons, founded in 1422.

Open Quadrangle: any reasonable time. For the chapel, please contact the keykeeper, Mrs D. Holyoak, 12 Lancaster St, Higham Ferrers.

Tel 01933 314157 (Site managed by East Northamptonshire Council.)

Entry Free.

Access In Higham Ferrers, on A6. (OS Map 153; ref SP 960687.)

Bus Stagecoach United Counties 46/A, X94 from Wellingborough. Tel 01604 620077.

Train Wellingborough 5m.

(restricted areas)

✚ Eleanor Cross, Geddington

Northamptonshire (p. 236, 9L)
One of a series of famous crosses
erected by Edward I to mark
the resting places of the body
of his wife, Eleanor, when brought
for burial from Harby in
Nottinghamshire to Westminster
Abbey.

Open Any reasonable time.
Entry Free.
Access In Geddington, off A43
between Kettering and Corby.
(OS Map 141; ref SP 896830.)
Bus Stagecoach United
Counties 8 Kettering– Corby.
Tel 01604 620077.
Train Kettering 4m. 🐾

⊕ Gainsborough Old Hall

❻ *Lincolnshire (p. 236, 12L)*
A large medieval house with a
magnificent Great Hall and suites
of rooms. A collection of historic
furniture and a recreated medieval
kitchen are on display.
Open Easter Sunday–31 Oct: 10am–
5pm Mon–Sat; 2pm–5.30pm Sun. 1

Nov–Easter Saturday 2001: 10am–
5pm Mon–Sat. Closed Good Friday,
24–26 Dec, and 1 Jan 2001.
(Property managed by Lincolnshire
County Council.)
Entry £2.50/£1.50/£1 (no reduction
for students/ unemployed). Small
charge on Special Event Days for
English Heritage members.

Tel 01427 612669
Access In Gainsborough, opposite
the Library. (OS Map 121; ref SK
815895.)
Bus From surrounding areas.
Tel 01522 553135.
Train Gainsborough Central ½m,
Gainsborough Lea Road 1m.
🚻 🎧 ♿(most of ground floor 🖼️🐾

✚ Geddington, Eleanor Cross

See Eleanor Cross above.

♡ Hardwick Old Hall

⊕ *Derbyshire (p. 236/239, 11K)*

Hardwick Old Hall was the family
home of Bess of Hardwick, one of
the most remarkable women of the
Elizabethan age, who during her
lifetime embarked on several grand
building projects to display her
immense wealth and authority.

This large ruined house, finished
in 1591, lies on the crest of the hill
next door to the stupendous 'New'
Hall she built in the 1590s. The Old
Hall displays Bess of Hardwick's
innovative planning and interesting
decorative plasterwork. The views
from the top floor over the country
park and 'New' Hall are spectacular.
• Audio tour telling the 'Bess
  of Hardwick' story.
Open 1 April–30 Sep: 11am–6pm
Wed–Sun. 1–31 Oct: 11am–5pm
Wed–Sun. 1 Nov–31 March 2001:
11am–4pm Sat–Sun.
Entry £2.60/£2/£1.30. National
Trust members admitted free, but
small charge at English Heritage
events. (Site maintained and
managed by English Heritage, and
owned by the National Trust.

Tickets for the New Hall and joint
tickets for both properties are
available at extra cost).
Tel 01246 850431
Access 9½m SE of Chesterfield,
off A6175, from J29 of M1.
(OS Map 120; ref SK 463638.)
Bus Cosy Coaches C1 from Worksop
to Hall (Sun, June–Aug only)
Stagecoach E Midland 737, 747
Sheffield/Chesterfield–Nottingham;
48 Chesterfield–Bolsover (local
buses link with 🚆 Chesterfield)
alight Glapwell 'Young Vanish'
2½m. Tel 01332 292200.
Train Chesterfield 8m.
Bolsover Heritage Services
(see Bolsover Castle for details).
🅿️ 🖼️ 📷 🐾 🎧
🚻 (in National Trust car park)

149

Kirby Hall

Built of the local Weldon stone, Kirby Hall was begun in 1570 by Sir Humphrey Stafford, and completed by Sir Christopher Hatton, one of Elizabeth I's most talented courtiers. It is an outstanding example of an Elizabethan mansion, including two courtyards, long galleries and a Great Hall. By the end of the 17th century the Hall's wonderful gardens were renowned as amongst the finest in England.

🎬 *Mansfield Park* was filmed here. 'Mansfield Park' tours take place on 22, 23, 24 April and 30 April/1 May 2000.

• Come to 'History in Action V' – the most spectacular historical event of its kind in Europe. Over 2,500 performers, from the Romans to WWII, bring history to life with displays and living history, on 12–13 August.

Open 1 April–30 Sep: 10am–6pm daily. 1–31 Oct: 10am–5pm daily. 1 Nov–31 March 2001: 10am–4pm, Sat–Sun.

Closed 24–26 Dec and 1 Jan 2001.
Entry £2.70/£2/£1.40.
Tel 01536 203230
Access On unclassified road off A43, 4m NE of Corby. (OS Map 141; ref SP 926927.)
Local Tourist Information Corby (Tel 01536 407507).
P 🚻 🏪 🎁 🎧
♿(grounds, gardens & ground floor only)⚠(restricted areas)

Left, view through the forecourt entrance towards the Inner Court gateway. Top, the west front and parterre. Main picture, detail of the parterre.

◕ Hob Hurst's House
Derbyshire (p. 236/239, 11J)
A square prehistoric burial chamber with an earthwork ditch and outer bank.

Open Any reasonable time. (Site managed by the Peak District National Park Authority.)
Entry Free.
Access From unclassified road off B5057, 9m W of Chesterfield.

(OS Map 119; ref SK 287692.)
Bus Hulleys 170, Ringwood X67 from Chesterfield to within 2m. Tel 01332 292200.
Train Chesterfield 9m.

◔ Jewry Wall
Leicestershire (p. 236, 9K)
A length of Roman wall over 9 metres (30 feet) high.

Open 10am–5.30pm Mon–Sat and 2–5.30pm Sun.
Entry Free.
Tel 0116 247 3021 (Jewry Wall Museum)
Access In St Nicholas St,

W of Church of St Nicholas. (OS Map 140; ref SK 583044.)
Bus From surrounding areas Tel 0116 251 1411.
Train Leicester ¼ m.

◔ Kirby Hall
Northamptonshire (p. 236, 9L)
See opposite page for full details.

◔ Kirby Muxloe Castle
Leicestershire (p. 236, 9K)
Picturesque, moated, brick-built castle begun in 1480 by William, Lord Hastings.

Open 1 April–31 Oct: noon–5pm Sat–Sun and Bank Holiday Mon.
Entry £1.95/£1.50/£1.
Tel 01162 386886
Access 4m W of Leicester off B5380,

close to junction 21A, M1. (OS Map 140; ref SK 524046.)
Bus Arriva Fox County 63, 152–4 from Leicester. Tel 0116 251 1411.
Train Leicester 5m.

⊕ Lyddington Bede House
Rutland (p. 236, 9L)
The Bede House was originally a wing of a medieval rural palace of the Bishops of Lincoln. In 1600 the building was converted into an almshouse for twelve poor men, two women and a warden, and remained a home for pensioners until the 1930s. Among the things to see on its three floors are the bedemen's rooms with tiny windows and fireplaces, and the Great Chamber with an exceptionally beautiful ceiling cornice.

An audio tour allows you to relive the changes over the last 700 years as if you were there – do not miss the experience!

• **New for 2000** 1600 'Anniversary Tours' on 8–9 April.
Open 1 April–30 Sep: 10am–6pm daily. 1–31 Oct: 10am–5pm daily.
Entry £2.60/£2/£1.30.
Tel 01572 822438
Access In Lyddington, 6m N of Corby, 1m E of A6003

next to church. (OS Map 141; ref SP 875970.)
Bus 'Rutland Flyer' Corby–Melton Mowbray (passes close ⇌ Oakham) Tel 0116 251 1411.
(ground-floor rooms only)

Lincoln Medieval Bishops' Palace

In the shadow of Lincoln Cathedral is the Medieval Bishops' Palace, the administrative centre of the largest diocese in medieval England, begun in the 1150s and abandoned after the Civil War of the 1640s when it was sacked.

The East Hall range, with its great vaulted undercroft, was built by Bishop St Hugh (who also built the choir of the cathedral) before 1200 as the bishop's private residence; the public West Hall and its kitchen, also begun by St Hugh, was completed in the 1220s by Bishop Hugh of Wells (who continued the rebuilding of the cathedral); and the chapel range and entrance tower were built by Bishop William Alnwick who modernised the palace in the 1430s. Together they form perhaps the most impressive bishop's house in England.

Built on terraces on the Lincoln hillside, the palace provides a wonderful panorama of the Roman, medieval, and modern city while retaining its aura of enclosure and privacy.

Open 1 April–30 Sep: 10am–6pm daily. 1–31 Oct: 10am–5pm daily. 1 Nov–31 March 2001: 10am–4pm Sat–Sun. Closed 24–26 Dec and 1 Jan 2001. Open daily for Lincoln Christmas Market.
Entry £1.90/£1.40/£1.
Tel 01522 527468
Access S side of Lincoln Cathedral.
(OS Map 121; ref SK 981717.)
Bus From surrounding areas. Tel 01522 553135.
Train Lincoln 1m.

✠ **Lincoln Medieval**
Bishops' Palace

Lincolnshire (p. 236/241, 11L)
See opposite page for full details.

✠ **Mattersey Priory**

Nottinghamshire
(p. 236/239/241, 11K)
Remains of a small Gilbertine
monastery founded in 1185.

Open Any reasonable time.
Entry Free.
Access Rough access down drive
¾m long, 1m E of Mattersey

off B6045, 7m N of East Retford.
(OS Map 112; ref SK 704896.)
Train Retford 7m.

⬢ **Nine Ladies Stone Circle**

Derbyshire (p. 236/239, 11J)
This Early Bronze Age circle
(pictured right), once part of a burial
site for 300–400 people, is 15 metres
(50 feet) across. It is adjacent to a
Bronze Age Cemetery and other
religious sites.

Open Any reasonable time.
(Site managed by the Peak District
National Park Authority.)
Entry Free.
Access From unclassified road
off A6, 5m SE of Bakewell.
(OS Map 119; ref SK 249635.)
Bus Hulleys 170 Matlock–Bakewell

to within 1m. Tel 01332 292200.
Train Matlock 4½m.

⚬ **Peveril Castle**
◑ *Derbyshire (p. 236/239, 11J)*

See p. 154 for full details.

✠ **Rufford Abbey**

Nottinghamshire (p. 236/239, 11K)
The remains of a 17th-century
country house, built on the
foundations of a 12th-century
Cistercian abbey, set in the Rufford
Country Park.

Open 1 April–31 Oct: 10am–5pm
daily. 1 Nov–31 March 2001:
10am–4pm daily. Closed 24–26 Dec
and 1 Jan 2001. (Site managed by
Nottinghamshire County Council.)
Entry Free. Parking charge applies.
Tel 01623 822944

Access 2m S of Ollerton off A614.
(OS Map 120; ref SK 645646.)
Bus Stagecoach E Midland 33
Nottingham–Worksop, also X33,
136, 233 from Nottingham.
Tel 0115 924 0000.
🚻 P 🍴 ⬚ (craft centre) ♿ ✖

✠ **Rushton Triangular Lodge**

Northamptonshire (p. 236, 9L)
An extraordinary building built by
the Roman Catholic Sir Thomas
Tresham on his return from
imprisonment for his religious
beliefs. Completed in 1597,
it symbolizes the Holy Trinity –
it has three sides, three floors,
trefoil windows and three triangular
gables on each side. Other buildings
with Tresham connections can be
explored on the 'Tresham Trail'.
Ring for details of guided tours.

Open 1 April–30 Sep: 10am–6pm
daily. 1–31 Oct: 10am–5pm daily.
Entry £1.50/£1.10/80p.
Tel 01536 710761
Access 1m W of Rushton,
on unclassified road 3m from
Desborough on A6.
(OS Map 141; ref SP 830831.)
Bus Stagecoach United Counties 19
Kettering–Market Harborough,
alight Desborough, thence 2m.
Tel 01604 620077.
Train Kettering 5m.
🐴 (restricted areas) ⬚ ⬚ ⬚

Peveril Castle

This castle, perched high above the pretty village of Castleton, offers breathtaking views of the Peak District. Founded soon after the Norman Conquest of 1066 by one of King William's most trusted knights, William Peverel, the castle played an important role in guarding the Peak Forest area which was valuable for its lead, and the silver that could be refined from it, and as hunting country bound by Forest Law. Some of the earliest herringbone masonry still to be seen belongs to this earliest castle.

When 'Castle Peak', as it was known in the Middle Ages, passed into the hands of Henry II in 1155, he made various additions to it, most notably the great square tower, built in 1176, which today stands almost to its original height. Fragments remain to show how elegant the keep once was, with shallow buttresses and round-headed windows.

Improvements were made to the castle during the 13th century, and it was also during this time that Peveril saw action when it was forcibly seized by the Earl of Derby. However it gradually fell into disrepair, until renewed interest in castles in the 19th century led to renovations.

• Picnic spot of exceptional beauty.

• Free Children's Activity Sheet available.

Open 1 April–30 Sep: 10am–6pm daily. 1–31 Oct: 10am–5pm daily. 1 Nov–31 March 2001: 10am–4pm Wed–Sun. Closed 24–26 Dec and 1 Jan 2001.
Entry £2.20/£1.70/£1.10.
Tel 01433 620613
Access On S side of Castleton, 15m W of Sheffield on A6187. (OS Map 110; ref SK 150827.)
Bus First Mainline/Stagecoach E Midland 272/4 ⇌ Sheffield–Castleton, thence 1m. Tel 01332 292200.
Train Hope 2½m.
Ⓟ (in town) 🚻 (in town)

● Sibsey Trader Windmill

Lincolnshire (p. 236/241, 11M)

An impressive tower mill built in 1877, with its machinery and six sails intact. Flour milled on the spot can be bought here.

Open 11am–5pm for Milling

Sundays; 23 & 30 April; 14 & 28 May; 11 & 25 June; 9 & 23 July; 13 & 27 Aug; and 9 & 10 Sep.

(Site managed by Mr & Mrs Bent.)

Entry £1.70/£1.30/90p.

Tel 01205 820065

Access ½m W of village of Sibsey, off A16 5m N of Boston.

(OS Map 122; ref TF 345511.)

Bus Various services and operators from Boston to Sibsey, thence ½m. Tel 01522 553135.

Train Boston 5m.

🅿 🚻 ♿ (exterior only) ✈ 🍴

○ Sutton Scarsdale Hall

Derbyshire (p. 236/239, 11K)

The dramatic hilltop shell of a great early 18th-century baroque mansion.

Open 10am–5/6pm daily.

Entry Free.

Access Between Chesterfield and Bolsover, 1½m S of Arkwright Town. (OS Map 120; ref SK 441690.)

Bus Stagecoach E Midland 48 Chesterfield–Bolsover. Tel 01332 292200.

Train Chesterfield 5m. 🅿 ♿ ✈

⊕ Tattershall College

Lincolnshire (p. 236, 11M)

Remains of a grammar school for church choristers, built in the mid-15th century by Ralph, Lord Cromwell, the builder of nearby Tattershall Castle.

Open Any reasonable time.

(Site managed by Heritage Lincolnshire.)

Entry Free.

Access In Tattershall (off Market Place) 14m NE of Sleaford on A153. (OS Map 122; ref TF 213577.)

Bus Road Car Brylaine 5 Boston–Lincoln (passing close ⇌ Boston and Lincoln). Tel 01522 553135.

Train Ruskington 10m.

✈

○ Wingfield Manor

Derbyshire (p. 236/239, 11J)

Huge, ruined country mansion built in the mid-15th century. Mary Queen of Scots was imprisoned here in 1569, 1584 and 1585. Although unoccupied since the 1770s, the manor's late-Gothic Great Hall and the 'High Tower' are fine testaments to Wingfield Manor in its heyday.

🎬 The manor has been used as a film location for *Peak Practice* and Zeffirelli's *Jane Eyre*.

Open 1 April–30 Sep: 10am–6pm Wed–Sun. 1–31 Oct: 10am–5pm Wed–Sun. 1 Nov–31 March 2001: 10am–1pm, 2–4pm Sat–Sun.

Also open Bank Holiday Mon. Closed 24–26 Dec and 1 Jan 2001.

Entry £3/£2.30/£1.50.

Tel 01773 832060

Access 17m N of Derby, 11m S of Chesterfield on B5035 ½m S of South Wingfield. From M1 – J28, W on A38, A615 (Matlock Road) at Alfreton and turn onto B5035 after

1½m. (OS Map 119; ref SK 374548.)

Bus Stagecoach E Midland 140, 254 Matlock–Alfreton. Tel 01332 292200.

Train Alfreton 4m.

🏠 🏠 🏠 ♿ (not suitable) ✈

Orientation guide available. Car parking only available for disabled visitors.

The manor contains a private working farm. Visitors are requested to respect the privacy of the owners, to keep to visitor routes and refrain from visiting outside official opening hours.

West Midlands

Left, in the background, the spire of Rotherwas Chapel, in
Herefordshire; in the foreground, Charles II, who made Boscobel
House famous when he chose to hide there to escape Cromwell's
troops in 1651; behind him, Boscobel House, in Shropshire, view
from the west; right, the south front of Witley Court, in
Worcestershire.

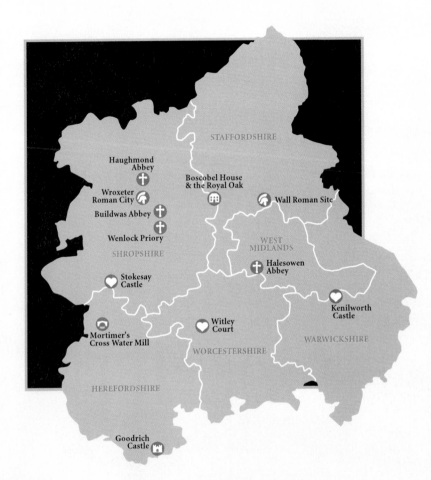

STAFFORDSHIRE

Haughmond
Abbey

Boscobel House
& the Royal Oak

Wall Roman Site

Wroxeter
Roman City

Buildwas Abbey

WEST
MIDLANDS

Wenlock Priory

SHROPSHIRE

Halesowen
Abbey

Stokesay
Castle

Kenilworth
Castle

Mortimer's
Cross Water Mill

Witley
Court

WARWICKSHIRE

WORCESTERSHIRE

HEREFORDSHIRE

Goodrich
Castle

Boscobel House and the Royal Oak

For one brief moment this modest timber-framed hunting lodge held history in its hand when King Charles II hid in the house and the nearby Royal Oak to avoid capture by Cromwell's troops, after his defeat at the Battle of Worcester in 1651.

The house is today fully furnished and restored. The panelled rooms, secret hiding

*Top, portraits of
Oliver Cromwell (right)
and Charles II (left).
Above right, general
view. Main picture,
interior of the house.*

places, and pretty gardens lend the place a truly romantic character.

• Free Children's Activity Sheet available.

Open 1 April–30 Sep: 10am–6pm daily. 1–31 Oct: 10am–5pm daily. 1–30 Nov: 10am–4pm Wed–Sun. 1–31 Dec: 10am–4pm Sat–Sun. Closed 1 Jan–31 March 2001. Admission to the house by guided tour only. Last admission 45 minutes before closing.

Entry £4.30/£3.20/£2.20.

Tel 01902 850244

Access On minor road from A41 to A5, 8m NW of Wolverhampton. Five-minute drive from junction 3, M54.(OS Map 127; ref SJ 837083.)

Train Cosford 3m.

P ⚇ E ⬚ ⬚ ⬚ ✖ ♿ (gardens only) 🍴 (Boscobel House Tearoom: April–Sep: Tue–Sun. Oct: Sun only.)

Charles II

It was the destiny of Charles II to be born into an age of great constitutional unrest. When, in 1642, the increasingly volatile relations between the monarchy and parliament led to the outbreak of civil war, the then young Prince could not know that the next decade would see the execution of his father, Charles I, and the necessity for him, himself, to flee the country as a fugitive.

In 1651, the twenty-year-old Charles's hopes of reclaiming his inheritance were crushed at Worcester in the final conflict of the civil war, and with his life in danger, it became imperative that he secure a passage to the continent.

Arriving at Boscobel House on 6 September 1651, Charles is said to have spent some time in a secret hiding place in the attic there but was compelled to leave the house for fear of detection. It was decided that the safest place to hide would be in the branches of a large oak tree nearby, and thus the famous episode of the Royal Oak, as it came to be known, was born. Journeying to Bristol from Boscobel disguised as a servant, Charles eventually made his way to Shoreham where on the morning of 15 October, he sailed secretly to France, remaining in exile until 1660 when he was restored as king.

Following the turbulent events of the preceding years, England

was delighted to have a monarch once more. Charles proved to be a tolerant king, no more remarkably so than in his treatment of those conspirators who had condemned his father to death; only nine of them were finally executed.

Although his interest in affairs of state was somewhat lacking, Charles was a popular and intelligent ruler and a patron of both the arts and of scientific research. His final years were spent securing his Catholic brother's claim to the throne, and in 1685, on his deathbed, Charles himself converted to the Roman Catholic faith.

Above, Charles II in Boscobel Wood, by Isaac Fuller (1606–1672). Left, portrait of Charles II c. 1680, by Thomas Hawker (d. 1722).

⊘ Acton Burnell Castle

Shropshire (p. 239, 9G)

The warm red sandstone shell of a fortified 13th-century manor house.

Open Any reasonable time.
Entry Free.
Access In Acton Burnell, on unclassified road 8m S of Shrewsbury.
(OS Map 126; ref SJ 534019.)

Bus Boultons/Arriva North Midlands Church Stretton–Shrewsbury (Tue, Sat only). Tel 0345 056785.
Train Shrewsbury or Church Stretton, both 8m.

⊘ Arthur's Stone

Herefordshire (p. 239, 7F)

Stunning prehistoric burial chamber formed of large blocks of stone.

Open Any reasonable time.
Entry Free.
Access 7m E of Hay-on-Wye off B4348 near Dorstone.

(OS Map 148; ref SO 319431.)
Bus Stagecoach Red & White 39 Hereford–Brecon to within ¼m. Tel 01633 266336.

⊕ Boscobel House
⊛ and the Royal Oak

Shropshire (p. 239, 9H)
See p. 158 for full details.

⊕ Buildwas Abbey

Shropshire (p. 239, 9G)

Set beside the River Severn, against a backdrop of wooded grounds, are the extensive remains of this Cistercian abbey founded in 1135.

Open 1 April–30 Sep: 10am–6pm daily. 1–31 Oct: 10am–5pm daily.
Entry £1.95/£1.50/£1.
Tel 01952 433274
Access On S bank of River Severn on A4169, 2m W of Ironbridge. (OS Map 127; ref SJ 642044.)
Bus Elcock Reison 96 Telford–Shrewsbury (passes close ⇌ Telford Central). Tel 0345 056785.
Train Telford Central 6m.

Left, interior of the chapter house.
Far left, aerial view of the abbey.

⊘ Cantlop Bridge

Shropshire (p. 239, 9G)

Single-span cast-iron road bridge over the Cound Brook, designed by the great engineer Thomas Telford.

Open Any reasonable time.
Entry Free.
Access ¼m SW of Berrington on unclassified road off A458. (OS Map 126; ref SJ 517062.)
Train Shrewsbury 5m.

⊘ Clun Castle

Shropshire (p. 239, 8F)

The remains of a four-storey keep and other buildings of this border castle.

Open Any reasonable time.
Entry Free.

Access In Clun, off A488, 18m W of Ludlow. (OS Map 137; ref SO 299809.)
Bus Shropshire Bus 741–5 from Ludlow (pass close ⇌Ludlow). Tel 0345 056785.
Train Hopton Heath 6 ½m; Knighton 6½m.

✠ Croxden Abbey

Staffordshire (p. 236/239, 10J)
Remains of a Cistercian abbey
founded in 1176.

Open 10am–5pm.
Entry Free.
Access 5m NW of Uttoxeter off A522.
(OS Map 128; ref SK 065397.)

Train Uttoxeter 6m.

✠ Edvin Loach Old Church

Herefordshire (p. 239, 8G)
Peaceful and isolated 11th-century
church remains.

Open Any reasonable time.
Entry Free.

Access 4m N of Bromyard on
unclassified road off B4203.
(OS Map 149; ref SO 663585.)
P 🐕

✪ Goodrich Castle

Herefordshire (p. 239, 7G)
Superbly sited, high above the
River Wye, Goodrich Castle was a
fortified baronial palace. Still largely
intact, this magnificent red sandstone castle, with a 12th-century
keep standing three storeys high
and extensive remains from the 13th
and 14th centuries, is protected by
wide and deep ditches cut into rock.
• Free Children's Activity Sheet
  available.

Open 1 April–30 Sep: 10am–6pm
daily. 1–31 Oct: 10am–5pm daily.
1 Nov–31 March 2001: 10am–1pm,
2–4pm daily. Closed 24–26 Dec and
1 Jan 2001.
Entry £3.20/£2.40/£1.60.
Tel 01600 890538
Access 5m S of Ross-on-Wye off
A40. (OS Map 162; ref SO 579199.)
Bus Stagecoach Red & White 34
Monmouth–Gloucester to within
½ m (passes close ⇌ Gloucester).
Tel 0345 125436.

P 400 m from car park to castle

✠ Halesowen Abbey

West Midlands (p. 239, 8H)
Remains of an abbey founded
by King John in the 13th century,
now incorporated into
a 19th-century farm.

Open 11 June, 16 July and 20 August
10am–6pm.
Entry £1.50/£1.20/80p.
Access Off A456 Kidderminster
road, ½m W of Junction 3, M5, 6m
W of Birmingham city centre. (OS
Map 139; ref SO 975828.)

Bus Travel West Midlands 9
Birmingham–Stourbridge.
Tel 0121 2002700.
Train Old Hill 2½m.
P ♿ (rough grass between
church and infirmary) 🐕

✠ Haughmond Abbey

Shropshire (p. 239, 9G)
The extensive remains of this 12th-
century Augustinian abbey include

the chapter house, which retains
its late-medieval timber ceiling,
and some fine medieval sculpture.
Open 1 April–30 Sep: 10am–6pm

daily. 1–31 Oct: 10am–5pm daily.
Entry £1.95/£1.50/£1.
Tel 01743 709661
Access 3m NE of Shrewsbury
off B5062. (OS Map 126; ref SJ 542152.)
Bus Arriva North Midlands 519
Shrewsbury–Newport.
Tel 0345 056785.
Train Shrewsbury 3½m.

◉ Iron Bridge
Shropshire (p. 239, 9G)

See opposite page for full details.

♡ Kenilworth Castle
◉ *Warwickshire (p. 239, 8J)*

See p. 164-165 for full details.

✟ Langley Chapel
Shropshire (p. 239, 9G)
This small chapel, standing alone in a field, contains a complete set of early 17th-century wooden fittings and furniture.

Open Any reasonable time. Closed 24–26 Dec and 1 Jan 2001. **Entry** Free. **Access** 1½m S of Acton Burnell, on unclassified road off A49, 9½m S of Shrewsbury.

(OS Map 126; ref SJ 538001.) **Bus** Boultons/Arriva North Midlands Church Stretton–Shrewsbury (Tue, Sat only) to within 1½m. Tel 0345 056785. **Train** Shrewsbury 7½m. ⊠

◉ Leigh Court Barn
◉ *Worcestershire (p. 239, 8H)*
Magnificent 14th-century timber-framed barn, built for the monks of Pershore Abbey. It is the largest of its kind in Britain.

Open 1 April–30 Sep: 10am–6pm Thu–Sun. **Entry** Free. **Access** 5m W of Worcester on unclassified road off A4103. (OS Map 150; ref 784534.)

Bus First Midland Red 417, 421/2/3/5 from Worcester to within 1m. Tel 0345 125436. **Train** Worcester Foregate St 5m. ⊠

✟ Lilleshall Abbey
Shropshire (p. 239, 9H)
Extensive and evocative ruins of an abbey of Augustinian canons, including remains of the 12th- and 13th-century church and the cloister buildings, surrounded by green lawns and ancient yew trees.
Open Any reasonable time but closed 1 Nov–31 March 2001.
Entry Free.

Tel 01604 730320 (regional office) **Access** On unclassified road off A518, 4m N of Oakengates. (OS Map 127; ref SJ 738142.) **Bus** Arriva North Midlands 80–3, 481 Telford–Stafford (pass close ⇌Telford Central and Stafford) to within 1m. Tel 0345 056785. **Train** Oakengates 4½m.
🔲 🔳 ⊠

Iron Bridge

The world's first iron bridge was cast by local ironmaster Abraham Darby and was erected over the River Severn in 1779. Set in a spectacular wooded gorge, Iron Bridge is now Britain's best-known industrial monument and a World Heritage Site.

Iron Bridge is the perfect place to start a tour of the many industrial, ceramic, decorative arts, and living history museums in the area. It is also a delightful spot for fishing. A boat can take you on a trip up the Severn during the summer months.

Open Any reasonable time.
Entry Free.
Access In Ironbridge, adjacent to A4169. (OS Map 127; ref SJ 672034.)
Bus Frequent from Telford (pass close ⇌Telford Central or Wellington Telford West). Tel 0345 056785.
Train Telford Central 5m.

Kenilworth Castle

Kenilworth Castle has been intimately linked with some of the most important names in English history. Today, with its Tudor gardens, its impressive Norman 'keep' and John of Gaunt's Great Hall, it is the largest castle ruin in England.

The first castle at Kenilworth was built 50 years after the Norman conquest. Henry II took over the castle 50 years later, to counter an attack from his son's rebel army. It was then radically extended by King John, who also transformed the mere (great lake) into one of its most glorious features.

Kenilworth stayed in royal hands until 1253, when it was given to Simon de Montfort by Henry III. The de Montforts turned against the Crown in the Barons' War in 1266, and the castle was besieged. Well-stocked with food, it managed to hold out for almost nine months before disease took its toll and surrender came.

Later, Edward II was briefly imprisoned here, before being taken to Berkeley Castle and hideously murdered in 1326. Henry V retired here after defeating the French at the Battle of Agincourt in 1415. He built himself a banqueting house, The Pleasaunce, on the other side of the lake.

The castle took centre stage again in the 16th century, when it was acquired by the Dudley family. John Dudley, Duke of Northumberland and effectively ruler of England in the reign of the boy-king Edward VI, was executed for trying to place his daughter-in-law, Lady Jane Grey, on the throne in 1553. His son, Robert, was a great favourite of Elizabeth I. Kenilworth was given back to him and he

transformed it into a place fit for her to visit.

Tales woven by Sir Walter Scott, in his novel *Kenilworth* (1821),

around Dudley, his wife (who died in mysterious circumstances) and the Virgin Queen still give extra glamour to the castle.

Kenilworth never saw such glories again. After the Civil War it was partially demolished by Parliamentary troops. Over the years it was allowed to fall further into ruin, and the lake drained away. The castle was saved for the nation in 1938. It remains a powerful reminder of great men, their glories, pleasures and rebellions, and offers glorious views over a countryside now at peace.

- **New for 2000** Basement rooms and ground floor of Leicester's Gatehouse reopen in April 2000 following consolidation works.
- Tearoom in Leicester's Barn (summer months).
- Interactive model
- Waymarked trails from castle to Pleasaunce and Old Kenilworth.
- Free Children's Activity Sheet available.

Open 1 April–30 Sep: 10am–6pm daily. 1–31 Oct: 10am–5pm daily. 1 Nov–31 March 2001: 10am–4pm daily. Closed 24–26 Dec and 1 Jan 2001.

Entry £3.50/£2.60/£1.80.

Tel 01926 852078

Access In Kenilworth. (OS Map 140; ref SP 278723.)

Local Tourist Information Kenilworth (Tel 01926 852595).

Bus Stagecoach Midland Red X18 Coventry–Stratford upon Avon calls Castle; otherwise X12/14/16/17/18, Travel West Midlands 12, 112 Coventry–Leamington Spa to within a few mins' walk (all pass close ⇌ Coventry–Leamington Spa). Tel 01926 414140.

Train Warwick 5m.

🅿 🚻 🍴 (Kenilworth Castle Tea Room, April–Oct daily) ♿ 🎧 (also available for the visually impaired and those with learning difficulties and in French, German and Japanese) 🖼 🏪 ⊘ 🖼 🐕 (allowed on leads)

Opposite page top, aerial view of Kenilworth Castle. Below the battlemented porch and the entrance to Leicester's Gatehouse. This page, above, general view

❶ Longtown Castle

Herefordshire (p. 239, 7F)

An unusual cylindrical keep built c.1200, with walls 4.5 metres (15 feet) thick. There are magnificent views to the Black Mountains.

Open Any reasonable time.

Entry Free.

Access 4m WSW of Abbey Dore. (OS Map 161; ref SO 321291.)

❷ Mitchell's Fold Stone Circle

Shropshire (p. 239, 9F)

An air of mystery surrounds this Bronze Age stone circle, set in dramatic moorland and consisting of some 30 stones, of which 15 are visible.

Open Any reasonable time. (Site managed by Shropshire County Council.)

Entry Free.

Access 16m SW of Shrewsbury, W of A488. (OS Map 137; ref SO 306984.)

Bus Minsterley 553 Shrewsbury–Bishop's Castle (pass close ⮞ Shrewsbury) to within 1m.

Tel 0345 056785.

Train Welshpool 10m.

❸ Moreton Corbet Castle

Shropshire (p. 239, 10G)

See opposite page for full details.

Right, detail of a Norman window, Moreton Corbet .

❹ Mortimer's Cross Water Mill

Herefordshire (p. 239, 8G)

Intriguing 18th-century mill, still in working order, showing the process of corn milling.

Open 1 April–30 Sep: 2–5.30pm Thu, Sun & Bank Holidays.

Entry £2/£1.50/£1.

Tel 01568 708820

Access 7m NW of Leominster on B4362. (OS Map 148; ref SO 426637.)

Train Leominster 7½m.

🦽(exterior & ground floor only)

❺ Old Oswestry Hill Fort

Shropshire (p. 239, 10F)

An impressive Iron Age fort of 68 acres defended by a series of five ramparts, with an elaborate western entrance and unusual earthwork cisterns.

Open Any reasonable time.

Entry Free.

Access 1m N of Oswestry, accessible from unclassified road off A483. (OS Map 126; ref SJ 295310.)

Bus Arriva North Midlands 2, D23, D63 from ⮞ Gobowen.

Tel 0345 056785.

Train Gobowen 2m.

❻ Rotherwas Chapel

Herefordshire (p. 239, 7G)

This Roman Catholic chapel dates from the 14th and 16th centuries and features an interesting mid-Victorian side chapel and High Altar.

Open Any reasonable time. Keykeeper at nearby filling station.

Entry Free.

Access 1½m SE of Hereford on B4399. (OS Map 149; ref SO 537383.)

Bus First Midland Red 110/1/8 from city centre.

Tel 0345 125436.

Train Hereford 3½m.

P 🦽(kissing gate)

Moreton Corbet Castle

Moreton Corbet Castle stands some eight miles to the north of Shrewsbury. A fortification probably stood here in the time of Domesday (1086) when two English brothers, Hunning and Wulfgeat, lived here. They were succeeded by the Torets who held the castle until 1235, losing it briefly to the great Earl William Marshall of Pembroke who besieged and took the castle in February 1216.

In 1235 the Corbets of Wattlesborough inherited Moreton Corbet and probably remodelled the great keep which may have been already standing for over 100 years. In 1282 Sir Robert Corbet was one of those involved in the death of Prince Llywelyn of Wales. In the 16th century the castle was extensively remodelled and then partially demolished to make way for a great Elizabethan mansion house.

In the English Civil War house and castle changed hands four times in vicious fighting of which traces still show in the ruined walls. The castle and mansion stand today as one of the most picturesque ruins of the Shropshire Marches.

Main picture and right, general views of Moreton Corbet Castle. Above right detail of the south-west corner.

Open Any reasonable time.
Entry Free.
Access In Moreton Corbet off B5063, 7m NE of Shrewsbury. (OS Map 126; ref SJ 562232.)
Bus Arriva North Midlands/First PMT X64 Shrewsbury–Hanley (passes close ⇌ Shrewsbury and Stoke on Trent). Tel 0345 056785.
Train Yorton 4m.

P & ♿ ⛲

Stokesay Castle

Stokesay Castle is the finest and best-preserved 13th-century fortified manor house in England, and it offers a unique glimpse into a distant age when strength and elegance combined.

It nestles in peaceful countryside near the Welsh border in a picturesque group with its timber-framed Jacobean gatehouse and the parish church. The Great Hall, almost untouched since medieval times, contains its original staircase, an open octagonal hearth and an innovative timber roof. Across the courtyard the delightful gatehouse, built in 1620, has carved animal heads decorating its gateposts.

The audio tour will help you imagine the castle as the centre of medieval life. Nowadays you can also stroll through the delightful cottage-style gardens.

Open 1 April–30 Sep: 10am–6pm daily. 1–31 Oct: 10am–5pm daily. 1 Nov–31 March 2001: 10am–1pm,

2–4pm Wed–Sun. Closed 24–26 Dec and 1 Jan 2001.

Entry £3.50/£2.60/£1.80.

Tel 01588 672544

Access 7m NW of Ludlow off A49. (OS Map 137; ref SO 436817.)

Local Tourist Information

Ludlow (Tel 01584 875053).

Bus Shropshire Bus 435 Shrewsbury–Ludlow. Tel 0345 056785.

Train Craven Arms 1m.

🅿 🛆🔒📷🚻♿ (call custodian for details) ☕ (refreshments, summer season only) ✗

• Opening in 2000 in Craven Arms (1 m away) the 'Shropshire Hills Discovery Centre'.

Top, general view of the castle from the east. Above, exterior of Stokesay. Above left, a carved oak corbel.

Wenlock Priory

The ruins of a large Cluniac priory in an attractive garden setting featuring delightful topiary. There are substantial remains of the early 13th-century church and Norman chapter house.

The priory is the resting place of St Milburga, the first Abbess, whose bones were found during rebuilding in 1101, and in whose memory a shrine was built. In 1685 the remains of a rare late Norman Lavatorium – a separate building for washing – were uncovered. Its carved panels have been replaced by accurate replicas.

Open 1 April–30 Sep: 10am–6pm daily. 1–31 Oct: 10am–5pm daily. 1 Nov–31 March 2001: 10am–1pm, 2–4pm Wed–Sun.
Closed 24–26 Dec and 1 Jan 2001.
Entry £2.70/£2/£1.40.
Tel 01952 727466
Access In Much Wenlock.
(OS Map 127; ref SJ 625001.)
Bus Shropshire Bus 436/7 Shrewsbury–Bridgnorth (pass close ⇌Shrewsbury). Tel 0345 056 785.
Train Telford Central 9m.
🅿 🚻 🎧 (also available for the visually impaired, those with learning difficulties, and in French and German)
🛉 🛉 🛒 ✚

Top and bottom pictures, general views of Wenlock Priory. Middle picture, the topiary.

Wigmore Castle

Wigmore Castle, one of the major fortresses of the Welsh Marches and the principal castle of the Mortimer dynasty, is one of the most remarkable ruins in England.

Abandoned and dismantled before the Civil War of the 17th century, it was simply left to collapse naturally. Today, its buildings are buried to first floor level by their fallen upper floors, but its towers and curtain walls survive to full height, almost as they appeared when they were first recorded in the 1730s. The natural grass capping, rich in wild plants and rare ferns, that has protected the fragile masonry so well for more than four centuries has been retained, and the castle remains the 'romantic ruin' the Secretary of State took into guardianship in 1995.

The ruins that survive represent a rebuilding of the castle by Roger Mortimer, first earl of March,

in the early 14th century. He was the lover of Queen Isabella and responsible for the murder in 1327 of her husband Edward II. He was himself executed on Edward III's order in 1330, having failed to seize the crown for himself. His buildings sit on top of two earlier castles, a stone fortress of the early 13th century, and a timber castle of the early 12th century.

Within the castle there are up to 8m (26ft) of buried archaeological deposits, containing evidence of daily life, a remarkable resource for future archaeologists. In 1322, for instance, the castle contained 'three springholds or machines for casting great stones or metal quarrels (heavy arrows); crossbows of horn and wood, some fitted with stirrup irons for the purpose of winding up the bows, others of simple construction; helmets for jousts and for real war, lances and spears, six tents and

pavilions, suits of armour and coats of mail; the Irish axe, Saracenic bows and arrows; ... a large chess board painted and gilt with chessmen, a board for tables and draughts; and in the courtyard five peacocks and a good store of grain and beasts.'

Overshadowed by nearby Ludlow Castle which the Mortimers had acquired by marriage in the late 13th century, Wigmore was little used from the late 14th century. Its one and only serious military action came in 1461 when the future Edward IV marched an army out to defeat a Welsh invasion at the Battle of Mortimers Cross. In 1534 it was described as 'utterly decayed', but continued to be used as a prison until it was sold by Elizabeth I in 1601 to Thomas Harley. His son Robert, born in the castle in 1579, was a

leading Parliamentarian, and in the run up to the Civil War, his wife, charged with stopping the Royalists taking the castle, dismantled its defences.

Open Any reasonable time.

Entry Free

Access 8m W of Ludlow on A4110. (OS Map 137; ref SO40906918). Only accessible via public footpath, $^3/_4$ m from the village centre on the Mortimer Way.

Bus daily (not Sun or Bank Hol). Return bus service from Ludlow to Wigmore (nos 736, 738).

Train Ludlow 10m; Buckrell 8m.

P Signposted in village

⛨ (including facilities for the disabled) at the Village Hall and also, by arrangement, with the Landlord of the Compasses Hotel (Tel 01568 770705).

🐕 (allowed on lead)

Warning Wigmore Castle has steep steps to the summit, which are hazardous in icy conditions. Children must be kept under close control and should not be allowed to climb the walls or banks. Strong footwear is recommended. There is no custodial presence.

Witley Court

An early Jacobean manor house, Witley Court was converted in the 19th century into a vast Italianate mansion with porticoes by John Nash. The spectacular ruins of this once-great house are surrounded by magnificent landscaped gardens – the 'Monster Work' of William Nesfield – which still contain immense stone fountains.

fountains and woodlands are currently being restored to their former glory.
• The Jerwood Foundation Sculpture Park at Witley Court consists of modern British sculptures situated in historic parkland.
• Call for details of special 'Cellar Tours'.

Entry £3.50/£2.60/£1.80.
Tel 01299 896636
Access 10m NW of Worcester on A443. (OS Map 150; ref 769649.)
Local Tourist Information
Droitwich Spa (Tel 01905 774312).
Bus Yarranton 758 Worcester–Tenbury Wells (passes close ⇌Worcester Foregate St).
Tel 0345 125436.

The largest of them, representing Perseus and Andromeda, once shot water 120 feet skywards, with 'the noise of an express train'.

Step back in time with a personal audio tour to relive the Court's Victorian heyday and hear stories of the extravagant parties and the 'upstairs, downstairs' lifestyle – perhaps you will even find yourself waltzing romantically across the ballroom! The landscaped grounds,

• Partial firing of Perseus and Andromeda Fountain at 2pm: Easter Sun & Mon (23 & 24 April); also May Bank Holiday Mons (1 & 29 May).
• Stroll along the woodland walks.
• Superb Gift Shop.
Open 1 April-30 Sep: 10am-6pm daily. 1–31 Oct: 10am-5pm daily. 1 Nov-31 March 2001: 10am-4pm Wed–Sun. Closed 24-26 Dec and 1 Jan 2001.

Train Droitwich Spa 8½m.
P ⛏ 🍴 📷 🛍 🐕
♿ (exterior & grounds only)
📷 (not managed by English Heritage)

Above, the south front and the Perseus and Andromeda Fountain. Above right, a sample of the Jerwood Foundation Sculpture Park: 'Walking Man' by Dame Elisabeth Frink (1930–1993). Far right, the Perseus and Andromeda Fountain. Right, part of the magnificent woodlands.

☯ Stokesay Castle
⚜ *Shropshire (p. 239, 8G)*
∅ *See p. 168 for full details.*

☉ Wall Roman Site (Letocetum)
Staffordshire (p. 236/239, 9J)

Wall was an important staging post on Watling Street, the Roman military road to North Wales. It provided overnight accomodation and a change of horse for travelling Roman officials and imperial messengers. Its Roman name *Letocetum* is thought to derive from the Celtic British word for 'grey woods'. Foundations of an inn and bath house can be seen, and many of the excavated finds are displayed in the museum on site.

Open 1 April–30 Sep: 10am–6pm daily. 1–31 Oct: 10am–5pm daily.

Entry £2.30/£1.70/£1.20. National Trust members admitted free, but small charge on English Heritage Special Events days. (Site maintained and managed by English Heritage, and owned by the National Trust.)
Tel 01543 480768

Access Off A5 at Wall near Lichfield.
(OS Map 139; ref SK 099067.)
Train Shenstone 1½m.
Ⓟ 🚻 🎧 (£1 for National Trust members) 🏠 Ⓓ 🛍 🔲 ⛱

✠ Wenlock Priory
⚜ *Shropshire (p. 239, 9G)*
See p. 169 for full details.

✠ White Ladies Priory
Shropshire (p. 239, 9H)
The ruins of the late 12th-century church of a small priory of Augustinian canonesses.

Open Any reasonable time.
Entry Free.
Access 1m SW of Boscobel House off unclassified road between A41 and A5, 8m NW of

Wolverhampton. (OS Map 127; ref SJ 826076.)
Train Cosford 2½m.
🐕

☯ Wigmore Castle
Herefordshire (p. 239, 8G)

See p. 170-171 for full details.

☾ Witley Court
⚙ *Worcestershire (p. 239, 8H)*

See p. 172-173 for full details.

☉ Wroxeter Roman City
Shropshire (p. 239, 9G)

See opposite page for full details.

Wroxeter Roman City

The excavated centre of the fourth largest city in Roman Britain is also the largest to have escaped subsequent development. The city was originally home to some 6,000 men and several hundred horses, but later became the focus of a thriving settlement attracting traders and retired legionaries.

The most impressive features are the 2nd-century municipal baths and the remains of the huge wall dividing the exercise hall from the baths.

There is a site museum in which many finds are displayed, from past excavations to recent work carried out by the Birmingham Field Archaeological Unit.

- Roman Fun for all the family on 22/23 July 2000.
- Regular guided tours by Hinterland project team. Call for details.
- Virtual reality Wroxeter visit.
- Free Children's Activity Sheet available.

Open 1 April–30 Sep: 10am–6pm daily. 1–31 Oct: 10am–5pm daily. 1 Nov–31 March 2001: 10am–1pm, 2–4pm Wed–Sun. Closed 24–26 Dec and 1 Jan 2001. **Entry** £3.20/£2.40/£1.60. **Tel** 01743 761330 **Access** At Wroxeter, 5m E of Shrewsbury on B4380. (OS Map 126; ref SJ 568088.)

Bus Elcock Reison 96 Telford–Shrewsbury (passes close ⇌ Telford Central). Tel 0345 056 785. **Train** Shrewsbury 5½m; Wellington Telford West 6m.

Ｐ ⑪ ⓬ Ｅ ⑪ ⑪ ⑫ ✕

Above, recontruction drawing of the city. Above left, a carved Venus figurine found during excavations. Below, the baths.

Yorkshire

Left, Fountains Abbey, in North Yorkshire; below, Thomas Cromwell (c 1485–1540), who was responsible for the dissolution of around 800 monasteries in England and Wales from 1536 to 1539, thus allowing Henry VIII to confiscate their contents and boost royal income. Amongst these monasteries were the magnificent abbeys of Rievaulx and Whitby, both in North Yorkshire; right, one of Charles Thellusson's collections of Italian white marble figures, bought in 1865. This one, *Education*, by Giuseppe Lazzerini, is among the most impressive and stands at the foot of the staircase, in the entrance hall of Brodsworth Hall.

Whitby Abbey

Richmond Castle

Mount Grace Priory

Helmsley Castle

Scarborough Castle

Middleham Castle

Rievaulx Abbey

NORTH YORKSHIRE

Byland Abbey

Pickering Castle

Fountains Abbey & Studley Royal

Aldborough Roman Site

Kirkham Priory

Clifford's Tower

EAST RIDING OF YORKSHIRE

WEST YORKSHIRE

NORTH LINCOLNSHIRE

NE LINC.

Brodsworth Hall and Gardens

Conisbrough Castle

SOUTH YORKSHIRE

Roche Abbey

177

Brodsworth Hall and Gardens

One of England's most beautiful Victorian country houses, Brodsworth Hall was reopened by English Heritage in 1995 following a major programme of restoration and conservation.

incorporating both formal and informal features was created, all contained within magnificent parkland.

If the exterior of the house seems a little pompous, the interior is screen of Corinthian columns, red silk damask on the walls, chandeliers and gilding, is a grand monument to Thellusson's ambitions. The Dining Room contains some of the finest paintings in the house. Away from the finery of the reception rooms are the more intimate spaces of the Library and Morning Room. Each has original wallpaper, a hand-painted pattern of roses and trellises resembling leather wallcoverings.

When Charles Thellusson acquired Brodsworth in the early 1860s he at once commissioned Chevalier Casentini, whom he had met in Italy, to build him a suitably impressive house. The result is formal, Italianate, four-square and lacks any fanciful detail. Casentini's designs were executed by a little-known English architect, Philip Wilkinson. It is said that Casentini never came to Yorkshire to view what he had designed, fearing the cold and a setting wholly different from the pastoral landscape and blue skies he had drawn. At the same time, a new garden

Brodsworth's chief glory. The Entrance Hall, with its gold, red and marbled walls, is a prelude to the splendours of the inner halls and reception rooms. Another of the house's remarkable features is the processional succession of white marble statues which runs from the Entrance Hall to the pillared South Hall. Of all the sculptures, Argenti's *Sleeping Venus* is particularly memorable.

Rich, decorative schemes appear everywhere in the house. The Drawing Room, with a dividing

When Brodsworth was first built and occupied, it amply fulfilled its role as a grand residence. Parties were conducted in sumptuous style, and in the evenings the gentlemen would relax in the Billiard Room, which has survived remarkably intact.

The servants were housed in a wing abutting the house's main block. Their domain, the Victorian Kitchen, is delightful. Its 'Eagle Range' by Farr and Sons of Doncaster and its grained dressers

still contain a vast range of cooking utensils.

Gradually, after World War I, with spiralling costs, parts of the house were shut away and, almost inadvertently, house and contents were preserved for the future.

The gardens are now largely restored to their original design. They include croquet lawns and a large formal flower garden; a quarry garden and a formal rose garden, with a special collection of old rose varieties.

★ Voted winner of the NPI Awards 1999 for the Northern Counties.

• Exhibitions at Brodsworth include: 'Family Life', 'Serving the House', 'The Gardens' and 'Before Britannia' a history of yachting during the Edwardian period and beyond.

• Free Children's Activity Sheet available.

Open House: 1 April–5 Nov: 1–6pm Tue–Sun and Bank Holidays (last admission 5pm).

Gardens, tearoom, shop: 1 April–5 Nov: noon–6pm.

Gardens only: 1 Nov–26 March 2001: 11am–4pm, weekends only. Pre-booked guided tours from 10am, 1 April–5 Nov only.

Entry £5/£3.80/£2.50. Gardens: £2.60/£2/ £1.30 (summer); £1.60/£1.20/80p (winter).

Tel 01302 722598

Access In Brodsworth, 5m NW of Doncaster off A635 Barnsley Road, from junction 37 of A1(M). (OS Map 111; ref SE 507071.)

Local Tourist Information Doncaster (Tel 01302 734309).

Bus Yorkshire Traction 211 Doncaster–Barnsley; Arriva Yorkshire 497/8 Doncaster–Wakefield (all passing close ⇌ Doncaster and passing ⇌ South Elmsall & Moorthorpe). Tel 01709 515151. Alight at Pickburn, Five Lanes End, thence ½m walk.

Train Doncaster 5½m, South Elmsall 4m, Moorthorpe 4½m.

P ⬚ ⬚ ⬚ E ⬚ ⬚ (colour)

⬚ (house and formal gardens)
⬚ (Brodsworth Hall Tearoom)
⬚ ⬚ Pushchairs, prams and back carriers for babies are regrettably not permitted in the fragile interiors of the house, but the property will provide suitable buggies and child slings.

Opposite page, the gardens and one of the garden statues.
This page, top right, the Drawing Room, with many of the original furnishings from Lapworths. Top left, the Entrance Hall. Above the Kitchen, and insert, part of the large collection of iron and copper pots and pans.

⊙ Aldborough Roman Site

North Yorkshire (p. 241, 14K)

The principal town of the Brigantes, the largest tribe in Roman Britain. These remains include parts of the Roman defences and two mosaic pavements. The museum displays local Roman finds.

Open 1 April–30 Sep: 10am–1pm, 2–6pm daily. 1–31 Oct: 10am–1pm, 2–5pm daily.

Entry £1.70/£1.30/90p.

Tel 01423 322768

Access In Aldborough, ¾m SE of Boroughbridge, on minor road off

B6265 within 1m of junction of A1 and A6055.
(OS Map 99; ref SE 405661.)
Bus Proctors/Harrogate & District 142 ⇌ York–Ripon.
Tel 01423 566061.
🛉 (summer only) 🅿 📷 🎪
🐕 (restricted areas)

Mosaic pavement with central star decoration, and pottery vessels.

⊕ Barton-upon-Humber, St Peter's Church

See St Peter's Church, p. 190

⊕ Brodsworth Hall and Gardens

✿ *South Yorkshire (p. 236, 12K)*

🅰 *See p. 178-179 for full details.*

Right, the Library at Brodsworth Hall.

⊙ Burton Agnes Manor House

East Riding of Yorkshire (p. 241, 14L)

Rare example of a Norman house, altered and encased in brick in the 17th and 18th centuries.

Open 1 April–31 Oct: 11am–5pm daily (the nearby Burton Agnes Hall and Gardens are privately owned and occupied, and not managed by English Heritage).

Entry Free.

Access In Burton Agnes village, 5m SW of Bridlington on A166. (OS Map 101; ref TA 103633.)
Bus E Yorkshire 744 ⇌ York–Bridlington. Tel 01482 222222.
Train Nafferton 5m. 🐕

⊕ Byland Abbey

North Yorkshire (p. 241, 14K)

A beautiful ruin set in peaceful meadows in the shadow of the Hambleton Hills. It illustrates the later development of Cistercian churches.

Open 1 April–30 Sep: 10am–1pm, 2–6pm daily. 1–31 Oct: 10am–1pm, 2–5pm daily.

Entry £1.60/£1.20/80p.

Tel 01347 868614

Access 2m S of A170 between Thirsk and Helmsley, near Coxwold village.
(OS Map 100; ref SE 549789.)
🅿 🅿 🛉🦽 (including toilets)
🎪🐕

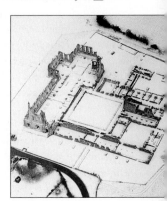

❶ Clifford's Tower

North Yorkshire (p. 241, 13K)
Standing high on its mound, the
11th-century Clifford's Tower is
the last remaining part of York
Castle, built by William the
Conqueror to establish his control
in the North.

• Tactile model with Braille text.
Open 1 April–30 Sep: 10am–6pm
daily (9.30am–7pm July–Aug).
1–31 Oct: 10am–5pm daily. 1 Nov–
31 March 2001: 10am–4pm daily.
Closed 24–26 Dec and 1 Jan 2001.
Entry £1.80/£1.40/90p.

Tel 01904 646940
Access In Tower St, York.
(OS Map 105; ref SE 605515.)
Local Tourist Information
York (Tel 01904 621756 or
01904 620557).

Bus From surrounding areas.
Tel 01904 551400.
Train York 1m.
Ⓟ (council; fee charged)

❷ Conisbrough Castle

South Yorkshire (p. 236/241, 12K)
The spectacular white keep of
this 12th-century castle, made of
magnesian limestone, is the oldest
circular keep in England. Recently
restored, it is now also one of the
finest medieval buildings.
Conisbrough was made famous
in Walter Scott's *Ivanhoe*.
Open 1 April–30 Sep: 10am–5pm
daily (6pm on Sun). 1 Oct–
31 March 2001: 10am–4pm daily.
Closed 24–26 Dec and 1 Jan 2001.
Last admission 40 minutes before
closing. (Castle managed by the
Ivanhoe Trust.)
Entry £2.80/£1.80/£1. Family ticket
£6.75. English Heritage members
admitted free. Discount for group
bookings of over 20 people. Guided

tours available. Castle available for
private hire and special events
outside general opening hours.
Please call before visiting on a
Saturday during Summer: the
Castle may close early for private
function.
Tel 01709 863329

Access NE of Conisbrough town
centre off A630, 4½m SW
of Doncaster. (OS Map 111;
ref SK 515989.)
Bus From surrounding areas.
Tel 01709 515151.
Train Conisbrough ½m.
Ⓟ ♿ (limited access)

❸ Easby Abbey

North Yorkshire (p. 240/242, 15J)
Substantial remains of the medieval
abbey buildings stand in a beautiful
setting by the River Swale near
Richmond. The abbey can be

reached by a pleasant riverside
walk from Richmond Castle.
Open Any reasonable time.
Entry Free.
Access 1m SE of Richmond off
B6271. (OS Map 92; ref NZ 185003.)

Bus Arriva North East X27, 27/8
Darlington–Richmond (pass close
≥Darlington) thence 1½m.
Tel 0345 124125.
Ⓟ

Fountains Abbey and Studley Royal

Fountains Abbey has been described as the 'crown and glory of all that monasticism has left us in England'. 800 years of history are there to be explored in the 320-hectare estate, which combines architectural and landscape features of outstanding historical and aesthetic importance.

The ruins of the Cistercian Abbey, founded in 1132 by 13 monks, are the largest such remains in Europe. They provide a dramatic focal point for the landscape garden laid out during the first half of the 18th century by John Aislabie. Visitors can lose themselves in the criss-crossing paths that wind past elegant ponds, cascades, follies and classical temples by centuries-old trees.

Other features within the estate are St Mary's Church (a master-piece of Victorian Gothic design, *see p. 184*) and Fountains Hall – an Elizabethan mansion built partly with stone from the Abbey.

Fountains Abbey was acquired by the National Trust in 1983 and declared a World Heritage Site in 1987. It remains today one of the most popular attractions in the North.

Open Fountains Abbey and Water Garden: 1 April–30 Sep: 10am–7pm daily (4pm on 7–8 July). 1 Oct–31 March 2001: 10am–5pm daily. Closed Fri in Nov, Dec, Jan. Closed 24–25 Dec. **Throughout the year, last admission: one hour before closing.** Deer Park: free of charge, open daily during daylight.
Entry Fountains Abbey and Water Garden £4.30/£2.10. Family ticket (2 adults & 3 children) £10.50. **English Heritage members admitted free.**
Tel 01765 608888
Reduction for groups if booked in advance. Guided tours available. Call for details on **01765 601005** (Mon–Fri).
• For Special Events call the Box Office on **01765 609999.**
Access 4m W of Ripon off B6265. (OS Map 99; ref SE 278703.)

Bus Harrogate & District 802 Bradford–Ripon, Sun in June–Aug only (Tel 01423 566061); otherwise Arriva North East 145 from Ripon (with connections from ≢Harrogate) Thur and Sat only. Tel 01609 780 780.
🅿🚻🔾🚼📷🏠🚲🅿🅴🚻♿ (not suitable for three-wheel battery cars. Call for details. Braille and large print guides available. Tactile wall frieze.)

Fountains Abbey and Studley Royal

North Yorkshire (p. 236/241, 14J)
See opposite page for full details.

Gainsthorpe Medieval Village

North Lincolnshire (p. 236/241, 12L)
Originally discovered and still best seen from the air, this hidden village comprises earthworks of peasant houses, gardens and streets.
Open Any reasonable time.
Entry Free.
Access On minor road W of A15 S of Hibaldstow 5m SW of Brigg (no directional signs).
(OS Map 112; ref SK 955012.)
Train Kirton Lindsey 3m.

Helmsley Castle

North Yorkshire (p. 241, 14K)
Spectacular earthworks surround the great ruined keep of this 12th-century castle. There is an exhibition on the history of the castle in Elizabethan buildings.
Open 1 April–30 Sep: 10am–6pm daily. 1–31 Oct: 10am–5pm daily.

1 Nov–31 March 2001: 10am–4pm Wed–Sun. Closed 1–2pm through the year, 24–26 Dec and 1 Jan 2001.

Entry £2.30/£1.70/£1.20.
Tel 01439 770442
Access Near town centre.
(OS Map 100; ref SE 611836.)
Bus Scarborough & District 128 from Scarborough (Tel 01723 375463). Stephensons from York (Tel 01347 838990).

P (large car park N of castle; charge payable) ⬚ ⬚
🚻 (in car park and in town centre)

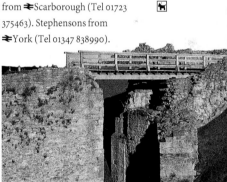

Howden Minster

East Riding of Yorkshire (p. 241, 13L)
A large, cathedral-like church dating from the 14th century. The chancel and octagonal chapter house are managed by Howden Minster Parochial Church Council and may be viewed from the outside only.
Open Any reasonable time. Closed 24–26 Dec.
Entry Free.
Access In Howden, 23m W of Kingston Upon Hull, 25m SE of York, near junction of A63 & A614. (OS Map 106; ref SE 748283.)
Bus East Yorkshire 155 Goole–Hull. Tel 01482 222222.
Train Howden 1½m.
P (street parking nearby)

183

⊕ Kirkham Priory

North Yorkshire (p. 241, 14K)
The ruins of an Augustinian priory,
set in a peaceful valley by the River
Derwent.

Open 1 April–30 Sep: 10am–6pm
daily. 1–31 Oct: 10am–5pm daily.
Entry £1.60/£1.20/80p.
Tel 01653 618768
Access 5m SW of Malton
on minor road off A64.
(OS Map 100; ref SE 735657.)

Bus Yorkshire Coastliner 840/2/3
Leeds–Scarborough
(pass ⇌ York and Malton)
to within ¾m. Tel 01653 692556.
Train Malton 6m.
🅿 ♿ 🐕 🚻 (summer only)

◉ Marmion Tower

North Yorkshire (p. 241, 14J)
A medieval gatehouse with a fine
oriel window.

Open Any reasonable time.
Closed 24–26 Dec.
Entry Free.
Access N of Ripon on A6108 in

West Tanfield.
(OS Map 99; ref SE 267787.)
Train Thirsk 10m.
🐕

⊛ Middleham Castle

North Yorkshire (p. 240, 14J)
See opposite page for full details.

⊕ Monk Bretton Priory

South Yorkshire (p. 236/241, 12K)
Sandstone ruins of a Cluniac
monastery founded in 1153 with
extensive remains of the fully
restored 14th-century gatehouse.

Open 1 April–30 Sep: 10am–6pm
daily. 1–31 Oct: 10am–5pm daily.
1 Nov–31 March 2001: 10am–4pm
daily. (Managed by a keykeeper.)
Entry Free.
Access 1m E of Barnsley town

centre off A633.
(OS Map 111; ref SE 373065.)
Bus From surrounding areas.
Tel 01709 515151.
Train Barnsley 2½m.
🅿 ♿ 🚻 🐕

Middleham Castle

This impressive fortress, built in the 12th century, was the childhood home of Richard III who made it his principal castle in the north of England. It was here that the future king, under the care of Richard Nevill, Earl of Warwick, learned the military skills and courtly manners appropriate to a young man of his rank. His only son, Edward, was born and lived his short life at the castle.

Before the present castle was built, a Norman motte-and-bailey fortification made from earth and timber existed at Middleham. The earthworks of this 11th-century fortification still survive on the high ground to the south-west of the existing castle. The principal building on the new site was a formidable stone keep, one of the largest in England, which today commands stunning views of the surrounding countryside from the battlements.

During the 15th century, extensive improvements and additions were made to the castle which reflected the dignity and status of its owners. Middleham became a centre of patronage and influence, a military headquarters, and a focus of social life, serving the needs of three of the greatest lords of the century, Salisbury, Warwick and Gloucester.

• Viewing gallery.

• See a replica of the fabulous medieval pendant, the Middleham Jewel.

🎥 *James Herriot's Yorkshire* was filmed at Middleham.

Open 1 April–30 Sep: 10am–6pm daily. 1–31 Oct: 10am–5pm daily. 1 Nov–31 Dec: 10am–1pm, 2–4pm daily. 2 Jan–31 March 2001 10am–1pm, 2–4pm Wed–Sun. Closed 24–26 Dec and 1 Jan 2001.

Entry £2.30/£1.70/£1.20.

Tel 01969 6238

Access At Middleham, 2m S of Leyburn on A6108. (OS Map 99; ref SE 128875.)

Bus Dales and District 159 Ripon–Richmond. Tel 01677 425203

Local Tourist Information

Richmond (Tel 01748 850252).

♿ (except tower)

🚻 (in town centre) 🏛 🖼 ⛺ ♿

✚ Mount Grace Priory

North Yorkshire (p. 241/242, 15K)
Mount Grace Priory is the best-preserved Carthusian monastery in Britain. Founded in 1398, it is

beautifully situated amongst attractive woodlands. The monks lived as virtual hermits in their own cells, only congregating for services in the monastery's small church. Today, you can see what life must have been like there in the 15th century by viewing the specially reconstructed cell and wandering through the remains of the Great Cloister, outer court, as well as the extensive gardens.

- Picnic spot of exceptional beauty.
- Nature trail.
- Free Children's Activity Sheet and nature trail leaflet available.

Open 1 April–30 Sep: 10am–6pm daily. 1–31 Oct: 10am–5pm daily. 1 Nov–31 March 2001: 10am–1pm, 2–4pm Wed–Sun. Last admission 30 minutes before closing time. Closed 24–26 Dec and 1 Jan 2001.
Entry £2.80/£2.10/£1.40.
National Trust members admitted free except when Special Events.. (Site owned by the National Trust, maintained and managed by English Heritage.)
Tel 01609 883494
Access 12m N of Thirsk, 7m NE of Northallerton on A19. (OS Map 99; ref SE 449985.)
Local Tourist Information
Northallerton (Tel 01609 776864).
Bus SSB Coaches Stokesley–Middlesbrough (pass close ≋ Northallerton) to within ½m. Tel 01609 778132.
Train Northallerton 6m.

P ⑪ ♿ ☐ ☐ ⊞ ✖

◎ Pickering Castle

North Yorkshire (p. 241, 14L)
A splendid motte and bailey castle, once a royal hunting lodge. It is well preserved, with much of the original walls, towers and keep, and spectacular views over the surrounding countryside.
- Exhibition.
- Free Children's Activity Sheet available.

Open 1 April–30 Sep: 10am–6pm daily. 1–31 Oct: 10am–5pm daily. 1 Nov–31 March 2001: 10am–4pm Wed–Sun. Closed 1–2pm through the year, 24–26 Dec and 1 Jan 2001.
Entry £2.30/£1.70/£1.20.
Tel 01751 474989
Access In Pickering 15m SW of Scarborough. (OS Map 100; ref SE 800845.)
Bus Yorkshire Coastliner 840/2

from ≋Malton (Tel 01653 692556); Scarborough & District 128 from ≋Scarborough (Tel 01723 375463).
Train Malton 9m; Pickering (N. York Moors Railway) ¼m.

P ⑪ ♿ (except motte)
E (prebook) ☐ ☐ ⊞ ✖

⊙ Piercebridge Roman Bridge

North Yorkshire (p. 240/242, 15J)
Remains of the stone piers and abutment of a Roman timber bridge over the River Tees.

Open Any reasonable time.
Entry Free.
Access At Piercebridge, 4m W of Darlington on B6275. (OS Map 93; ref NZ 214154.)
Bus Arriva North East 75, X75

Darlington–Barnard Castle (pass close ⇌ Darlington).
Tel 0345 124125.
Train Darlington 5m. 🖼

⊙ Richmond Castle

North Yorkshire (p. 240/242, 15J)
Hugely dramatic Norman fortress, built by William the Conqueror in his quest to quell the rebellious North. William's close ally, Alan of Brittany, chose the site for his principal castle and residence. The 11th-century remains of the curtain wall and domestic buildings are combined with the 30-metre (100-foot) high keep with its massive thick walls, added in the 12th century. There are magnificent views over the River Swale from the keep and there is a delightful riverside walk to Easby Abbey.

• **New for 2000** New exhibitions opening in Summer.
• **New for 2000** New gift shop opening in Summer.
• Free Children's Activity Sheet available.

Open 1 April–30 Sep: 10am–6pm daily. 1–31 Oct: 10am–5pm daily. 1 Nov–31 March 2001: 10am–1pm, 2–4pm. Closed 24–26 Dec

and 1 Jan 2001.
Entry £2.50/£2/£1.30.
Tel 01748 822493
Access In Richmond. (OS Map 92; ref NZ 174006.)
Bus Arriva North East X27, 27/8 Darlington–Richmond (pass close ⇌ Darlington). Tel 0345 124125.
🖼🖼🖼🖼🖼

⊕ Rievaulx Abbey

North Yorkshire (p. 241, 14K)

See p. 188-189 for full details.

⊕ Roche Abbey

South Yorkshire (p. 236/241, 11K)
A Cistercian monastery, founded in 1147, which is set in an enchanting valley landscaped by Capability Brown. Excavation has revealed the complete layout of the abbey.
Open 1 April–30 Sep: 10am–6pm daily. 1–31 Oct: 10am–5pm daily.
Entry £1.60/£1.20/80p.
Tel 01709 812739
Access 1½m S of Maltby off A634. (OS Map 111; ref SK 544898.)
Bus First Mainline 100-2, Powell 122 Rotherham–Maltby, thence

1½m. Tel 01709 515151.
Train Conisbrough 7m.
🖼🖼🖼🖼🖼🖼

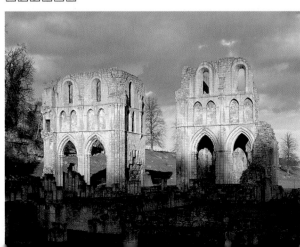

Rievaulx Abbey

'Everywhere peace, everywhere serenity, and a marvellous freedom from the tumult of the world.' Those words could describe Rievaulx today, for it is one of the most atmospheric of all the ruined abbeys of the North. In fact, these words were written over eight centuries ago by St Aelred, the monastery's third abbot. Although much of what was built by the monks is in ruins, most of the spectacular presbytery, the great eastern part of the abbey church, stands virtually to its full height. Built in the 13th century, its soaring beauty conveys the glory and splendour that Rievaulx once possessed.

Rievaulx was founded directly by the holy St Bernard of Clairvaux, as part of the missionary effort to bring Christianity to western Europe. Twelve Clairvaux monks

came to Rievaulx in 1132, and from these modest beginnings sprang one of the wealthiest monasteries of medieval England and the first Cistercian monastery in the North.

In the Middle Ages, wealthy families vied with each other in founding churches. Rievaulx enjoyed the protection and endowment of Walter Espec, who provided much of the abbey's land. The monks of Byland Abbey, over the river, co-operated with the Cistercians in agreeing to divert the course of the River Rye. You can still make out traces of the old river, and the channels dug by the monks.

A steady stream of monks came to Aelred, author and preacher, who was regarded then, and since, as a wise and saintly man. After his death in 1167 the monks sought his canonisation and, in the 1220s, rebuilt the east part of their church in a much more elaborate style for his tomb. Rievaulx was still a vibrant community when Henry VIII dissolved it in 1538. Its new owner, Thomas Manners, first Earl of Rutland, swiftly began the systematic destruction of the buildings. What he left was one of the most eloquent of all monastic sites, free 'from the tumult of the world'.

- **New for 2000** Exciting new exhibition: "The Work of God and Man".
- Superb gift shop.

Open 1 April–30 Sep: 10am–6pm daily (9.30am–7pm in July–Aug). 1–31 Oct: 10am–5pm daily. 1 Nov–31 March 2001: 10am–4pm daily.

Closed 24–26 Dec and 1 Jan 2001. **Entry** £3.40/£2.60/£1.70. **Tel 01439 798228**

Access In Rievaulx, 2¼m W of Helmsley on minor road off B1257. (OS Map 100; ref SE 577849.)

Local Tourist Information Helmsley (Tel 01439 770173). **Bus** Moorsbus from Helmsley (connections from ⇌Scarborough) Sun, June–Sep plus daily in Aug; otherwise Scarborough & District 128 from Scarborough (Tel 01723 375463), Stephensons 57 from ⇌York (Tel 01347 838990), alighting Helmsley, thence 2 ½m.

🅿 👬🔽♿🔊📷📺

🎧 (also available for the visually impaired, those with learning difficulties and in French, Swedish and Japanese) 🔲 🔲

Opposite page, main picture, general view of the abbey. Top, an engraving of Rievaulx by George Hawkins, 1843, after William Richardson (1842–77) This page, top, general view of the abbey. Left, the south side of the early 13th-century presbytery, one of the finest monastic churches in the north of England.

✛ St Mary's Church,
✷ Studley Royal

North Yorkshire (p. 241, 14J)
Magnificent church, designed by
William Burges in the 1870s, with a
highly decorated interior. Coloured
marble, stained glass, gilded and
painted figures and a splendid
organ remain in their original glory.
See also Fountains Abbey p. 182

*Below, the chuch's interior; right,
and below right, details.*

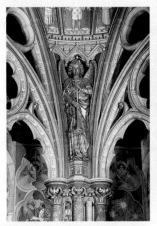

Open 1 April–30 Sep: 1–5pm daily.
(English Heritage property
managed by the National Trust as
part of the Studley Royal Estate.)
Entry Free.
Tel 01765 608888
Access 2½m W of Ripon off
B6265, in grounds of Studley Royal
estate. (OS Map 99; ref SE 278703.)
Bus Harrogate & District 802
Bradford–Ripon, Sun June–Aug
only (Tel 01423 566061); otherwise
145 from Ripon (with connections
from ⇌Harrogate) Thur and Sat
only. Tel 01609 780 780.
P (free at visitor centre) ♿ 🐕

✛ St Peter's Church

North Lincolnshire (p. 241, 12L)
A fine 15th-century former parish
church, with an Anglo-Saxon
tower and baptistry.

Open 2–4pm daily.
Closed 25–26 Dec and 1 Jan 2001.
Entry Free.
Tel 01652 632516
Access In Barton-upon-Humber.

(OS Map 112;
ref TA 034220.)
Bus Road Car/E York 350
Hull–Scunthorpe. Tel 01724 297444.
Train Barton-upon-Humber ½m. 🚋

Deserted medieval villages

In patches of rumpled ground, clumps of nettles and grassy hollows, lie clues to medieval communities which have disappeared. Time and the plough have blurred their outlines – the traces of houses, yards, trackways, mills, graveyards and orchards are easy to miss – which partly explains why until the 1950s many historians doubted their existence. But historical research, archaeology and the aerial camera have since found thousands of them.

Lost places tell us much. From the excavation of settlements like Wharram Percy and the analytical mapping of medieval fields we are beginning to suspect that parts of lowland England were overwritten by a great replanning which began in the late 9th or 10th century, and shaped many aspects of the landscape we subsconsciously regard as 'English'.

On a more detailed level, the investigation of houses in which peasants lived, and the graveyards in which they were buried, illuminates topics which range from health and diet to the history of privacy. The houses themselves emerge as sturdier and more structurally efficient than was once supposed. From the 13th century their fabrics reflect the growth of professional craftsmanship to which peasants had access, and which built some thousands of houses that are still lived in today.

Why were villages deserted? It used to be thought that they

Aerial view of Hound Tor Deserted Medieval Village in Devon. Below, aerial view of Wharram Percy Deserted Medieval Village in North Yorkshire

were hit by crisis, like the Black Death of 1348–9. In fact, abandonment was rarely sudden, and while a catastrophe could hasten an existing trend it seldom by itself caused one.

In looking for underlying reasons we should rather reflect that change is settlement's natural condition. Medieval England was not a uniform, stagnant place but a dynamic landscape of localities in flux, wherein settlements grew, shrank moved or dissolved in reaction to economic opportunities and pressures, to which factors like climatic change, disease, war or natural catastrophe added further co-varying rhythms.

Vanished villages are places of silenced lullabies, where the motion, gossip and labour of ordinary people half a millennium ago may be sensed. Their archaeology opens windows into England's personality, and your surroundings, tomorrow.

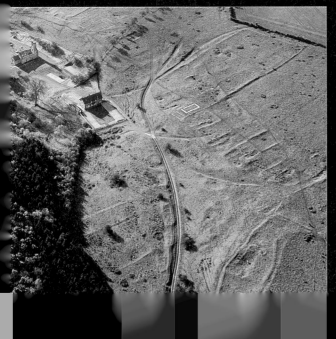

Scarborough Castle

North Yorkshire (p. 241, 14L)

There are spectacular coastal views from the buttressed walls of this enormous 12th-century castle. The remains of the great rectangular stone keep still stand over three storeys high. There is also the site of a 4th-century Roman signal station.

• Free Children's Activity Sheet available.

Open 1 April–30 Sep: 10am–6pm daily (9.30am–7pm in July & Aug) 1–31 Oct: 10am–5pm daily. 1 Nov–31 March 2001: 10am–4pm Wed–Sun. Closed 24–26 Dec and 1 Jan 2001.

Entry £2.30/£1.70/£1.20.

Tel 01723 372451

Access Castle Rd, E of town centre. (OS Map 101; ref TA 050893.)

Bus From surrounding areas. Tel 01723 375463.

Train Scarborough 1m.

 (also available for the visually impaired and those with learning difficulties) (except keep)

Skipsea Castle

East Riding of Yorkshire (p. 241, 13M)

The remaining earthworks of a Norman motte and bailey castle.

Open Any reasonable time.

Entry Free.

Access 8m S of Bridlington, W of Skipsea village. (OS Map 107; ref TA 163551.)

Train Bridlington 9m.

Spofforth Castle

North Yorkshire (p. 241, 13J)

This manor house has some fascinating features including an undercroft built into the rock. It was once owned by the Percy family.

Open 1 April–30 Sep: 10am–6pm daily. 1 Oct–31 March 2001: 10am–4pm daily. Closed 24–26 Dec. Keykeeper. (Site managed by Spofforth-with-Stockeld Parish Council.)

Entry Free.

Access 3 ½m SE of Harrogate, off A661 at Spofforth. (OS Map 104; ref SE 360511.)

Bus Harrogate & District 79 Harrogate–York. Tel 01423 566061.

Train Pannal 4m.

Stanwick Iron Age Fortifications

North Yorkshire (p. 240/242, 15J)

The tribal stronghold of the Brigantes, whose vast earthworks cover some 850 acres. Today you can see an excavated section of the ditch, cut into the rock, and the rampart.

Open Any reasonable time.

Entry Free.

Access On minor road off A6274 at Forcett Village. (OS Map 92; ref NZ 178124.)

Bus Burell's 78/A from Darlington (passes close ≥Darlington) Tel 0191 383 3337.

Train Darlington 10m.

Thornton Abbey and Gatehouse

Set in a remote corner of Humberside are the remains of this impressive abbey, founded in 1139 for a community of Augustinian canons. Its founder, William le Gros, Earl of Yorkshire, was buried here.

Those buildings which survive reflect the extent to which this house, when reconstructed in the 1260s, was a truly magnificent structure, belonging to a rich and prestigious community. The imposing 14th-century gatehouse is faced partly in brick and partly in stone, a decorative style new to England at this time, and would have contained the abbot's court and exchequer. The beautiful octagonal chapterhouse, with its elaborate 'window tracery', is an example of only a small number of

similar buildings either existing or known to have existed in Britain, and is entirely unrepresented elsewhere.

Thornton Abbey's ruins are associated with a local legend which tells the story of the remains of

canon having been found immured in a room here, seated at a table with a book, pen and ink – a tale woven into the fabric of the abbey's history since the 16th century.

Open Abbey grounds: any reasonable time. Gatehouse: 1 April–30 Sep: noon–6pm , 1st & 3rd Sun of the month. 1 Oct– 31 March 2001: noon–4pm, 3rd Sun of the month.

Entry Free.

Access 18m NE of Scunthorpe on minor road N of A160; 7m SE of Humber Bridge on minor road E off A1077. (OS Map 113; ref TA 115190.)

Train Thornton Abbey ¼m.

🅿️ ♿ (except interior of gatehouse and part of chapter house ruins) 🚻 (restricted areas) ⛩

Left, the chapterhouse. Above, the abbey's gatehouse from the west.

Wharram Percy Deserted Medieval Village

Nestling in a valley near Malton in North Yorkshire is Wharram Percy, the extraordinary site of one of the most famous 'deserted medieval villages'.

As one of about 3000 villages thought to have been abandoned between the 11th and 18th centuries, many of which contain only scant traces of the medieval settlements which once occupied them, Wharram Percy is of special interest; still standing are the remains of the medieval church and farm cottages, and the foundations of over thirty medieval peasant houses can be clearly seen.

What is perhaps most fascinating about Wharram Percy is that during the forty years that it came under excavation, between 1950 and 1990, evidence was discovered of Stone Age occupation of the area, and of a settlement on the site dating back to the Bronze Age, with Roman farms and a wealthy Anglo-Saxon estate.

The careful preservation and reconstruction of many fragments of items found at Wharram Percy – such as the rings, brooches and candlesticks discovered at the sites which housed medieval peasant farmers – offer a unique insight into the lives of the some of the countless generations who lived here.

Open Any reasonable time.
Entry Free.
Access 6m SE of Malton, on minor road from B1248 ½m S of Wharram le Street. (OS Map 100; ref SE 859645.)
Train Malton 8m.
P (at Bella Farm, ¼ m walk to site)

◉ Steeton Hall Gateway

North Yorkshire (p. 241, 13K)
A fine example of a small, well-preserved 14th-century gatehouse.

Open 10am–5pm daily (exterior only).
Entry Free.
Access 4m NE of Castleford, on minor road off A162 at South Milford.
(OS Map 105; ref SE 484314.)
Train South Milford 1m.

⊕ Thornton Abbey and Gatehouse

North Lincolnshire (p. 241, 12M)
See page 193 for full details.

◉ Wharram Percy Deserted Medieval Village

North Yorkshire (p. 241, 14L)
See opposite page for full details.

Right, a reconstruction drawing.

◉ Wheeldale Roman Road

North Yorkshire (p. 241, 15L)
This mile-long stretch of Roman road, still with its hardcore and drainage ditches, runs across isolated moorland.

Open Any reasonable time. (Site managed by North York Moors National Park.)
Entry Free.
Access S of Goathland, W of A169, 7m S of Whitby.
(OS Map 94; ref SE 805975.)
Train Goathland (N York Moors Railway) 4m.

⊕ Whitby Abbey

North Yorkshire (p. 241, 15L)
See p. 196-197 for full details.

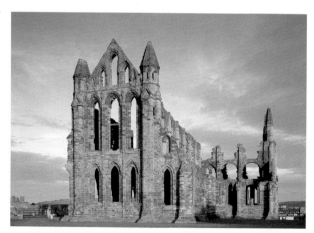

Whitby Abbey

Whitby Abbey is a magnificent reminder of the early church's power and dedication; it contained the shrine of St Hilda, the foundress who died in 680, and it symbolised the continuing Christian tradition in the north.

Set high on a North Yorkshire clifftop, its remains overlook a picturesque town and harbour with associations ranging from Victorian jewellery and whaling to Count Dracula. The abbey is today a gaunt and moving ruin and those who choose to approach it up the 199 steps from Whitby town also know the meaning of dedication.

St Hilda brought monks and nuns, including the poet Caedmon, to found a religious house on the coastal headland in 657. Because of her reputation, the Synod of 664 was held there and the two branches of early English Christianity, the Celtic and Roman churches, buried many differences in practice and doctrine. The matter that had most divided them was the date of Easter, and the Synod decided in favour of the Roman tradition.

When the Vikings invaded Northumbria in 867, the abbey was destroyed and its wealth pillaged. A Norman invader, Reinfrid, revived Whitby Abbey in the late 1070s; he also resettled Jarrow, home of Bede, whose writings had

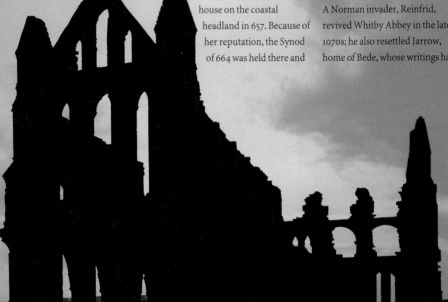

kept alive the memory of the early holy places, and refounded Whitby. The Norman church proved inadequate under the pressure of pilgrims, and in the 1220s rebuilding commenced. Since its dissolution in 1538, Whitby's dramatic location has attracted 18th-century painters and engravers. They helped begin the appreciation of the grandeur of these ruins, which has led to their continued preservation.

📹 The abbey has been used as the setting for the popular TV series, *Heartbeat* .

• Activity book for children available.

Open 1 April–30 Sep: 10am–6pm daily. 1–31 Oct: 10am–5pm daily. 1 Nov–31 March 2001: 10am–4pm daily. Closed 24–26 Dec and 1 Jan 2001.

Entry £1.70/£1.30/90p.

Tel 01947 603568

Access On cliff top E of Whitby. (OS Map 94; ref NZ 904115.)

Local Tourist Information
Whitby (Tel 01947 602674).

Bus From surrounding areas. Tel 01947 602146.

Train Whitby ½ m.

🖼️🖼️Ⓟ (both local council; charge payable) 🚻♿ (we regret that access for wheelchairs is at present unsuitable.) 🖼️🖼️

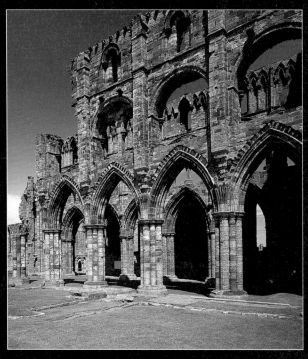

Top, the north transept windows. Right, Whitby Abbey by Alfred William Rich (1856–1921). Opposite page top, the abbey and parish church, perched above the town and harbour.

North West

Left, the Sandbach Crosses, in Cheshire; in the background, Brough
Castle, in Cumbria; in the foreground, find out about life as a Roman
soldier serving the Emperor Hadrian. Each year, there are numerous
special events happening along the 73-mile wall which Hadrian built
when he came to Britain in AD 122. The wall, stretching across
Northern England from Bowness-on-Solway in the west to
Newcastle-upon-Tyne in the east, is now a World Heritage Site;
right, the outer gatehouse of Carlisle Castle, in Cumbria.

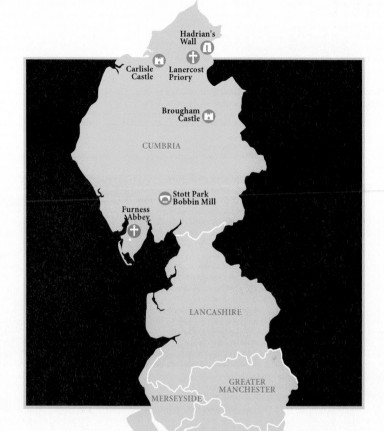

Hadrian's Wall

Carlisle Castle

Lanercost Priory

Brougham Castle

CUMBRIA

Stott Park Bobbin Mill

Furness Abbey

LANCASHIRE

GREATER MANCHESTER

MERSEYSIDE

CHESHIRE

Beeston Castle

⊘ Ambleside Roman Fort
⬠ *Cumbria (p. 240/242, 15G)*
The remains of this 1st- and 2nd-century fort were built to guard the Roman road from Brougham to Ravenglass.

Open Any reasonable time.
(Site managed by the National Trust.)
Entry Free.
Access 200 yds W of Waterhead car park, Ambleside.
(OS Map 90; ref NY 376033.)

Bus Stagecoach Cumberland 555/6/9 from Windermere.
Tel 01946 63222.
Train Windermere 5m.

⬠ Arthur's Round Table
Cumbria (p. 240/242, 15G)
Prehistoric circular earthwork bounded by a ditch and an outer bank.

Open Any reasonable time.
Entry Free.
Access At Eamont Bridge, 1m S of Penrith.

(OS Map 90; ref NY 523284.)
Train Penrith 1½m.

⊘ Beeston Castle
○ *Cheshire (p. 239/240, 11G)*
Standing majestically on sheer, rocky crags, Beeston has perhaps the most stunning views from any castle in England. Its history stretches back over 4,000 years, to when it was a Bronze Age hill fort.

The huge castle was built from 1226 and soon became a royal stronghold, only falling centuries later during the English Civil War.
• 'The Castle of the Rock' exhibition outlines the history of this strategic site from prehistoric times, through the Middle Ages to the Civil War.
• Free Children's Activity Sheet.
Open 1 April–30 Sep: 10am–6pm daily. 1–31 Oct: 10am–5pm daily. 1 Nov–31 March 2001: 10am–4pm daily. Closed 24–26 Dec and 1 Jan 2001.
Entry £2.80/£2.10/£1.40.
Tel 01829 260464
Access 11m SE of Chester on minor

road off A49 or A41.(OS Map 117; ref SJ 537593.)
Local Tourist Information
Nantwich (Tel 01270 610983).

Bus Huxley C83 from Chester.
Tel 01244 602666.
Train Chester 10m.

⊘ Bow Bridge
⬠ *Cumbria (p. 240, 14F)*
Late medieval stone bridge across Mill Beck, carrying a route to nearby Furness Abbey *(see p. 204)*.

Open Any reasonable time.
Entry Free.
Access ½m N of Barrow-in-Furness, on minor road off A590 near Furness Abbey.

(OS Map 96; ref SD 224715.)
Bus Stagecoach Cumberland 6/A Barrow-in-Furness–Dalton to within ¾m. Tel 01946 63222.
Train Barrow-in-Furness 1½m.

Carlisle Castle

A rich and colourful history spanning over 900 years is waiting to be explored at this impressive castle. Once commanding the western end of the Anglo-Scottish border, Carlisle Castle has witnessed, over the centuries, the conflict of countless sieges as both the English and Scots made their successive claims to it.

It was under the orders of Henry I, in 1122, that the existing defences at Carlisle were re-fashioned and work on the first buildings in stone began. The city walls and the stone keep were constructed over the next decade, the keep surviving today as the oldest building in the fortress. In a small cell there are elaborate wall-carvings, probably made by the prisoners of Richard of Gloucester in about 1480.

These weren't the last prisoners to be held within Carlisle Castle's walls. Mary Queen of Scots was confined here in 1568, following her abdication from the Scottish throne. It was also here, in 1746, that Bonnie Prince Charlie's supporters locked themselves, trying to fight back the Hanoverian Army. After a few days, they hung out the white flag and the castle became their prison. Some were hanged, others were sentenced to exile.

The keep also houses a large model of the city in 1745, and an exhibition about Bonnie Prince Charlie and the Jacobite Rising of 1745.

• See the legendary 'licking stones' in the dungeon, where the Jacobite prisoners found enough moisture to stay alive before their execution.
• Visit the King's Own Royal Border Regimental Museum.
• Free Children's Activity Sheet available.

Open 1 April–30 Sep: 9.30am–6pm daily. 1–31 Oct: 10am–5pm daily. 1 Nov–31 March 2001: 10am–4pm daily. Closed 24–26 Dec and 1 Jan 2001. Guided tours available at a small extra charge. Tours are daily, June–Oct; weekends in May. Please call for times.

Entry £3/£2.30/£1.50.

Tel 01228 591922

Access In Carlisle city centre. (OS Map 85; ref NY 397563.)

Local Tourist Information
Carlisle (Tel 01228 512444).

Bus From surrounding areas. Tel 01228 606000.

Train Carlisle ½m.

P (disabled only). Car parking in nearby city car parks (signposted).

& (except interiors of buildings)

(restricted areas)

◎ Brough Castle

Cumbria (p. 240/242, 15H)

Dating from Roman times, the 12th-century keep replaced an earlier stronghold destroyed by the Scots in 1174. It was restored by Lady Anne Clifford in the 17th century.

Open 1 April–30 Sep: 10am–6pm daily. 1–31 Oct: 10am–5pm daily. 1 Nov–31 March 2001: 10am–4pm daily.

Entry Free.

Access 8m SE of Appleby S of A66. (OS Map 91; ref NY 791141.)

Bus Woof 564 Kendal–Brough (passing ⇌ Kirkby Stephen and Oxenholme); Stagecoach Cumberland 563 Penrith–Brough (passing ⇌ Penrith).
Tel 01228 606000.

Train Kirkby Stephen 6m. 🐕 🅿

◎ Brougham Castle

Cumbria (p. 240/242, 15G)

These impressive ruins on the banks of the River Eamont include an early 13th-century keep and later buildings. Its one-time owner Lady Anne Clifford restored the castle in the 17th century *(see also Countess Pillar, opposite page)*. An introductory exhibition includes carved stones from the nearby Roman fort.

Open 1 April–30 Sep: 10am–6pm daily. 1–31 Oct: 10am–5pm daily.

Entry £2/£1.50/£1.

Tel 01768 862488

Access 1½m SE of Penrith on minor road off A66. (OS Map 90; ref NY 537290.)

Train Penrith 2m.

🅿 ⛪ ♿ (excluding keep) 📷 🏕 🐕

◎ Carlisle Castle

Cumbria (p. 240/242, 16G)

See p. 201 for full details.

◉ Castlerigg Stone Circle

Cumbria (p. 240/242, 15F)

This is possibly one of the earliest Neolithic stone circles in Britain. Its 33 stones stand in a beautiful setting.

Open Any reasonable time. (Site managed by the National Trust.)

Entry Free.

Access 1½m E of Keswick. (OS Map 90; ref NY 293236.)

Bus Stagecoach Cumberland X4/5 from ⇌ Penrith to within 1m.
Tel 01946 63222.

Train Penrith 16m.

● Chester Castle: Agricola Tower
● and Castle Walls

Cheshire (p. 239/240, 11G)
Set in the angle of the city walls, this
12th-century tower contains a fine
vaulted chapel.

Open Castle walls open any
reasonable time; cell block open
1 April–30 Sep: 10am–5pm daily.
1 Oct–31 March 2001: 10am–4pm
daily. Closed 24–26 Dec and
1 Jan 2001.
Entry Free. (Site managed
by Chester City Council).

Access Access via Assizes Court
car park on Grosvenor St.
(OS Map 117; ref SJ 405658.)
Bus From surrounding areas.
Tel 01244 602666.
Train Chester 1m.
♿(parts) ⌕

● Chester Roman Amphitheatre

Cheshire (p. 239/240, 11G)
The largest Roman amphitheatre in
Britain, partially excavated. It was
used for entertainment and military
training by the 20th Legion, based
at the fortress of Deva.

Open Any reasonable time.
Entry Free. (Site managed by
Chester City Council).
Access On Vicars Lane beyond
Newgate, Chester.
(OS Map 117; ref SJ 404660.)

Bus From surrounding areas.
Tel 01244 602666.
Train Chester ¼m.
♿(no access to amphitheatre
floor) ⌕

● Clifton Hall

Cumbria (p. 240/242, 15G)
The surviving tower block of
a 15th-century manor house.

Open Any reasonable time.
Closed 24–26 Dec and 1 Jan 2001.
Entry Free. (Please call at Hall Farm
for keys.)

Access In Clifton next to Clifton
Hall Farm, 2m S of Penrith on A6.
(OS Map 90; ref NY 530271.)
Train Penrith 2½m. ⌕

● Countess Pillar

Cumbria (p. 240/242, 15G)
An unusual monument, bearing
sundials and family crests, erected
in 1656 by Lady Anne Clifford to

commemorate her parting with
her mother in 1616 *(see also*
Brougham Castle, opposite page).
Open Any reasonable time.
Entry Free.

Access 1m SE of Brougham on A66.
(OS Map 90; ref NY 546289.)
Train Penrith 2½m.
⌕

● Furness Abbey

Cumbria (p. 240, 14F)
See p. 203 for full details.

Below, Furness Abbey as it may have
looked in the early 16th century.

Furness Abbey

In a secluded valley in the Vale of Nightshade are the extensive remains of the beautiful abbey of St Mary of Furness.

Founded in 1123 by Stephen, later King of England, Furness originally belonged to the small Order of Savigny and then, in 1147, to the Cistercians. It became a powerful and important religious house and, before the Dissolution, was the second richest Cistercian monastery in England after Fountains Abbey in Yorkshire.

On entering the site the large open area on view would once have been filled with buildings, and is now marked out by a series of low walls, the earliest of which date from the 12th century. Beyond lie the impressive ruins of the church.

The Savigniac order had built a small, Romanesque, highly ornate church but the Cistercians gradually rebuilt and enlarged it in an early Gothic, more austere manner. This second church was itself extensively remodelled in the 15th century. However, the early

Savigniac style survives in many parts of the red sandstone building – such as in the south transept – and bears witness to the abbey's rich history. The presbytery is of particular interest, as the Furness sedilia is recognised as one of the most magnificent in the country.

An extensive exhibition about the remarkable history of Furness is housed at the visitor centre. On display are various pillars and pieces of stone recovered from the abbey and engravings of effigies from the church nave.

Open 1 April–30 Sep: 10am–6pm daily. 1–31 Oct: 10am–5pm daily. 1 Nov–31 March 2001: 10am–1pm, 2–4pm Wed–Sun. Closed 24–26 Dec and 1 Jan 2001. Please phone to confirm if open in winter.

Entry £2.60/£2/£1.30.
Tel 01229 823420
Access 1½ m N of Barrow-in-Furness, on minor road off A590. (OS Map 96; ref SD 218717.)
Bus Stagecoach Cumberland 6/A Barrow-in-Furness–Dalton to within ¼ m. Tel 01946 63222.
Train Barrow-in-Furness 2m.

 (also available for the visually impaired and those with learning difficulties) (restricted areas)

✪ Goodshaw Chapel

Lancashire (p. 240, 13H)
A restored 18th-century Baptist chapel with all its furnishings.
Open Keykeeper. Call **0161 242 1400** for details.

Entry Free.
Access In Crawshawbooth, 2m N of Rawtenstall, in Goodshaw Avenue off A682.
(OS Map 103; ref SD 815263.)

Bus Rossendale; Stagecoach Ribble 273 Burnley–Bolton (pass ⇌Burnley Manchester Rd).
Tel 0870 608 2608.
Train Burnley Manchester Rd 4½m.

✪ Hadrian's Wall

See p. 210-215 for full details.

Right, sunrise over Housesteads Roman Fort, in winter.

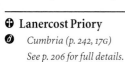

✪ Hardknott Roman Fort

Cumbria (p. 240/242, 15F)
One of the most dramatic Roman sites in Britain, with stunning views across the Lakeland fells. The fort, built between AD 120 and 138, controlled the road from Ravenglass to Ambleside. There are visible remains of granaries, the headquarters building and the

commandant's house, with a bath house and parade ground outside the fort.
Open Any reasonable time. Access may be hazardous in winter. (Site managed by the National Trust.)

Access 9m NE of Ravenglass, at W end of Hardknott Pass.
(OS Map 96; ref NY 218015.)
Train Eskdale (Dalegarth) (Ravenglass & Eskdale Railway) 3m.

✪ Lanercost Priory

Cumbria (p. 242, 17G)
See p. 206 for full details.

✪ Mayburgh Earthwork

Cumbria (p. 240/242, 16G)
An impressive prehistoric circular earthwork, with banks up to 4.5 metres (15 feet) high, enclosing a

central area of one and a half acres containing a single large stone.
Open Any reasonable time.
Entry Free.
Access At Eamont Bridge,

1m S of Penrith off A6.
(OS Map 90; ref NY 519285.)
Train Penrith 1½m.

✪ Penrith Castle

Cumbria (p. 240/242, 16G)
A 14th-century castle set in a park on the edge of the town.

Open Park: 7.30am–9pm summer; 7.30am–4.30pm winter.
Entry Free.
Access Opposite Penrith

railway station.
(OS Map 90; ref NY 513299.)
Train Penrith, adjacent.

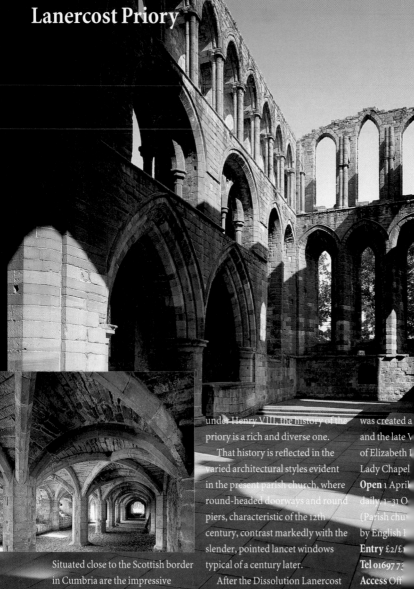

Lanercost Priory

Situated close to the Scottish border in Cumbria are the impressive remains of this 12th-century Augustinian priory. From the relative tranquillity of Lanercost's life as a monastic house to its involvement in the turbulent Anglo-Scottish wars of the 14th century and eventual dissolution under Henry VIII, the history of the priory is a rich and diverse one.

That history is reflected in the varied architectural styles evident in the present parish church, where round-headed doorways and round piers, characteristic of the 12th century, contrast markedly with the slender, pointed lancet windows typical of a century later.

After the Dissolution Lanercost was granted to the Dacres and remained home to this powerful and prosperous local family until the 18th century. Among the fine tombs housed in the ruined church are those of Sir Thomas Dacre, who fought at the Battle of Flodden and

was created a
and the late V
of Elizabeth I
Lady Chapel

Open 1 April
daily, 1–31 O
(Parish chu
by English I
Entry £2/£
Tel 01697 7:
Access Off
Lanercost,
(OS Map 8
Bus Stage
Carlisle–
within 1½
Train Bra

➤ Piel Castle

Cumbria (p. 240, 14F)

The ruins of a 14th-century castle, accessible by boat from Roa Island, with a massive keep, inner and outer baileys, and curtain walls and towers.

Open Any reasonable time. Access by small boat from Roa Island during summer, subject to tides and weather. For information call **01229 833609** or **01229 870156**.
Entry Free.
Access On Piel Island, 3¼m SE of Barrow. (OS Map 96; ref SD 233636.)
Bus Stagecoach Cumberland 11/12 Barrow-in-Furness–Roa Island. Tel 01946 63222.
Train Barrow-in-Furness 4m to Roa Island.

⊘ Ravenglass Roman Bath House

Cumbria (p. 240, 15F)

The walls of the bath house are among the most complete Roman remains in Britain.

Open Any reasonable time. (Site managed by Lake District National Park Authority.)
Entry Free.
Access ¼m E of Ravenglass, off minor road leading to A595. (OS Map 96; ref NY 088961.)
Train Ravenglass, adjacent.

✛ Salley Abbey

Lancashire (p. 240, 13H)

The remains of a Cistercian abbey founded in 1147.

Open 1 April–30 Sep: 10am–6pm daily. 1–31 Oct: 10am–5pm daily. 1 Nov–31 March 2001: 10am–4pm daily. (Site managed by Heritage Trust for the North West.)
Entry Free.
Access At Sawley 3½m N of Clitheroe off A59. (OS Map 103; ref SD 776464.)
Train Clitheroe 4m.

✛ Sandbach Crosses

Cheshire (p. 239/240, 11H)

Rare Saxon stone crosses from the 9th century, carved with animals, dragons and biblical scenes, in the centre of the market square.

Open Any reasonable time.
Entry Free.
Access Market square, Sandbach. (OS Map 118; ref SJ 758608.)
Bus Tel 01244 602666.
Train Sandbach 1½m.

✛ Shap Abbey

Cumbria (p. 240/242, 15G)

The striking tower and other remains of this Premonstratensian abbey stand in a remote and isolated location.

Open Any reasonable time.
Entry Free. (Site managed by the Lake District National Park).
Access 1½m W of Shap on bank of River Lowther. (OS Map 90; ref NY 548153.)
Bus Stagecoach Cumberland 107 Penrith–Kendal, to within 1½m. Tel 01946 63222.
Train Penrith 10m.

⊙ Stott Park Bobbin Mill

Cumbria (p. 240, 14G)

A working mill built in 1835, Stott Park created the wooden bobbins vital to the spinning and weaving industries of Lancashire. Although Stott Park worked continuously until 1971, it remains almost identical to its Victorian appearance of a hundred years ago, making it a unique and important monument.

Open 1 April–30 Sep: 10am–6pm daily. 1–31 Oct: 10am–5pm daily. Guided tours lasting 45 minutes are included in admission charge. Last tour starts 1 hour before closure.

Entry £3/£2.30/£1.50.

Tel 01539 531087

Access 1½m N of Newby Bridge, off A590.

(OS Map 96; ref SD 373883.)

Local Tourist Information Hawkshead (Tel 01539 436525).

Bus Stagecoach Cumberland 534 from ⇌ Grange-over-Sands, summer only; otherwise Windermere ferry from Ambleside or Bowners to Lakeside, thence 1m. Tel 01228 606000.

Train Grange-over-Sands 8m.

🅿 🚻 ♿ (ground floor only) 🏠 🏠 📷 🍴

⊕ Warton Old Rectory

Lancashire (p. 240, 14G)

Rare medieval stone house with remains of the hall, chambers and domestic offices.

Open 1 April–30 Sep: 10am–6pm daily. 1–31 Oct: 10am–5pm daily. 1 Nov–31 March 2001: 10am–4pm daily. Closed 24–26 Dec and 1 Jan 2001. (Site managed by Heritage Trust for the North West.)

Entry Free.

Access At Warton, 1m N of Carnforth on minor road off A6. (OS Map 97; ref SD 499723.)

Bus Stagecoach Lancaster 55/A Lancaster–Warton (pass ⇌ Carnforth). Tel 0870 608 2608.

Train Carnforth 1m. 🐕 ♿

⊕ Wetheral Priory Gatehouse

Cumbria (p. 240/242, 16G)

A Benedictine priory gatehouse, preserved after the Dissolution by serving as the vicarage for the parish church.

Open 1 April–30 Sep: 10am–6pm daily. 1–31 Oct: 10am–5pm daily. 1 Nov–31 March 2001: 10am–4pm daily. Closed 24–26 Dec and 1 Jan 2001.

Entry Free.

Access On minor road in Wetheral village, 6m E of Carlisle on B6263. (OS Map 86; ref NY 469542.)

Bus Stagecoach Cumberland 74/5 Carlisle–Wetherall. Tel 01946 63222.

Train Wetherall ½m. 🐕

⊕ Whalley Abbey Gatehouse

Lancashire (p. 240, 13H)

The outer gatehouse of the nearby Cistercian abbey. There was originally a chapel on the first floor.

Open Any reasonable time. (Site managed by Whalley Abbey Council).

Entry Free.

Access In Whalley, 6m NE of Blackburn on minor road off A59.

(OS Map 103; ref SD 730360.)

Bus Stagecoach Ribble 225 ⇌ Blackburn–Clitheroe. Tel 01254 886633.

Train Whalley ¼m. 🐕 ♿

Thatching

Left, below left and below, work on the thatching of Falmer Tithe Barn , in Sussex.
Far left, an early 20th-century photograph of thatched hay in Norfolk,

Thatch is probably the oldest type of roofing material still in use in England. We know that at one time or another almost every long-stemmed plant found in abundance has been used, and recent archaeological work for English Heritage has shown how skilful medieval thatching was, while revealing much about the agriculture of the time from the smoke-blackened underlayers of surviving roofs.

Most of these astonishing survivals are of wheat straw, which is still the predominant material today, laid either in 'long straw' fashion or as 'combed wheat reed'. The latter should not be confused with water reed, the other modern thatching material, which in this country is harvested chiefly on the Norfolk Broads.

As organic materials, straw and water reed are a valuable sustainable resource. Thatched roofs contribute enormously to the enduring visual appeal of the English countryside. Fortunately, the overall decline in the numbers of thatched roofs has been stemmed in recent years, and some 24,000 thatched buildings are listed. There are now few in northern England, and the lion's share of thatched roofs lies in a broad swathe of counties from Devon to Norfolk. Of the million or so buildings believed to have been thatched in 1800, more than half were ancillary buildings, but the fraction that survives consists almost entirely of houses. Thatched houses are today very popular, but there is a threat to the character of some of these buildings and areas from the replacement of one thatching material with another.

English Heritage believes in fostering well established local traditions. We are using our grant schemes to achieve this, at buildings like Falmer Barn.

Whatever material is used, thatching demands great skill to make a durable roof out of material which nature intended to degrade. Thatchers are among the last true rural craftsmen, adapting technique to the demands of each roof. The aim is to lay the material in such a way that water flows off as swiftly as possible: the alignment of the stems, the pitch of the coat, and the shaping of valleys and eaves are all made to contribute to this end.

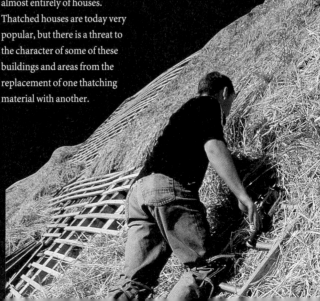

Hadrian's Wall

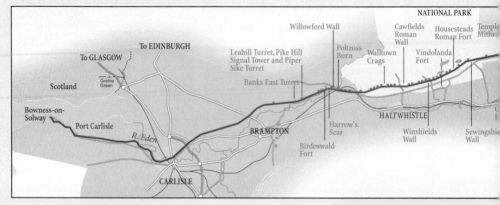

NATIONAL PARK

Willowford Wall · Cawfields Roman Wall · Housesteads Roman Fort · Temple Mithra

To EDINBURGH · Leahill Turret, Pike Hill Signal Tower and Piper Sike Turret · Poltross Burn · Walltown Crags · Vindolanda Fort

To GLASGOW · Banks East Turret

Scotland · Gretna Green

Bowness-on-Solway · Port Carlisle · R. Eden · BRAMPTON · Harrow's Scar · HALTWHISTLE · Winshields Wall · Sewingshi Wall

Birdoswald Fort

CARLISLE

Most of us leave something behind us when we go but few can boast a monument the size of Hadrian's Wall. Stretching 73 miles (80 Roman miles) from coast to coast across Northern England from the Solway to the Tyne, it today spans nearly 2,000 years of history.

The Wall was built by order of the Emperor Hadrian who came to Britain in AD122. His purpose was to mark the boundary of the Roman Empire and divide the 'civilised' world from the tribes beyond or, as Hadrian's biographer put it, 'to separate the Romans from the Barbarians'.

At some points it is as stark and inspiring as it would have been in Hadrian's time. Elsewhere it has mellowed into the landscape or is tucked into hidden corners of the towns and cities which run its length.

Hadrian's Wall is, of course, much more than a wall. Small forts a mile apart ('milecastles'), temples and turrets appear all along its line and museums, visitors centres and reconstructions bring the frontier to life.

Fortified lines once marked many of the Roman Empire's boundaries along the Rhine, the Danube and in the Middle East. These, along with Hadrian's Wall and the Antonine Wall in Britain were the outposts of the empire.

Above, stone head and frieze, found at Corbridge Roman Site.
Below left, Cawfields Roman Wall.

Of them all, Hadrian's Wall, now a World Heritage Site, is by far the best-preserved and being there can still evoke a sense of standing on the edge of the world.

Access West of Hexham, the Wall runs roughly parallel to the A69 Carlisle–Newcastle-Upon-Tyne road, lying between 1 and 4 miles north of it, close to the B6318.

Bus This road carries an hourly bus service: Arriva Northumbria/ Stagecoach Cumberland 685 Newcastle-Carlisle.

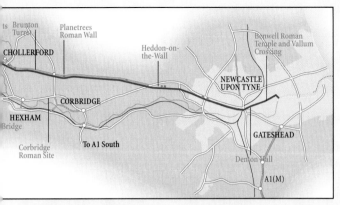

Above, a group of four intaglii, found at Birdoswald Fort.

Cumbria County Council on behalf of English Heritage.)
Entry Free for English Heritage members.
Tel 01697 747602
Access 2¾m W of Greenhead, on minor road off B6318.
(OS Map 86; ref NY 615663).

The Hadrian's Wall Bus runs all year (27 May–1 Oct 2000 daily; 2 Oct–26 May 2001: reduced service) between Carlisle, Hexham, Haltwhistle, Brampton, Newcastle and all main Roman sites. Please call **01434 605555** or **01228 606003** for further details.

Train The Newcastle–Carlisle railway line also has stations at Hexham, Haydon Bridge, Bardon Mill, Haltwhistle, and Brampton. Closer access to the Wall is then available on special buses (Stagecoach Cumberland 682) from May to September linking ⇌Hexham, Haltwhistle and Carlisle and covering the section from Brunton Turret to Walltown Crags Turret on a hail-and-ride basis. For all train enquiries call **0345 484950.**

For all public transport information please call **01670 533128**

Local Tourist Information
Hexham (Tel 01434 605225) or Carlisle (Tel 01228 512444).

Banks East Turret
Well-preserved turret with adjoining stretches of Wall. (Site managed by Cumbria County Council.)
Access On minor road E of Banks village, 3½m NE of Brampton. (OS Map 86; ref NY 575647.)

Benwell Roman Temple and Vallum Crossing
Remains of small temple, and the sole remaining stone-built causeway across the Vallum earthwork.
Access Immediately S off A69 at Benwell in Broomridge Ave. (OS Map 88; ref NZ 217646.)
Bus Frequent from centre of Newcastle. Tel 0191 232 5325.
Train Newcastle 2m.

Birdoswald Fort
Almost on the edge of the Irthing escarpment, remains survive of granaries and the east gate, which is among the best preserved on the Wall.
Open 20 March–30 Nov: 10am–5.30pm daily. Winter season, exterior only. (Site managed by

Black Carts Turret
A 460-metre (500-yard) length of Wall and turret.
Access 2m W of Chollerford on B6318. (OS Map 87; ref NY 884712.)

Brunton Turret
Well-preserved 2.5-metre (8-foot) turret with a stretch of Wall.
Access ¼m S of Low Brunton on A6079.
(OS Map 87; ref NY 922698.)
Bus Stagecoach Cumberland 682 *(see p. 200)*; also Tyne Valley 880/2 from ⇌ Hexham. Tel 01670 533 128.
Train Hexham 4m.

Cawfields Roman Wall
Camps, turrets, a fortlet, and Milecastle 42 – along with a fine, consolidated stretch of the Wall.
Access 1¼m N of Haltwhistle off B6318. (OS Map 87; ref NY 716667.)

Chesters Bridge

The fragments of the bridge that carried Hadrian's Wall across the North Tyne are visible on both banks. The most impressive remains are on the east side.

Access ¼ m S of Low Brunton on A6079. (OS Map 87; ref NY 922698.)

The museum, which was built in 1896 soon after his death, houses the important Clayton Collection of altars and sculptures from all along Hadrian's Wall.

- Special Events: see the English Heritage *Events Diary 2000* or call Customer Services on 01793 414910.

Bus Stagecoach Cumberland 682 *(see p. 200)*; also Tyne Valley 880/2 from ⇌ Hexham to within ½ m. Tel 01670 533128.

Train Hexham 5½ m.

P 🏠 🚻 ♿ 🚐

📷 (not managed by English Heritage) 📷 (restricted areas)

Bus Stagecoach Cumberland 682 *(see p. 200)*; also Tyne Valley 880/2 from ⇌ Hexham to within ½ m. Tel 01670 533128.

Train Hexham 4½ m.

Chesters Roman Fort

Chesters, located between the 27th and 28th milecastles, is one of the best-preserved examples of a cavalry fort. Many parts are still visible, including the barracks and a finely preserved bath house. So much is known about this early fort because of the pioneering archaeological work of John Clayton, who inherited the local estate in 1832.

Open 1 April–30 Sep: 9.30am–6pm daily. 1–31 Oct: 10am–5pm daily. 1 Nov–31 March 2001: 10am–4pm daily. Closed 24–26 Dec and 1 Jan 2001.

Entry £2.80/£2.10/£1.40.

Tel 01434 681379

Access ¼ m W of Chollerford on B6318. (OS Map 87; ref NY 913701.)

Local Tourist Information

Hexham (Tel 01434 605225).

Corbridge Roman Site and Museum

Originally the site of a fort on the former patrol road, Corbridge evolved into a principal town of the Roman era, flourishing until the 5th century. The large granaries, with their ingenious ventilation system, are among its most impressive remains. Corbridge is an excellent starting point to explore the Wall. Its museum contains fascinating finds and remarkable sculptures.

- New 'Divine Silver' Exhibition.
- Special Events: see the English Heritage *Events Diary 2000* or call Customer Services on 01793 414910.
- Children's Activity Book available.

Open 1 April–30 Sep: 10am–6pm
daily. 1–31 Oct: 10am–5pm daily.
1 Nov–31 March 2001: 10am–1pm,
2–4pm Wed–Sun.
Closed 24–26 Dec and 1 Jan 2001.
Entry £2.80/£2.10/£1.40.
Tel 01434 632349
Access ½m NW of Corbridge on

Denton Hall Turret
The foundations of a turret and
65-metre (70-yard) section of Wall.
Access 4m W of Newcastle city
centre on A69.
(OS Map 88; ref NZ 195656.)
Bus Frequent from centre of
Newcastle. Tel 0191 232 5325.

Heddon-on-the-Wall
A stretch of Wall up to 3 metres
(10 feet) thick.
Access Immediately E of
Heddon village, S of A69.
(OS Map 88; ref NZ 36669.)
Bus Blue Bus 83, Go-Northern
684, Arriva Northumbria 685

minor road, signed Corbridge
Roman Site.
(OS Map 87; ref NY 983649.)
Local Tourist Information Hexham
(Tel 01434 605225).
Bus Northumbria 602, 685
Newcastle-upon-Tyne–Hexham
to within ½m. Tel 01670 533128.
Train Corbridge 1¼m.
🅿 🏛 🚻 ♿ 🚽 🎧 (also available for
the visually impaired and those with
learning difficulties) 🐕 (restricted
areas)
*Opposite page far left, statue of Victory
and bowl, found at Corbeidge Roman
Site. Right, aerial view of Chesters
Roman Fort. This page, above, remains
of the Fountain House at Corbridge
Roman Site. Right, Housesteads Fort.*

Train Blaydon 2m.
Hare Hill
A short length of Wall standing nine
feet high. (Site managed by
Cumbria County Council.
Access ¼m NE of Lanercost,
off minor road.
(OS Map 86; ref NY 562646.)

Harrow's Scar Milecastle
The most instructive mile section on
the whole length of Hadrian's Wall
linked to Birdoswald Fort.
(Site managed by Cumbria
County Council.)
Access ¼m E of Birdoswald, on
minor road off B6318.
(OS Map 86; ref NY 621664.)

from Newcastle-upon-Tyne.
Tel 0191 232 5325.
Train Wylam 3m.

Housesteads Roman Fort
Housesteads occupies a
commanding position on the
cliffs of the Whin Sill. One of
17 permanent forts built by
Hadrian c. AD124, it is the
most complete example of a
Roman fort in Britain. Its visible
remains include 4 gates with
towers between them, as well
as the principal buildings from
within an auxiliary fort. There are
also remains of the civilian settlement
that clustered at its gates.

From the archaeological record of Housesteads, we can glimpse the people who lived at the edge of the Empire. We know that cavalry from the modern Netherlands were stationed here in the 3rd century – flat-bottomed pottery and larger cooking pots found at the site are Frisian in origin.

Some of the Wall has been reconstructed by John Clayton in the late 19th century, to give one of the most vivid pictures of the Romans and their works in Britain.

• Childrens Activity Book available.

• A volunteer guide may be provided if requested in advance.

Open 1 April–30 Sep: 10am–6pm daily. 1–31 Oct: 10am–5pm daily. 1 Nov–31 March 2001: 10am–4pm daily. Closed 24–26 Dec and 1 Jan 2001.

Entry £2.80/£2.10/£1.40. National Trust members admitted free.

(Site owned by the National Trust, and maintained and managed by English Heritage.)

Tel 01434 344363

Access 2¼m NE of Bardon Mill on B6318.(OS Map 87; ref NY 790687.)

Local Tourist Information

Hexham (Tel 01434 605225).

Bus/Train *see p. 200.*

P ⛹ (both on main road, ½m walk to S, parking charge payable to National Park) Ⓞ 📷 🄴 ♿ (car park at site; enquire at information centre on main road) 🛏 (restricted areas)

Leahill Turret and Piper Sike Turret

Turrets west of Birdoswald. (Site managed by Cumbria County Council.)

Access On minor road 2m W of Birdoswald Fort. (OS Map 86; ref NY 585653.)

Pike Hill Signal Tower

Remains of a signal tower joined to the Wall at an angle of 45 degrees. (Site managed by Cumbria County Council.)

Access On minor road E of Banks village. (OS Map 86; ref NY 597648.)

Planetrees Roman Wall

A 15-metre (50-foot) length of narrow Wall on broad foundations.

Access 1m SE of Chollerford on B6318. (OS Map 87; ref NY 928696.)

Bus Stagecoach Cumberland 682 *(see p. 200)*; also Tyne Valley 880/2 from ⇌Hexham to within ¾m. Tel 01670 533128.

Train Hexham 5½m.

Poltross Burn Milecastle

One of the best-preserved milecastles with a flight of steps and remains of gates. (Site managed by Cumbria County Council.)

Opposite page, top right, Vindolanda Fort's bath house. Main picture, general view of Housesteads Roman Fort.

Access Immediately SW of Gilsland village by old railway station. (OS Map 86; ref NY 634662.)
P (near Station Hotel)

Sewingshields Wall

Largely unexcavated section of Wall, with remains of a milecastle.
Access N of B6318, 1½ m E of Housesteads Fort.
(OS Map 87; ref NY 813702.)

Temple of Mithras, Carrawburgh

A 3rd-century temple with facsimiles of altars found during excavation.
Access 3¾ m W of Chollerford on B6318. (OS Map 87; ref NY 869713.) **P**

Vindolanda Fort

A fort and well-excavated civil settlement. A museum there contains many unusual artefacts from everyday Roman life.

Open Mid Feb–mid November open at 10am daily. Seasonal closing times from 4pm to 6.30pm.
(Site owned and managed by Vindolanda Charitable Trust.)
Entry £3.80/£3.20/£2.80.
(**10% discount for English Heritage members** and groups of 15 or more.)
Tel 01434 344277
Access 1¼ m SE of Twice Brewed, on minor road off B6318.
(OS Map 87; ref NY 771664.)
Bus/Train *see p. 200.*

Walltown Crags

One of the best-preserved sections of the Wall, snaking over the crags to the turret on its summit.
Access 1m NE of Greenhead off B6318. (OS Map 87; ref NY 674664.)
P (nearby)

Willowford Wall, Turrets and Bridge

1,000 yards of Wall, including two turrets.
Open Access to bridge controlled by Willowford Farm; small charge levied.
Access W of minor road ¾ m W of Gilsland.
(OS Map 86; ref NY 629664.)

Winshields Wall

Rugged section of the Wall, including its highest point.
Access W of Steel Rigg car park, on minor road off B6318.
(OS Map 87; ref NY 745676.)

North East

Left, a modern sculpture of Saint Aidan, first bishop of the northern Northumbrians, who founded Lindisfarne Priory in 635; in the background, the ruins of Thomas of Lancaster's Gatehouse at Dunstanburgh Castle, which stands majestically on the coastal headland of Northumberland. Right, a modern version of Lindisfarne's Madonna and Child by Anton Stancnyk, at Lindisfarne Priory, in Northumberland.

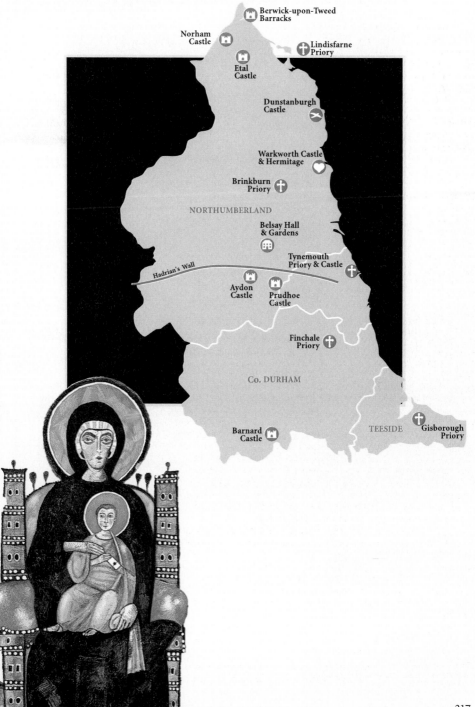

Berwick-upon-Tweed
Barracks

Norham
Castle

Lindisfarne
Priory

Etal
Castle

Dunstanburgh
Castle

Warkworth Castle
& Hermitage

Brinkburn
Priory

NORTHUMBERLAND

Belsay Hall
& Gardens

Tynemouth
Priory & Castle

Hadrian's Wall

Aydon
Castle

Prudhoe
Castle

Finchale
Priory

Co. DURHAM

Barnard
Castle

TEESIDE

Gisborough
Priory

Belsay Hall, Castle and Gardens

The thirty acres of magnificent landscaped grounds are Belsay's particular glory, and are deservedly listed Grade I in the Register of Gardens. They are largely the work of two members of the Middleton family, Sir Charles Monck (1779-1867) and his grandson Sir Arthur Middleton (1838-1933). Especially fine are the quarry garden and the Cragwood Walk where Sir Charles Monck, who also built the present hall, introduced many rare and fine specimens.

Succeeding generations extended the quarry and added to its planting. They made a green gorge, its sheer walls hung with exotic plants and the floor dotted with ferns. It is an adventure in itself to explore its paths and shady corners. Rhododendrons, among Belsay's great delights, grow in the quarry – some can be found

flowering as early as November –
as well as in the woodland
and rhododendron gardens created
later in the 19th century. These
wilder areas are separated from the
more formal terraces at the front of
the Hall, with their beds of roses,
lilies, lavender and other plants.
English Heritage has made great
efforts to return Belsay's gardens,
which suffered from neglect after
World War II, to their former state,
to complement the great house.

Sir Charles Monck built the Hall to
his own designs in 1810 after studying
Greek architecture. It resembles a
Greek temple, raised on a podium
with giant columns at the entrance
and pilasters on the walls. The
beautiful honey-coloured stone
from which the house is built came
from its own quarries which became
the garden.

A castle, built in the 14th century,
preceded the house, with a new
range attached in 1614. The family
moved into the New Hall in 1817.
**An exhibition of Sitooteries:
May–September 2000.** Twelve
contemporary summerhouses –
Sitooteries – have been created
by the country's most exciting
architects, designers and artists.
Please call for further details.
Plants are on sale in summer.
Open 1 April–30 Sep: 10am–6pm
daily. 1–31 Oct: 10am–5pm daily.
Nov–31 March 2001: 10am–4pm
daily. Closed 24-26 Dec and 1 Jan 2001.

Tel 01661 881636
Access In Belsay, 14m NW
of Newcastle on A696.
(OS Map 88; ref NZ 088785.)
Local Tourist Information
Morpeth (Tel 01670 511323).
Bus Snaith's 808 from Newcastle
(Tel 01670 533128); Arriva
Northumbria 508 from ⇌
Newcastle (summer Sun. only);
otherwise National Express
Newcastle– Edinburgh to within 1m.
Train Morpeth 10m.
🅿️ 🚻 ♿ 🏪 🗄️ Ⓔ ♿ (grounds,
tearoom and ground floor only;
toilets) 🍴 (Belsay Hall Tearoom
open daily April–Oct and weekends
in March.) 🚫 🚫 (restricted areas)

*Opposite page, Belsay Hall, view of
the east front. Main picture, Belsay
Castle.*
*This page, top, the Pillar Hall and
above, the Quarry Garden archway.*

⊙ Auckland Castle Deer House

Co. Durham (p. 240/242, 16J)
A charming building erected in 1760 in the park of the Bishops of Durham so that deer could shelter and find food.

Open Park: 1 April–30 Sep: 10am–6pm daily. 1 Oct–31 March 2001: 10am–4pm daily. Closed 24–26 Dec and 1 Jan 2001. (Site managed by the Church Commissioners for England.)
Entry Free. Castle not managed by English Heritage; separate charge for members.
Access In Auckland Park, Bishop Auckland, N of town centre on A68. (OS Map 93; ref NZ 216305.)
Train Bishop Auckland 1m.
🐕

◑ Aydon Castle

Northumberland (p. 242, 17H)
Overlooking the steep valley of the Cor Burn, Aydon Castle is one of the finest examples in England of a 13th-century manor house. It was originally built as an undefended house, during a time of unusual peace in the Borders. When peace ended, the house had to be fortified at once but even so, it was pillaged and burnt by the Scots in 1315, seized by English rebels two years later, and underwent frequent repairs and modifications. In the 17th century, the castle was converted into a farmhouse, and it remained so until 1966.

🎬 The blockbuster *Elizabeth* was filmed at Aydon.

Open 1 April–30 Sep: 10am–6pm daily. 1–31 Oct: 10am–5pm daily.

Entry £2/£1.50/£1.
Tel 01434 632450
Access 1m NE of Corbridge, on minor road off B6321 or A68. (OS Map 87; ref NZ 002663.)
Train Corbridge 4m – approach by Bridlepath from W side of Aydon Road, immediately N of Corbridge bypass.
🅿 🚻 ♿(ground floor)
⬛ ⬛ ⬛ ⬛ (restricted areas)

⊡ Barnard Castle

Co. Durham (p. 240/242, 15H)
Substantial remains of a large castle standing on a rugged escarpment .
Open 1 April–30 Sep: 10am–6pm daily. 1–31 Oct: 10am–5pm daily. 1 Nov–31 March 2001: 10am–4pm Wed–Sun. Closed 1–2pm through the year. Closed 24–26 Dec and 1 Jan 2001.

Entry £2.30/£1.70/£1.20.
Tel 01833 638212
Access In Barnard Castle. (OS Map 92; ref NZ 049165.)

Bus Arriva North East 75, X75 Darlington–Barnard Castle (pass close ⇌ Darlington). Tel 0345 124125.
🚻(in town)♿ ⬛ ⬛ ⬛ ⬛

◉ Belsay Hall Castle and Gardens

Northumberland (p. 242, 17I)
See p. 218-219 for full details.

Right, the Quarry Garden, Belsay Hall.

Dunstanburgh Castle

Dunstanburgh Castle, engraving by Charles Turner, 1808.

Outlined against the sky, on a basalt crag more than 30m (100 feet) high, stands the jagged silhouette of this magnificent 14th-century castle. The stormy seas which pound the rocky shoreline beneath the castle's walls and the screaming of the seabirds which echo under its cliffs lend the area a distinctly dramatic and romantic feel.

The background to the building of Dunstanburgh and the history of those associated with it is one of turmoil and unrest, as dramatic in itself as the castle's surroundings. Built at a time of political crisis and Anglo-Scottish conflict, the strained relations between King Edward II and his nephew, Thomas Earl of Lancaster, who built the castle, led eventually to rebellion and to the capture and execution of the Earl in 1322.

By the 16th century Dunstanburgh had fallen into decay. The castle which had been built on the grandest possible scale and had reflected the lavish tastes of the Earl, was by then perceived to be of no use and so left to ruin. Even at this time, however, Dunstanburgh retained its sense of the dramatic; a ballad told of a resident ghost, that of Sir Guy the Seeker, who, after having failed to rescue a beautiful lady held captive in a hall under the castle, was said to roam the castle ruins, moaning dismally to anyone who would listen.

Open 1 April–30 Sep: 10am–6pm daily. 1–31 Oct: 10am–5pm daily. 1 Nov–31 March 2001: 10am–4pm Wed–Sun. Closed 24–26 Dec and 1 Jan 2001. Last admission 30 minutes before closing time.

Entry £1.80/£1.40/90p. National Trust members admitted free. (Property owned by the National Trust, maintained and managed by English Heritage.)

Tel 01665 576231

Access 8m NE of Alnwick, on footpaths from Craster or Embleton (1½ m easy coastal walk). (OS Map 75; ref NU 258220.)

Bus Arriva Northumbria 401, 501 Alnwick– ≉ Berwick-upon-Tweed, with connections from Newcastle (passing Tyne & Wear Metro Haymarket), alight Craster, 1½ m. Tel 01670 533128.

Train Chathill 7m, Alnmouth 8m.

🚗🏠🚻

P (in Craster village, charge payable)

⚙ Berwick-upon-Tweed Barracks

Northumberland (p. 242, 19H)

Berwick Barracks were begun in 1717 and were among the first purpose-built barracks to be erected. Their design was based on a sketch by Nicolas Hawksmoor, architect of Blenheim Palace. When completed in 1725, they could house both single and married soldiers and their families. Today, the barracks house a number of attractions including the award-winning 'By Beat of Drum', an exhibition recreating the life of the British infantryman.

• Visit the Regimental Museum of the King's Own Scottish Borderers.

Open 1 April–30 Sep: 10am–6pm daily. 1–31 Oct: 10am–5pm daily. 1 Nov–31 March 2001: 10am–1pm, 2–4pm Wed–Sun. Closed 24–26 Dec and 1 Jan 2001. **Entry** £2.60/£2/£1.30. **Tel** 01289 304493

Access On the Parade, off Church St, Berwick town centre. (OS Map 75; ref NT 994535.) **Bus** From surrounding areas. Tel 01670 533128. **Train** Berwick-upon-Tweed ¼ m. **P** (in town) 🚻 ♿ 🅿 E 🛍 **🐕** (restricted areas)

⚙ Berwick-upon-Tweed Castle

Northumberland (p. 242, 19H)

Remains of a 13th–16th-century castle.

Open Any reasonable time.

Entry Free. **Access** Adjacent to Berwick railway station, W of town centre, accessible also from river bank. (OS Map 75; ref NT 994535.)

Bus From surrounding areas. Tel 01670 533128. **Train** Berwick-upon-Tweed adjacent. **🐕**

⚙ Berwick-upon-Tweed Main Guard

Northumberland (p. 242, 19H)

Georgian Guard House near the quay. 'The Story of a Border Garrison Town' is a permanent display of the history of the town and its fortifications.

Open 2–5 April, 1–3 May, 29 May–30 Sep: 1pm–5pm daily. Closed Wed. (Site managed by Berwick Civic Society.)

Entry Free. **Access** Berwick town centre on N bank of River Tweed. (OS Map 75; ref NT 994535.) **Bus/Train** *See Berwick-upon-Tweed Barracks.* ♿

⚙ Berwick-upon-Tweed Ramparts
♡
Northumberland (p. 242, 19H)

Remarkably complete 16th-century town fortifications, with gateways and projecting bastions.

Open Any reasonable time.

Entry Free.

Access Surrounding Berwick town centre on N bank of River Tweed. (OS Map 75; ref NT 994535.)

Bus/Train *see Berwick-upon-Tweed Barracks.*

🚻 & **P** (in town centre) ♿ 🐕

What do Hadrian's Wall, the Great Barrier Reef, Kathmandu, Iron Bridge and the Smashed-in-Head Buffalo Jump in Canada all have in common? They are all among the 582 places described by UNESCO as World Heritage Sites. As such they have been recognised as having 'outstanding universal significance' for the whole world.

The United Kingdom joined the World Heritage Convention in 1984. There are now 11 World Heritage Sites in England. Apart from Hadrian's Wall and Iron Bridge, they include Durham Castle and Cathedral, Fountains Abbey and Studley Royal Gardens, Bath, Blenheim Palace, Avebury and Stonehenge, the Palace and Abbey of Westminster, the Tower of London, Maritime Greenwich and Canterbury Cathedral, together with St Augustine's Abbey and St Martin's Church. Taken together, they represent a wide range of England's history and prehistory.

A new list of candidate sites that might be put forward over the next ten years was published in 1999. This concentrates less on monumental architecture and great buildings, and more on other aspects where Britain has made great contributions to the world. Therefore it includes sites such as the Derwent Valley, Saltaire, and the Cornish Mining Industry, which illustrate the development of industrialisation begun in Britain, Liverpool and Chatham which in different ways represent Britain's great maritime influence, and Down House and Kew, representing Britain's intellectual influence. Also included are the cultural landscapes of the Lake District and the New Forest which demonstrate the interaction between humanity and the natural environment.

English Heritage is working closely with the Government and with site owners, site managers and local communities on the development of Management Plans for all the existing sites and on the preparation of nominations for new sites. The proper care of World Heritage Sites on behalf both of ourselves and of the rest of the world is an important and growing responsibility which we gladly accept.

Above, Hadrian's Wall, and left, Iron Bridge, both World Heritage Sites. Below, Down House, which may become a World Heritage Site within the next ten years.

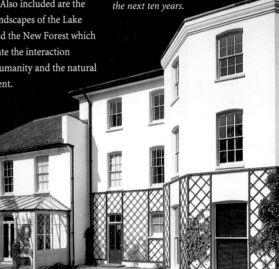

🌐 Bessie Surtees House

Tyne & Wear (p. 241/242, 16J)
Two 16th- and 17th-century
merchants' houses. One is
a remarkable and rare example
of Jacobean domestic architecture.
An exhibition about these buildings
is on the first floor.

Open 10am–4pm Mon–Fri
except Bank Holidays.
Entry Free.
Tel 0191 269 1200
Access 41–44 Sandhill, Newcastle.
(OS Map 88; ref NZ 252639.)
Bus From surrounding areas.
Tel 0191 232 5325.

Train Newcastle ½m.
Metro Central Station ½m.
🚻 ♿ ✗

🛕 Bishop Auckland Deer House

See Auckland Castle Deer House.

◐ Black Middens Bastle House

Northumberland (p. 242, 17H)
A 16th-century two-storey defended
farmhouse, set in splendid walking
country, on the Reivers Route.
Open Any reasonable time.
Entry Free.
Access 180 metres (200 yards) N of
minor road 7m NW of Bellingham
or along minor road from A68.
(OS Map 80; ref NY 774900.)
P ♿ ✗

◉ Bowes Castle

Co. Durham (p. 240, 15H)
Massive ruins of Henry II's tower
keep, three storeys high, set within
the earthworks of a Roman fort.

Open Any reasonable time.
Entry Free.
Access In Bowes Village just off
A66, 4m W of Barnard Castle.

(OS Map 92; ref NY 992135.)
Bus Primrose X69 from Newcastle,
Arriva North East 79 from Barnard
Castle. Tel 0191 383 3337. ✗

✚ Brinkburn Priory

Northumberland (p. 242, 17J)
This late 12th-century church is a fine
example of early Gothic architecture,
restored in 1858. It is set in a lovely
spot down a leafy lane, with a later
manor house.
Open 1 April–30 Sep: 10am–6pm
daily. 1–31 Oct: 10am–5pm daily.
Entry £1.60/£1.20/80p.
Tel 01665 570628
Access 4½m SE of Rothbury off
B6344. (OS Map 81; ref NZ 116984.)

Bus Arriva Northumbria 416
Morpeth–Rothbury to within ½m.
Tel 01670 533128.
Train Acklington 10m.
P ♿ ✗
(500 metres – 550 yards – from P)
✗ (restricted areas)

◕ Derwentcote Steel Furnace

Co. Durham (p. 240/242, 16J)
Built in the 18th century, the earliest
and most complete steel-making
furnace to have survived. Closed in
the 1870s, it has now been restored
and opened to the public.

Open 1 April–30 Sep: 1pm–5pm
1st & 3rd Sunday of every month.
Entry Free.
Tel 01207 562573
Access 10m SW of Newcastle on
A694 between Rowland's Gill
and Hamsterley.

(OS Map 88; ref NZ 131566.)
Bus GoNorthern 745 Newcastle-
upon-Tyne–Consett.
Tel 0845 6060260.
Train Metro Centre 7m.
P ✗ (restricted areas)

Etal Castle

The remains of this early 14th-century border castle dominate the picturesque village of Etal. Its transformation from a house into a small, yet impressive castle began in 1341, when Robert Manners was granted a licence to fortify his home. He added stone curtain walls, corner towers and a gatehouse to protect against the threat of attack from Scottish raiders.

The castle was thrust into the forefront of national events in 1513, when an army of 30,000 Scots led by James IV invaded England. Etal Castle fell to the Scots but in the bloody battle which ensued on Flodden Hill the invaders were defeated.

An award-winning exhibition tells the story of the Battle of Flodden and of the border warfare which existed here before the union of the English and Scottish crowns in 1603. The Manners family's connections with Etal ended in 1547 and the castle was transferred to Royal ownership, although by this time it had begun to fall into decay.

The beauty of Etal village today, with its well-kept cottages and charming inn, owes much to the Joicey family, who bought the castle and the neighbouring estate of Ford at the beginning of the 20th century. The conservation work initiated by them has ensured that both village and castle are a delight to the visitor.

Open 1 April–30 Sep: 10am–6pm daily. 1–31 Oct: 10am–5pm daily.
Entry £2.60/£2/£1.30.
Tel 01890 820332
Access In Etal village, 10m SW of Berwick. (OS Map 75; ref NT 925394.)
Bus Border Villages 267 Berwick-upon-Tweed–Wooler. Tel 01670 533128.
Train Berwick-upon-Tweed 10½m. 🅿️ 🚻 (in village) 📷 🎧 (the audio tour guides visitors around the castle and the exhibition) 🎪 ♿ (restricted areas)

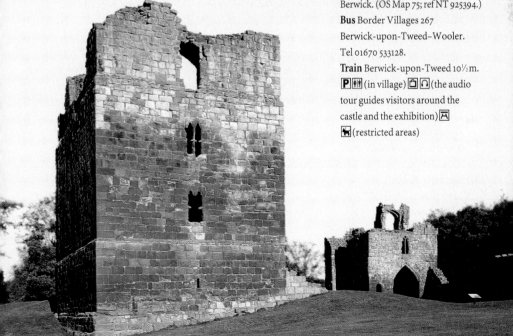

◕ Dunstanburgh Castle
◔ *Northumberland (p. 242, 18J)*

See p. 221 for full details.

◔ Edlingham Castle
Northumberland (p. 242, 18J)
Set in a beautiful valley, this complex ruin has defensive features spanning the 13th–15th centuries.

Open Any reasonable time. (Site managed by the Parochial Church Council St John the Baptist, Edlingham with Bolton Castle.) **Entry** Free. **Access** At E end of Edlingham

village, on minor road off B6341 6m SW of Alnwick. (OS Map 81; ref NU 115092.) **Train** Alnmouth 9m. 🥾 (waterproof footwear recommended)

⊕ Egglestone Abbey
Co. Durham (p. 240/242, 15J)
Picturesque remains of a 12th-century abbey. Substantial parts of the church and abbey buildings remain.

Open Any reasonable time. **Entry** Free. **Access** 1m S of Barnard Castle on minor road off B6277. (OS Map 92; ref NZ 062151.) **Bus** Arriva North East 75, X75

Darlington–Barnard Castle (pass close ⇌ Darlington, thence 1½ m, or 79 Richmond– Barnard Castle, thence ½ m. Tel 0345 124125.) Ⓟ ♿ 🏞 🥾

◕ Etal Castle
Northumberland (p. 242, 19H)

See p. 225 for full details.

⊕ Finchale Priory
𝟞 *Co. Durham (p. 241/242, 16J)*
Dating from the 13th century, these beautiful priory ruins are in a wooded setting beside the River Wear.
Open 1 April–30 Sep: 10am–6pm

daily. 1–31 Oct: 10am–5pm daily. **Entry** £1.30/£1/70p. **Tel 0191 386 3828** **Access** 3m NE of Durham, on minor road off A167. (OS Map 88; ref NZ 297471.)

Bus Go-Northern 37 Durham–Chester-le-Street (passes close ⇌ Durham). Tel 0845 60 60 260. **Train** Durham 5m. ⬜ Ⓟ (on south side of river, charge payable) 🥾

⊕ Gisborough Priory
Redcar & Cleveland (p. 241/242, 15K)
An Augustinian priory whose remains also include the gatehouse and the east end of an early 14th-century church.
Open 1 April–30 Sep: 9am–5pm Tue–Sun. 1 Oct–31 March 2001:

9am–5pm Wed–Sun. Closed 24 Dec–1 Jan 2001. (Property managed by Recar & Cleveland Borough Council). **Entry** 90p/65p/45p. Free to English Heritage Members. **Tel 01287 633801** **Access** In Guisborough town,

next to parish church. (OS Map 94; ref NZ 618163.) **Bus** Arriva North East X56, 65, 93, 765 from Middlesbrough (pass close ⇌ Middlesbrough) Tel 0345 484950. **Train** Marske 4½ m. 🚻 (in town) ♿ 🥾

◔ Hadrian's Wall

See p. 210–215 for full details.

◔ Hylton Castle
Tyne & Wear (p. 241/242, 16J)
A 15th-century keep-gatehouse, with a fine display of medieval heraldry adorning the facades.

Open Any reasonable time (access to grounds only). (Property managed by Sunderland City Council.) **Entry** Free.

Access 3¾ m W of Sunderland. (OS Map 88; ref NZ 358588.) **Bus** From surrounding areas. Tel 0191 232 5325. **Train** Seaburn 2½ m. Ⓟ ♿ (grounds only) 🥾

Lindisfarne Priory

Lindisfarne was the site of one of the most important early centres of Christianity in Anglo-Saxon England. St Aidan (right) founded Lindisfarne in 635. Austerity was the watchword of the community – a few monks and a simple wooden church. It was, however, to become a shrine when the corpse of the former bishop St Cuthbert was dug up in 698, 11 years after his burial, and found undecayed. Cuthbert was an exceedingly holy man who earlier withdrew to be a hermit on the lonely Farne Islands and later returned there to die. His relics survive in Durham Cathedral.

The island of Lindisfarne, with its wealthy monastery, was easy prey for Viking raiders from the end of the 8th century. Only in the 12th century did monks from Durham re-establish a religious house on Lindisfarne, or as it was then known, 'Holy Island'. The small community lived there until the dissolution of the monasteries in 1537.

Lindisfarne is still today a holy site and place of pilgrimage. However, going there requires prior knowledge of the tide tables. At high tide the causeway linking Holy Island to the Northumberland coast is submerged under water and the island is cut off from the mainland.

Today, in the award-winning museum, Anglo-Saxon carvings are displayed in a lively exhibition.

Oliver's Travels, starring Alan Bates, was filmed at Lindisfarne.
• Free Children's Activity Sheet.
Open 1 April–30 Sep: 10am–6pm daily. 1–31 Oct: 10am–5pm daily. 1 Nov–31 March 2001: 10am–4pm daily. Closed 24–26 Dec and 1 Jan 2001.
Entry £2.80/£2.10/£1.40.
Tel 01289 389200
Access On Holy Island, only reached at low tide across causeway (tide tables at each end or details from Berwick Tourist Information Centre Tel **01289 330733**). (OS Map 75; ref NU 126418.)
Bus Arriva Northumbria 477 from Berwick-upon-Tweed (passes close ≥Berwick-upon-Tweed). Times vary with tides. Tel 01670 533128.
Train Berwick-upon-Tweed 14m via causeway.
(restricted areas)

Norham Castle

Set on a promontory in a curve of the River Tweed, Norham was one of the strongest of the border castles. Built in the latter half of the 12th century, it came under siege on several occasions during its four hundred year history as a military stronghold. Its massive walls proved impenetrable during many of these attacks but when, in 1513, it was stormed by James IV, Norham fell and was largely destroyed.

The glory of the castle is the Great Tower, which shows signs of four building phases spanning the 12th to the 16th centuries. After the siege of 1513, extensive repairs were made to the castle and the Great Tower was re-roofed. Much of the castle that can be seen today dates from this time.

Following the union of the English and Scottish crowns in 1603, Tweed ceased to exist as a frontier, and Norham Castle became redundant as a defensive stronghold. However, its role as an active and important border castle was recognised in a poem by Sir Walter Scott, *Marmion*. The poem tells of a 14th-century Lincolnshire knight, Sir William Marmion, who, as an act of chivalrous devotion to his mistress, volunteers to serve in the most dangerous place in England. That place is Norham Castle.

Open 1 April–30 Sep: 10am–6pm daily. 1–31 Oct: 10am–5pm daily.
Entry £1.80/£1.40/90p.
Tel 01289 382329
Access Norham village, 6½m SW of Berwick-upon-Tweed on minor road off B6470 (from A698). (OS Map 75; ref NT 907476.)
Bus Swan/Arriva Northumbria/ First Edinburgh 23 ⇌ Berwick-upon-Tweed–Kelso. Tel 01670 533128.
Train Berwick-upon-Tweed 7 ½m.
♿ (excluding keep)

⊕ Lindisfarne Priory
○ *Northumberland (p. 242, 19J)*

See p. 227 for full details.

◍ Norham Castle
◉ *Northumberland (p. 242, 19H)*

See opposite page for full details.

◍ Prudhoe Castle
Northumberland (p. 240/242, 16J)

See p. 230 for full details.

⊕ St Paul's Monastery
Tyne & Wear (p. 242, 16J)

The home of the Venerable Bede, partly surviving as the chancel of the parish church. The monastery has become one of the best-understood

Anglo-Saxon monastic sites.
Open Monastery ruins, any reasonable time. (Property managed by Jarrow 700AD Ltd.)
Entry Free to Monastery ruins.
Tel 0191 489 2106

Access In Jarrow, on minor road N of A185. (OS Map 88; ref NZ339652)
Bus Go Coastline 527 Newcastle–South Shields. Tel 0845 606 0260.
Train Brockley Whins 2½ m.
Metro Bede ¾ m. **P**

⊕ Tynemouth Priory and Castle
Tyne & Wear (p. 242, 17J)

The castle walls and gatehouse enclose the substantial remains of a Benedictine priory founded c.1090 on a Saxon monastic site.

- Explore underground chambers beneath the World War I gun batteries.

Open 1 April–30 Sep: 10am–6pm daily. 1–31 Oct: 10am–5pm daily. 1 Nov–31 March 2001: 10am–1pm, 2–4pm Wed–Sun. Closed 24–26 Dec and 1 Jan 2001. Gun battery: April–Sep: Sat–Sun and Bank Holidays 10am–6pm.
Entry £1.80/£1.40/90p.
Tel 0191 257 1090

Access In Tynemouth, near North Pier. (OS Map 88; ref NZ 374695.)
Bus From surrounding areas. Tel 0191 232 5325.
Metro Tynemouth ½ m.
◻◻ (nearby; local council)
♿(priory) ⛔ ✘

○ Warkworth Castle
◓ and Hermitage
◍ *Northumberland (p. 242, 185)*

The magnificent eight-towered keep of Warkworth Castle stands on its hill above the River Coquet. A large, complex, and impressive stronghold, it was home to the Percy family who at times wielded more power in the North than the King himself.

🎬 *Elizabeth* was filmed here.

- Many chambers, passageways and dark staircases to explore.
- Free Children's Activity Sheet.

Open Castle: 1 April–30 Sep: 10am–6pm daily. 1–31 Oct: 10am–5pm daily. 1 Nov–31 March 2001: 10am–1pm,

2–4pm daily. Closed 24–26 Dec and 1 Jan 2001.
Hermitage: 1 April– 30 Sep: 11am–5pm Wed, Sun and Bank Holidays.
Entry Castle:£2.40/£1.80/£1.20. Hermitage: £1.60/£1.20/80p.
Tel 01665 711423
Access In Warkworth, 7 ½ m S of Alnwick on A1068. (OS Map 81; Castle ref NU 247057, Hermitage ref NU 242060).
Bus Arriva Northumbria 518 Newcastle–Alnwick. Tel 01670 533128.
Train Alnmouth 3½ m.
P ◻◻♿(limited access)
⛔◌ *small charge* (also available for the visually impaired and those

with hear-ing difficulties)
✘(restricted areas)

Prudhoe Castle

On a wooded hillside overlooking the River Tyne stand the remains of this formidable castle. Inside its defensive ditches and ramparts is the massive earthwork enclosure of the inner castle on which stand the masonry towers and curtain walls. Although Prudhoe Castle first appears in the historical records in the 12th century there is archaelogical evidence of a defended enclosure, consisting of earth ramparts and timber walls and palisades, having existed on the site as early as the mid-11th century.

In its later history the castle played an active part in the warfare between Scottish and English kings and was besieged on several occasions. The most notable of these sieges occurred in 1173 and 1174 when the King of Scotland attempted to seize the earldoms of Northumberland and Cumberland. Prudhoe Castle successfully resisted these attacks, the events of which were famously recorded by the contemporary chronicler, Jordan Fantosme.

Today the Georgian Manor House is a dominating feature. On the site of a medieval residential cross-range dividing the enclosure into two parts, the Manor House repeats a strong visual element separating the wards - the private from the more public portions of the castle. There is a small exhibition and video presentation.

• Beautiful picnic spot.
• Brass rubbing.

Open 1 April–30 Sep: 10am–6pm daily. 1–31 Oct: 10am–5pm daily.

Entry £1.80/£1.40/90p.

Tel 01661 833459

Access In Prudhoe, on minor road off A695. (OS Map 88; ref NZ 092634.)

Bus From surrounding areas. Tel 01670 533128.

Train Prudhoe ¼m.

🅿 🚻 🄾 🄴 🎍 🦽 (restricted areas)

A guide to maps

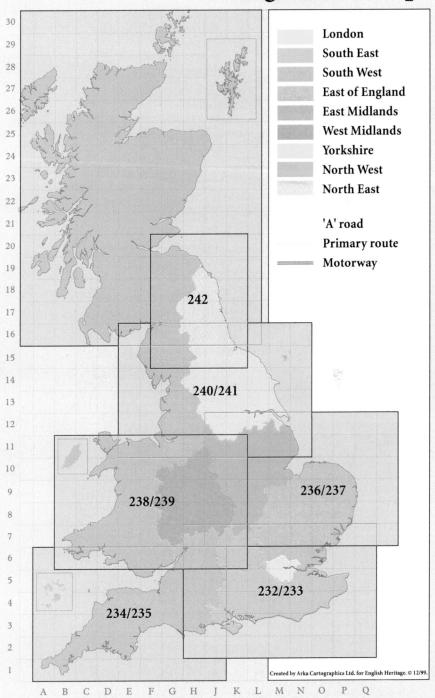

London
South East
South West
East of England
East Midlands
West Midlands
Yorkshire
North West
North East

'A' road
Primary route
Motorway

242

240/241

238/239

236/237

234/235

232/233

Created by Arka Cartographics Ltd. for English Heritage. © 12/99.

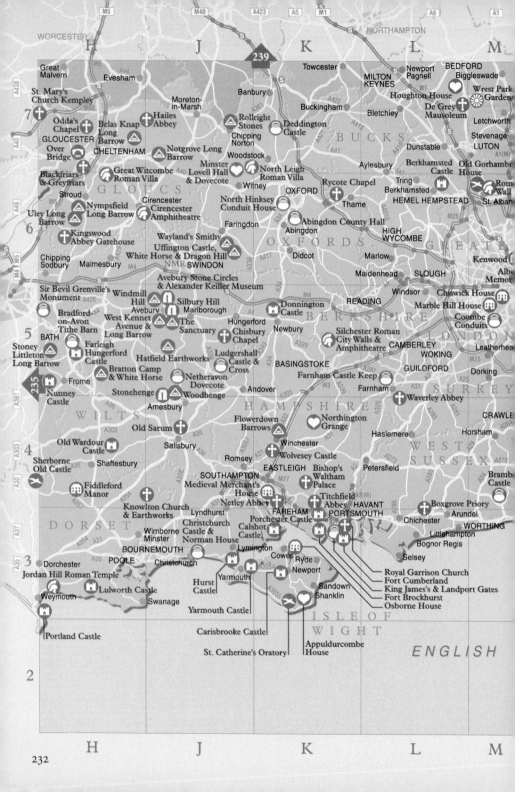

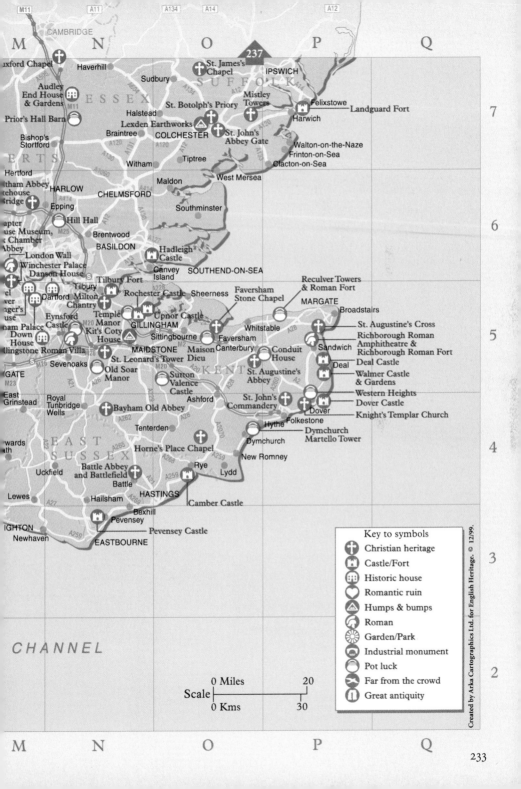

Map labels

Grid references (top): M11, A11, A134, A14, A12
Grid columns (top): M, N, O, P, Q
Grid rows (right): 7, 6, 5, 4, 3, 2

CAMBRIDGE

237

IPSWICH

SUFFOLK

ESSEX

Haverhill
Sudbury
St. James's Chapel
uxford Chapel
Audley End House & Gardens
Prior's Hall Barn
Halstead
St. Botolph's Priory
Mistley Towers
Felixstowe
Landguard Fort
Harwich
Bishop's Stortford
Braintree
Lexden Earthworks
COLCHESTER
St. John's Abbey Gate
Walton-on-the-Naze
Frinton-on-Sea
Clacton-on-Sea
RTS
Hertford
Witham
Tiptree
West Mersea
tham Abbey
tehouse
ridge
HARLOW
CHELMSFORD
Epping
Southminster
Maldon
apter
use Museum,
Chamber
Abbey
Hill Hall
Brentwood
BASILDON
Hadleigh Castle
SOUTHEND-ON-SEA
London Wall
Winchester Palace
Danson House
el
ver
ger's
use
Canvey Island
Tilbury Fort
Tilbury
Dartford
Milton Chantry
Rochester Castle
Sheerness
Faversham Stone Chapel
Reculver Towers & Roman Fort
MARGATE
Broadstairs
Temple Manor
Upnor Castle
ham Palace
Down
House
Eynsford Castle
Kit's Coty House
GILLINGHAM
Sittingbourne
Faversham
Whitstable
St. Augustine's Cross
Richborough Roman Amphitheatre & Richborough Roman Fort
llingstone Roman Villa
MAIDSTONE
Maison Dieu
Canterbury
Conduit House
Sandwich
Deal
Sevenoaks
St. Leonard's Tower
Old Soar Manor
KENT
St. Augustine's Abbey
Deal Castle
Walmer Castle & Gardens
GATE
Sutton Valence Castle
St. John's Commandery
Western Heights
Dover Castle
East Grinstead
Royal Tunbridge Wells
Bayham Old Abbey
Ashford
Dover
Knight's Templar Church
Hythe
Folkestone
Dymchurch Martello Tower
Tenterden
Horne's Place Chapel
Dymchurch
New Romney
EAST SUSSEX
Uckfield
Battle Abbey and Battlefield
Battle
Rye
Lydd
wards
th
Lewes
Hailsham
HASTINGS
Camber Castle
IGHTON
Newhaven
Bexhill
Pevensey
EASTBOURNE
Pevensey Castle

CHANNEL

Key to symbols

- Christian heritage
- Castle/Fort
- Historic house
- Romantic ruin
- Humps & bumps
- Roman
- Garden/Park
- Industrial monument
- Pot luck
- Far from the crowd
- Great antiquity

Scale
0 Miles — 20
0 Kms — 30

Created by Arka Cartographics Ltd. for English Heritage. © 12/99.

233

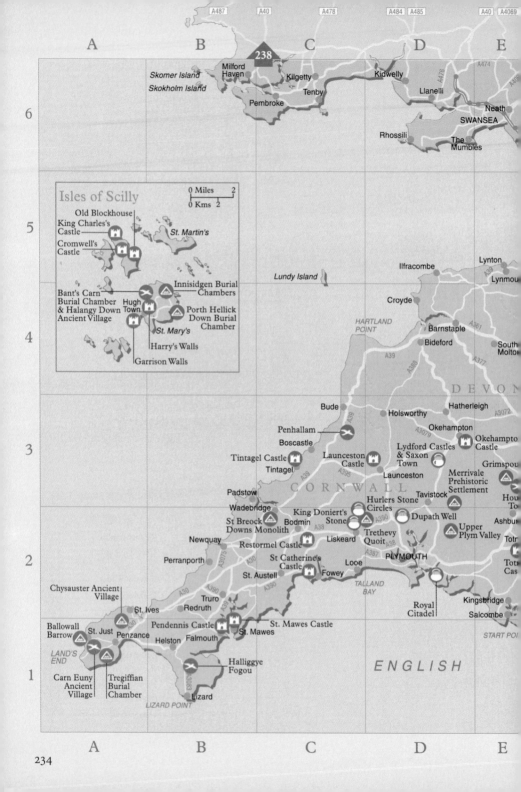

Map labels

E F G H J (top and bottom grid references)

A40 A470 A479 A465 A466 A49 A449 M50 A417 A38 M5 A435 A429 A44 A361

CHELTENHAM

239 GLOUCESTER

GLOUCS.

Monmouth
St Briavel's Castle   Stroud
Offa's Dyke
Raglan
Great Witcombe Roman Villa
Minster Lovell Hall and Dovecote

Aberdare
Uley Long Barrow
Nympsfield Long Barrow
Cirencester
Cirencester Amphitheatre
Lechlade
Wayland's Smithy

Maesteg
Chepstow
Kingswood Abbey Gatehouse

Caerphilly
Chipping Sodbury
Malmesbury
Uffington Castle, White Horse & Dragon Hill

NEWPORT
Avonmouth
Temple Church
Avebury Stone Circles & Alexander Keiller Museum
SWINDON

CARDIFF
Portishead
Sir Bevil Grenville's Monument
Windmill Hill
Silbury Hill
Marlborough

rthcawl
Penarth
BRISTOL
Avebury
Chisbury Chapel

Barry
BATH
West Kennet Avenue & Long Barrow
The Sanctuary

WESTON-SUPER-MARE
Stanton Drew Circles & Cove
Bradford-on-Avon Tithe Barn
Hungerford Castle
Farleigh
Ludgershall Castle & Cross

BRISTOL CHANNEL
Stoney Littleton Long Barrow
Hatfield Earthworks

nehead
Daws Castle
Burnham-on-Sea
Bratton Camp & White Horse
Netheravon Dovecote

Yarn Market Butter Cross
Cleeve Abbey
Wells
Nunney Castle
Frome
Stonehenge
Woodhenge

Gallox Bridge
Bridgwater
Meare Fish House
Glastonbury Tribunal
Amesbury

SOMERSET
Glastonbury
Old Sarum
Stockbridge

Taunton
Muchelney Abbey
Ilchester
Old Wardour Castle
Salisbury
Romsey

ampton
Ilminster
Sherborne
Shaftesbury
SOUTHAMPTON

erton
Yeovil
Sherborne Old Castle
WILTS.

Honiton
Axminster
Fiddleford Manor
Wimborne Minster
Christchurch Castle & Norman House

EXETER
Blackbury Camp
Lyme Regis
The Nine Stones
Maiden Castle
Knowlton Church & Earthworks
Lyndhurst
BOURNEMOUTH
POOLE
Christchurch

whill
Sidmouth
Winterbourne Poor Lot Barrows
Dorchester
DORSET

Exmouth
Kingston Russell Stone Circle
Abbotsbury
Jordan Hill Roman Temple
Lulworth Castle
Hurst Castle

Dawlish
Abbotsbury Abbey Remains
Weymouth
Swanage

Newton Abbot
St. Catherine's Chapel
Portland Castle

TORQUAY
Berry Pomeroy Castle
BILL OF PORTLAND

Kirkham House
Bayard's Cove Fort
Dartmouth

Dartmouth Castle

CHANNEL

Key to symbols

- Christian heritage
- Castle/Fort
- Historic house
- Romantic ruin
- Humps & bumps
- Roman
- Garden/Park
- Industrial monument
- Pot luck
- Far from the crowd
- Great antiquity

0 Miles 20
0 Kms 30

Created by Arka Cartographics Ltd. for English Heritage. © 12/99.

232

A650   A1   A19   A614   A1079

LEEDS   KINGSTON-UPON-HULL
BRADFORD   J   K   L   M   N

M62   WAKEFIELD   Barton-upon-Humber
HUDDERSFIELD   Hemsworth   St. Peter's   Immingham
Holmfirth   Monk Bretton   Church   Thornton   GRIMSBY
Priory   SCUNTHORPE   Abbey &   Cleethorpes
S. YORKS.   Brodsworth Hall   2   Gatehouse
BARNSLEY   DONCASTER   Gainsthorpe   Brigg
Conisbrough Castle   Medieval Village   1   Caistor
ROTHERHAM   Gainsborough Old Hall   Market Rasen
SHEFFIELD   Gainsborough   Louth
12   Roche Abbey   Mattersey Priory   Mablethorpe
Peveril Castle   Worksop   Sutton-on-Sea
Buxton   Sutton   Wragby
Nine Ladies   Scarsdale Hall   NOTTS   Lincoln   Horncastle   Ingoldmells
Stone Circle   CHESTERFIELD   Bolsover Castle   Medieval   Bolingbroke Castle
11   Hob   Ollerton   Bishop's   Skegness
Arbor Low   Hurst's   Rufford   Palace
Stone Circle &   House   Hardwick   Abbey   LINCOLN   Tattershall College   Sibsey
Gib Hill Barrow   Old Hall   Mansfield   Trader
Matlock   Newark-on-Trent   Coningsby   Windmill
Wingfield Manor   LINCOLNS.
DERBYS   NOTTINGHAM   Sleaford   THE
Ashbourne   WASH
Croxden   Grantham   Boston
10   Abbey   DERBY   Holbeach
Uttoxeter   Long
Melton   Spalding   Sutton
Ashby de   Loughborough   Mowbray   Wisbech
la Zouch   LEICS.   Stamford   Downham
Ashby   Castle   Oakham   Longthorpe   Market
de la Zouch   Kirby Muxloe   LEICESTER   A47   Tower
Wall Roman   Castle   Jewry Wall   PETERBOROUGH   March
9   Site   Lyddington   CAMBS.
TAMWORTH   Bede House   Kirby Hall   Chatteris
Hinckley   Market   Corby   Oundle
NUNEATON   Harborough   Rushton   Eleanor Cross   Ely
BIRMINGHAM   Lutterworth   Triangular Lodge   Kettering   Huntingdon
MIDLANDS   RUGBY   NORTH-   Chichele College   St. Neots   Denny Abbey
COVENTRY   AMPTONS   the Farmland
8   Kenilworth Castle   Kenilworth   NORTHAMPTON   Bushmead Priory   Museum
Warwick   CAMBRIDG
WARWICKS.   Daventry   BEDFORD   Duxford Chap
Stratford-   Towcester   Newport   Biggleswade
upon-Avon   Pagnell   BEDFORDS.
Moreton-   MILTON   Houghton House   Audley
in-Marsh   Banbury   KEYNES   Wrest Park   End House
7   Hailes Abbey   Rollright   Bletchley   De Grey   Gardens   & Gardens
Notgrove Long   Stones   Bucklingham   Mausoleum   Letchworth   HERTS.
Barrow   Chipping Norton   Deddington   BUCKS   Dunstable   Stevenage   Prior's Hall B
Minster   Castle   Aylesbury   LUTON   Bishop's
Lovell Hall   Woodstock   North Leigh Roman Villa   Hertford   Stortford
& Dovecote   232   HARLOW

OXFORD   J   K   M40   L   A4010   M   N   M11
A420   M25

KEY TO NUMBERS
1 NORTH EAST LINCOLNSHIRE
2 NORTH LINCOLNSHIRE
4 RUTLAND

Scale
0 Miles 20
0 Kms 30

12

NORTH SEA

11

10

9

8

7

Creake Abbey
Blakeney Guildhall
Wells-next-the-Sea
Sheringham
Cromer
Hunstanton
Holt
Binham Wayside Cross
Binham Priory
Baconsthorpe Castle
North Walsham
Castle Rising Castle
Fakenham
Aylsham
Castle Acre Bailey Gate
Castle Acre Castle
North Elmham Chapel
Castle Acre Priory
East Dereham
NORWICH
Cow Tower
Hemsby
Caister Roman Site
Great Yarmouth
Swaffham
Berney Arms Windmill
Row 111 Houses, Old Merchant's House & Greyfriar's Cloister
NORFOLK
Wymondham
Loddon
St. Olave's Priory
Burgh Castle
Grime's Graves
Attleborough
LOWESTOFT
Weeting Castle
Bungay
Thetford Warren Lodge
Beccles
Brandon
Thetford
Kessingland
Thetford Priory
Diss
Church of the Holy Sepulchre
Isleham Priory Church
Halesworth
Southwold
Newmarket
Framlingham Castle
Bury St. Edmunds
Saxtead Green Post Mill
Leiston Abbey
Moulton Packhorse Bridge
Bury St. Edmunds Abbey
Stowmarket
Aldeburgh
SUFFOLK
Woodbridge
Orford Castle
Orford
Haverhill
St. James's Chapel
IPSWICH
Sudbury
Mistley Towers
Felixstowe
ESSEX
St. Botolph's Priory
Landguard Fort
Halstead
Harwich
Lexden Earthworks
St. John's Abbey Gate
COLCHESTER
Braintree
Walton-on-the-Naze
Frinton-on-Sea
Witham
Tiptree
West Mersea
Clacton-on-Sea
CHELMSFORD

Key to symbols
Christian heritage
Castle/Fort
Historic house
Romantic ruin
Humps & bumps
Roman
Garden/Park
Industrial monument
Pot luck
Far from the crowd
Great antiquity

Created by Arka Cartographics Ltd. for English Heritage. © 12/99.

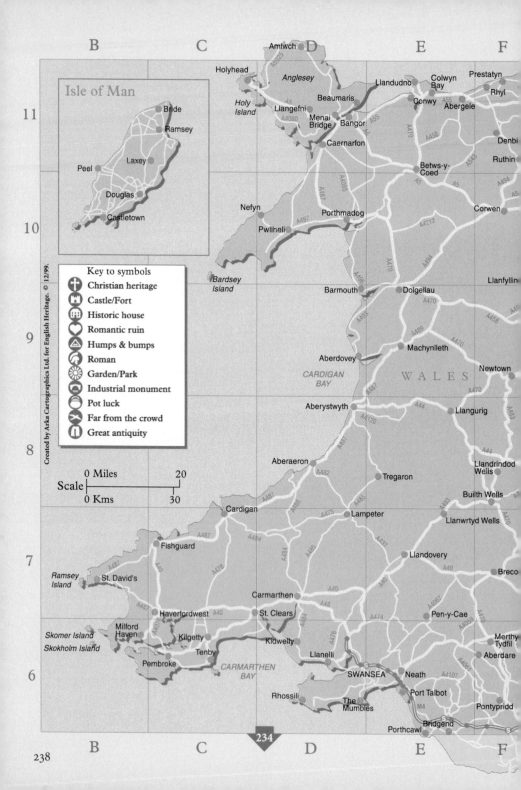

Amlwch

Holyhead

Anglesey

Llandudno   Colwyn
           Bay   Prestatyn

Beaumaris   Conwy   Rhyl

Holy
Island   Llangefni   Abergele

Menai   Bangor
Bridge

Caernarfon   Denbi

Betws-y-   Ruthin
Coed

Isle of Man

Bride

Ramsey

Laxey

Peel

Douglas

Castletown

Nefyn   Porthmadog   Corwen

Pwllheli

Llanfyllin

Bardsey
Island   Barmouth   Dolgellau

Key to symbols

✝ Christian heritage
🏰 Castle/Fort
🏛 Historic house
♥ Romantic ruin
△ Humps & bumps
🏛 Roman
⚙ Garden/Park
⚒ Industrial monument
☕ Pot luck
✈ Far from the crowd
🏛 Great antiquity

Machynlleth

Aberdovey   Newtown

CARDIGAN
BAY   W A L E S

Aberystwyth   Llangurig

Scale

0 Miles   20

0 Kms   30

Aberaeron   Llandrindod
                   Wells

Tregaron

Builth Wells

Cardigan   Lampeter   Llanwrtyd Wells

Fishguard   Llandovery   Breco

Ramsey
Island   St. David's   Carmarthen   Pen-y-Cae

Haverfordwest   St. Clears   Merthy
                              Tydfil

Skomer Island   Milford   Kilgetty   Kidwelly   Aberdare
           Haven

Skokholm Island   Tenby   Llanelli

Pembroke   *CARMARTHEN*   SWANSEA   Neath   Pontypridd
           BAY   Port Talbot

Rhossili   The   Bridgend
         Mumbles   Porthcawl

Created by Arka Cartographics Ltd. for English Heritage. © 12/99.

234

B   C   D   E   F

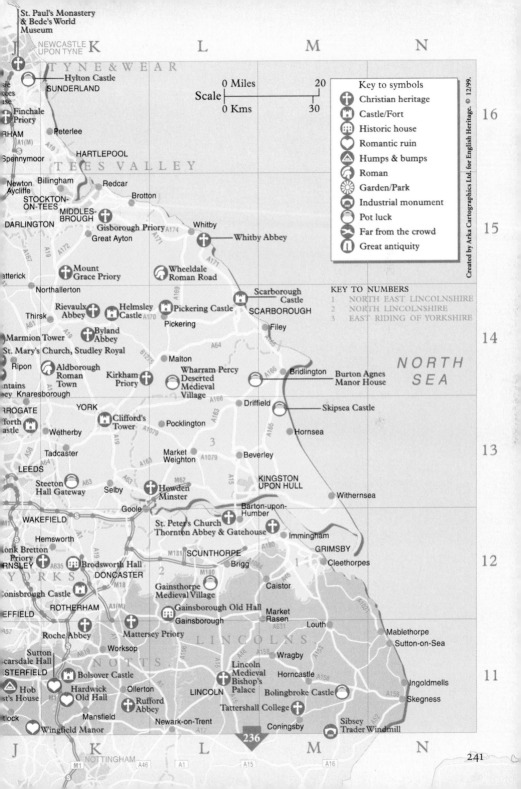

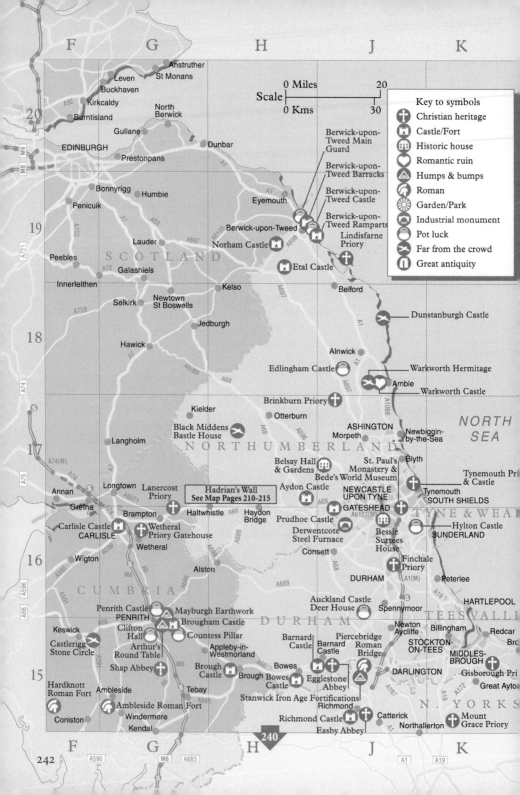

Scale

0 Miles 20

0 Kms 30

Key to symbols

- Christian heritage
- Castle/Fort
- Historic house
- Romantic ruin
- Humps & bumps
- Roman
- Garden/Park
- Industrial monument
- Pot luck
- Far from the crowd
- Great antiquity

Anstruther
St Monans
Leven
Buckhaven
Kirkcaldy
Burntisland
North Berwick
Gullane
Dunbar
EDINBURGH
Prestonpans
Bonnyrigg
Humbie
Penicuik
Eyemouth

Berwick-upon-Tweed Main Guard
Berwick-upon-Tweed Barracks
Berwick-upon-Tweed Castle
Berwick-upon-Tweed Ramparts
Berwick-upon-Tweed
Lindisfarne Priory

Peebles
Lauder
S C O T L A N D
Galashiels
Norham Castle
Etal Castle
Innerleithen
Selkirk
Newtown St Boswells
Kelso
Belford
Hawick
Jedburgh

Dunstanburgh Castle

Alnwick
Edlingham Castle
Warkworth Hermitage
Amble
Warkworth Castle

Kielder
Brinkburn Priory
Otterburn
Langholm
Black Middens Bastle House
N O R T H U M B E R L A N D
ASHINGTON
Morpeth
Newbiggin-by-the-Sea
Blyth

NORTH SEA

Belsay Hall & Gardens
St. Paul's Monastery & Bede's World Museum
Tynemouth Pri & Castle
Longtown
Lanercost Priory
Hadrian's Wall See Map Pages 210-215
Aydon Castle
Haltwhistle
Haydon Bridge
NEWCASTLE UPON TYNE
GATESHEAD
Tynemouth
SOUTH SHIELDS
Annan
Gretna
Brampton
Prudhoe Castle
Derwentcote Steel Furnace
T Y N E & W E A R
Hylton Castle
Carlisle Castle
CARLISLE
Wetheral Priory Gatehouse
Wetheral
Consett
Bessie Surtees House
SUNDERLAND
Wigton
Finchale Priory
DURHAM
Peterlee
Alston
HARTLEPOOL
C U M B R I A
Auckland Castle Deer House
Spennymoor
T E E S V A L L I
Penrith Castle
PENRITH
Mayburgh Earthwork
Brougham Castle
D U R H A M
Newton Aycliffe
Billingham
Redcar
Bro
Keswick
Clifton Hall
Countess Pillar
Barnard Castle
Piercebridge Roman Bridge
STOCKTON-ON-TEES
Castlerigg Stone Circle
Arthur's Round Table
Appleby-in-Westmorland
Barnard Castle
DARLINGTON
MIDDLES-BROUGH
Shap Abbey
Brough Castle
Bowes
Gisborough Pri
Great Ayto
Hardknott Roman Fort
Ambleside
Brough Bowes Castle
Egglestone Abbey
Stanwick Iron Age Fortifications
N . Y O R K S
Coniston
Ambleside Roman Fort
Windermere
Kendal
Richmond
Richmond Castle
Easby Abbey
Catterick
Northallerton
Mount Grace Priory

240

242

Other historic attractions

In addition to free admission to all the English Heritage properties featured in this Handbook, members are also entitled to free or reduced price entry to a host of other historic attractions throughout Britain.

Whether you're on holiday or simply live nearby, you can use your membership card to visit over one hundred more heritage attractions in Scotland, Wales and the Isle of Man. Members pay only half price. After your first year, it's free!

Monuments to visit include Edinburgh and Sterling Castles and Melrose Abbey in Scotland, Caerphilly Castle and Tintern Abbey in Wales and, on the Isle of Man, the Manx Museum and Cregneash Village Folk Museum.

Across England, you can use your membership card to gain free or reduced price entry to attractions such as the Flag Fen Excavations near Peterborough, one of Europe's most important archaeological sites, six magnificent historic sites in the care of Sussex Past, York's 14th-century Merchant Adventurers' Hall and the stunning Fountains Abbey, managed by the National Trust.

We are delighted that having received funding and support from English Heritage **Kensal Green Cemetery** in London, **Dover Museum** and **Duncombe Park** in Helmsley, North Yorkshire are now offering members discounted entry to their sites.

So, take full advantage of your membership and start visiting many of Britain's other historic attractions! And don't forget to take your membership cards with you!
Above left, Conwy Castle.
Below, Kidwelly Castle.

Members are entitled to free or reduced price entry to the following historic attractions:

Historic Scotland: **0131 668 8800**
Cadw: **029 20500200**
Manx National Heritage:
  01624 648000
Sussex Past: **01273 486 260**
Weald and Downland Open Air
  Museum, Sussex: **01243 811348**
Flag Fen, Lincolnshire:
  01733 313 414
Pendle Heritage Centre:
  01282 695 366
Fountains Abbey, North Yorkshire:
  01765 608888
Jorvik Viking Centre, Yorkshire:
  01904643211
Archaeological Resource Centre,
  Yorkshire: **01904 654324**
Merchant Adventurers' Hall,
  Yorkshire: **01904 654 818**
Kensal Green Cemetery, London:
  020 7402 2749
Dover Museum and The White
  Cliffs Experience: **01304 201066**
Duncombe Park, North Yorkshire:
  01439 770213

For an illustrated guide to these suites, call Customer Services on 01793 414910.

243

For each property the first number, in bold, gives the page of its entry; the second, the page and grid reference on the maps.

Picture credits

P. 12 *Elizabeth I* by an unknown artist and *Queen Victoria* by Bertha Muller (1848-1925) © By courtesy of the National Portrait Library, London. P. 13 Whitby Abbey, watercolour by John Spink © The Bridgeman Art Library. P. 15 Inn Sign © R M Edwards ARPS; New Tyne Bridge © DS Ridey LRPS; Belle Tout Lighthouse © Michael Nash. P. 42 William the Conqueror © The Bridgeman Art Library. P. 44 Battle Abbey, the Cloisters and Priors Hall © Derry Brabbs. P. 45 Battle Abbey, the Great Gatehouse © Derry Brabbs. P. 46 Bayeux Tapestry © Michael Holford; aerial view of Bayham Old Abbey © Skyscan Balloon Photography. P. 47 Aerial view of Bishop's Waltham Palace © Skyscan Balloon Photography. P. 48 Aerial view of Carisbrooke castle © Skyscan Balloon Photography. P. 50 Donnington Castle © Peter Ashley. P. 51 Aerial view of Farnham Castle Keep © Skyscan Balloon Photography. P. 52 *Henry II* and *Henry VIII* © By courtesy of the National Portrait Gallery, London. P. 61 Northington Grange © Peter Ashley. P. 62 Northington Grange (top) © Peter Ashley. P. 63 The Albert Memorial © Angelo Hornak; *Queen Victoria* © By courtesy of the National Portrait Gallery, London. P. 64 Aerial view of Osborne House © Skyscan Balloon Photography. P. 65 The Royal Family © By courtesy of the National Portrait Gallery, London. P. 67 *Queen Victoria and Princess Beatrice* © By courtesy of the National Portrait Gallery, London. P. 68 Aerial view of Pevensey Castle © Skyscan Balloon Photography. P. 69 Aerial view of Richborough Roman Fort © Skyscan Balloon Photography. P. 73 Aerial view of White Horse © Skyscan Balloon Photography. P. 74 Aerial view of Walmer Castle © Skyscan Balloon Photography. P. 77 Aerial view of Wolvesey Castle © Skyscan Balloon Photography. P. 85 Aerial views of Dartmouh Castle © Skyscan Balloon Photography. P. 87 Aerial views of Farleigh Hungerford Castle © Skyscan Balloon Photography. P. 93 Aerial view of Launceston Castle © Skyscan Balloon Photography. P. 94 Aerial view of Maiden Castle © Skyscan Balloon Photography. P. 94 Maiden Castle, insert © National Monuments Record Centre, Swindon; main picture © Skyscan Balloon Photography. P. 96 Aerial view of Mulcheney Abbey © Skyscan Balloon Photography. P. 97 May Garlands © National Monuments Record Centre, Swindon. P. 99 Aerial view of Okehampton Castle © Skyscan Balloon Photography. P. 100 Aerial view of Old Sarum © Skyscan Balloon Photography. P. 101 Aerial views of Old Wardour Castle and Portland Castle © Skyscan Balloon Photography. P. 102 Aerial view of Pendennis Castle © National Monuments Record Centre, Swindon. P. 105 Portland Castle, both pictures © National Monuments Record Centre, Swindon. P. 107 Aerial View of Sherborne Old Castle © Skyscan Balloon Photography. P. 109 All three pictures © John Mason. P. 112 Aerial of Stonehenge in the snow © Skyscan Balloon Photography. P. 126 Aerial view of Castle Rising Castle © Skyscan Balloon Photography. P. 127 Denny Abbey, top right © Peter Ashley. P.129 Aerial view of Framlingham Castle © Skyscan Balloon

Photography. P. 130 Aerial view of Grimes Grave © Skyscan Balloon Photography. P. 137 Aerial view of Saxtead Green Post Mill © Skyscan Balloon Photography. P. 138 Aerial view of Tilbury Fort © Skyscan Balloon Photography. P. 144 Aerial view of Bolsover Castle © Skyscan Balloon Photography. P. 148 Aerial view of Ashby de la Zouch Castle © Skyscan Balloon Photography. P. 158 Interior of Boscobel House © Peter Ashley. P. 159 *Charles II* and *Charles II in Boscobel Wood* © By courtesy of the National Portrait Gallery, London. P. 160 Aerial views of Buildwas Abbey and Clun Castle © Skyscan Balloon Photography. P. 161 Aerial view of Goodrich Castle © Skyscan Balloon Photography. P. 164 Aerial view of Kenilworth Castle © Skyscan Balloon Photography. P. 166 and 167 Moreton Corbet Castle, all pictures © Peter Ashley. P. 169 Aerial view of Wenlock Priory © Skyscan Balloon Photography. P. 170 Wigmore Castle, main picture and top left © Boris Baggs; top right © Peter Ashley. P. 180 Aerial view of Byland Abbey © National Monuments Record Centre, Swindon. P. 182 Fountains Abbey, top & middle pics © The National Trust Photographic Library/M. Antrobus; main pic. © The National Trust Photographic Library/Oliver Benn. P. 183 Fountains Abbey, left pic. © The National Trust Photographic Library/M. Antrobus; righ pic. © The National Trust Photographic Library/ Martin Dohrn. P. 184 Aerial view of Middleham Castle © Skyscan Balloon Photography. P. 188 Aerial view of Rievaulx Abbey © Skyscan Balloon Photography; Painting of Rievaulx Abbey © The Bridgeman Art Library. P. 191 Hounds Tor and Wharram Percy medieval villages © National Monuments Record Centre, Swindon. P. 193 Thornton Abbey, bottom pic. © Derry Brabbs. P. 197 *Whitby Abbey*, watercolour by John Spink © The Bridgeman Art Library. P. 202 Aerial view of Brough Castle © Skyscan Balloon Photography. P. 205 Aerial view of Lanercost Priory © Skyscan Balloon Photography. P. 208 Thatched hay in Norfolk © National Monuments Record Centre, Swindon. P. 210-11 map of Hadrian's Wall © Ann Rooke/Hadrian's Wall Tourism Partnership. P. 220 Aerial view of Aydon Castle © Skyscan Balloon Photography. P. 221 *Dunstanburgh Castle* © The Bridgeman Art Library. P. 228 Aerial view of Norham Castle © Skyscan Balloon Photography. P. 230 Aerial view of Prudhoe Castle © Skyscan Balloon Photography. *Prudhoe Castle* © The Bridgeman Art Library.

Front cover: Wigmore Castle © Peter Ashley.
Back cover: *Walking Man*, statue by Elisabeth Frink, photo. © National Monuments Record Centre, Swindon.

All Skyscan Balloon Photography pictures were sourced at the English Heritage Photographic Library.

Special thanks to Celia Sterne and Cathy Houghton from the English Heritage Photographic Library.